MIRACLES THROUGH MUSIC

MIRACLES THROUGH MUSIC

THE ODYSSEY OF A MUSIC HEALER

an Autobiographical Account by

Joel Andrews

Miracles Through Music, The Odyssey of a Music Healer
by Joel Andrews

© 2014 Joel Andrews. All rights reserved

No part of this book may be used or reproduced, stored in or introduced into a retrieval system, or transmitted in any form, or by any means (electronic or mechanical, photocopying, recording, or otherwise), without the prior written permission of the author, except in brief quotations embedded in critical articles or reviews. The scanning, uploading and distribution of this book via the Internet or any other means without the permission of the author is illegal and punishable by law.

For permission to quote from this book, address your inquiry to:
Golden Harp Enterprises
Web: www.harpofgold.com
Email: goldharp@jps.net

Published by Portal Center Press, Gleneden Beach, Oregon
www.portalcenterpress.com

ISBN: 978-1-62620-744-8
Library of Congress Control Number: 2013938452
1. Miracles with Sound 2. Music Therapy 3. Co-Creation with Spirit
4. Interspecies Communication 5. Plants and Animals 6. Love 7. Harp
8. The Emerging Age 9. Name Analysis 10. How We Learn

Printed in the United States of America by LightningSource, Inc.

Cover Design by Dale Moyer
First Edition 2014

DEDICATION

With deepest gratitude and everlasting love,
To the One Source of all Consciousness.

To all the patient, emissaries of Light
with whom I've co-created over the years,
and especially those who have overseen the work reported herein;

To my own shining guardians
and indwelling Gift of Spirit;

To my beloved wife, friend, and creative partner, Serafina,
For support of the completion and publication of this research.

To all those who helped, some of whom are listed on the next page.

To the thousands of clients who came for help on The Path;

And finally to the musicians, healers, channels,
and students of the Spiritual Renaissance
who enjoyed *A Harp Full of Stars*
and have waited for this book.

The Divine in me salutes The Divine in you.

ACKNOWLEDGEMENTS

My deepest gratitude to my beloved wife, Serafina. She not only supported the writing of this book for five years but had a number of valuable suggestions along the way. Heartfelt thanks to the over 100 clients who offered their moving testimonies of healing of various kinds. Thanks go also to the many Centers of Light, in many countries, that set up concerts, workshops and reading sessions. Without their belief in the potential of healing through co-created music, or at least open minds, this book would probably never have come into being.

Included in these thanks must be the mentors who encouraged my exploration of these relatively uncharted waters in the early '70s: Kay Ortmans for early encouragement, Johann Blomeyer for ongoing reinforcement, Ellen Spies for her channeling of the symbolism of the alphabet, Bella Karish for valuable tips on the art of channeling and effective affirmations, and Dr. C. Norman Shealy for his work in expanding holistic medicine, his support of my work, and the Forward to my first book, *A Harp Full of Stars*. And finally, for editing and production, deep thanks to Barbara Wilson, fine author in her own right, Dale Moyer for cover design, Portal Center Press for publishing, and Kathleen Thormod Carr for the back cover photo.

Disclaimer: No process in this book is to be construed as to guarantee healing. All of these techniques can be conducive to healing and many have brought about significant improvement in conditions and even complete remission. If you have a condition which could be serious we recommend you consult a trained health practitioner. If you do, healing music can certainly then provide therapeutic support. The attitude the author would like to take here is that true holistic medicine means all the health practitioners working together for the optimum health of us all.

A brief biography and bibliography of Joel Andrews is to be found at the end of the book.

TABLE OF CONTENTS

PART ONE

1. PRELUDE.. 1
   Welcome to a feast of miracles, please pull up a throne—A stranger arrives at my door (my guide and companion for the book)—Background for this book—Recent research— What is a miracle—A basic question: Is the universe alive?—laws of a Higher Order—New theory about how we learn—My general background as a healer—Comment on organized religion—This book presents a totally positive, informative and inspiring view of life, so is a kind of manual for living a spiritual life—What's in this book—I realize who my guide is—Introducing Serafina, my partner and wife.

2. ODYSSEY TO EUROPE 11
   First, you are invited on an odyssey of Europe taken from diaries of 16 tours—Jomanda, world-class healer in Holland—200 spirit doctors work through her with an audience of 3,000—Time and space no obstacles—Scars from inner-plane operations disappear quickly—Garden for past-life memory—Jomanda touches 13,000 in one day—The spirit doctors oversee my hip operation with miraculous success—What we learned—Jomanda cleanses the healing energies at world-famous Lourdes—Serafina receives higher guidance to write a whole book of poems—I prepare for an unusual concert in Antwerp—In the park a flock of honking swans chases us—Heading south for Provence—A unique bed-and-breakfast—Overnight with a friend among the lavender fields near Apt: French dinner and dancing—Leaving the perfume factory in Grasse, we head south enveloped in a green cloud of "Herbs de Provence."

3. EUROPEAN ODYSSEY CONTINUES 23
   On to Assisi, Italy, the home of St. Francis—His three churches and the basilica—Serafina's miracle with keys—Ascended masters and their appearances in human form. Revelation as I meditate on a Jesus on the Cross, Smiling—The artwork of the ancient city of Pompeii appears freshly painted—Sorrento and Capri—I chant overtones in a vacant sanctuary—I explain the Overtone Series (the scale of nature) and contrast it with the Tempered Scale—Two nights in Venice and a special concert—The night before we

leave Venice I meet, on the Street, a former student from California—Off through the Alps to Basel, Switzerland. A concert overlooking the Rhine River: Swiss airs, Dixieland, and a Beatles song—We visit a butterfly sanctuary on its last day of the season—One more miracle with keys as we retrieve our luggage.

4. RESPONSES FROM CLIENTS.. 31
My process of co-creating music with my sources for a client—Four sensitivities I developed: clairaudience, clairvoyance, clairsentience, and telepathy—General CDs reviewed—A church—Concerts—College—Lecture—Concert-Lecture—Music for a relationship—Creativity with children- *A Harp Full of Stars*, my first book—Manifesting a love partner—Comment by an intuitive—Appearance of a Guardian Seraphim—Ascended Masters—Crystal effects on DNA—My deep gratitude for the confirmation of my work in these testimonials.

5. DEEPER TESTIMONIALS OF HEALING 47
Explanation of how music acts for healing—Physical healing—Personal past-life readings: *Soul-Path Re-Alignments*—Major life changes—Mykael and I discuss the testimonials in this chapter.

6. MORE CLIENT RESPONSES: THE SPECTRUM WIDENS 63
My destiny fulfilled—Headaches, migraines, spinal and neck, personal healing—Clients in Holland, the general CDs—Music from the ascended masters Kuthumi and St. Germaine—Spiritual enlightenment—Emotional cleansing—Name analysis—Doctors—After concerts—Yoga—Tai Chi—Childbirth—Massage—Dentistry—Ray Stanford's comment—Responses to my book *A Harp Full of Stars* —My comments—I'm kept young and active by these healings—We all have a unique Work to do.

7 CORNERSTONE OF THE SPIRITUAL RENAISSANCE: CO-CREATION 75
The Aquarian Age of Oneness—The Dropping of barriers—Cooperation between an individual's different aspects—Co-creation with the minerals, the plants, the animals, humans, and the angels—Angels taken out of the Bible to strengthen the story of Jesus—The polygraph and the emotions of plants—Elementals helping plants to grow—Transmigration of Souls—The ascension career.

8. INTERSPECIES COMMUNICATION: TALKING TO PLANTS AND TREES 85
A potted plant reaches out—The peace of trees—Music from a sacred cedar—Conversation with a Ponderosa Pine—I am gifted a

Christmas Tree—Music from a giant cypress—A cork oak donates the perfect cork—A live oak curious about traffic—Questioning plants by muscle-testing their outer bodies.

9. INTERSPECIES COMMUNICATION: TALKING TO ANIMALS 95

The origin of some Basic Selves in animals—A cat deals with a nightmare—How to love an untamed cat—A spider moves its web—Gophers in my vegetable garden—Inter-species communication conference—A robin and a cat patch it up—San Diego zoo crisis—Dolphins—Retuning my harp to an Overtone Series scale wakes a flock of birds—Whales.

10. NEW METHOD FOR ACCESSING THE SUBCONSCIOUS WITH KINESIOLOGY... 107

Talking to your subconscious with muscle-testing—What you can explore—How many Basic Selves?—Their origin?—Masculine and feminine?—Their jobs?—Their positioning?—Their names?—Testing yourself—Making agreements—Replacements and higher destiny. Strange answers—Split personality—A brighter future for Basic Selves.

PART TWO

11. BEFORE THE BEGINNING THERE WERE MIRACLES AND STORIES 121

My grandmother Myra—She opens the ball with the King of England—She sweeps a famous pianist off the bench—Paderewzki gives her a piano—My Grandmother Lilia, a painter, bought my first large harp—My father, Loring, and his adventures in the Cook Islands—A mandolin gives him music—A date with the Queen of England—Life in the cave—My first harp lessons—Brother Oliver, painter and contemporary sculptor—Brother Gavin, writer and national scrabble player.

12 EARLY PREPARATION AS A HEALER 131

Childhood—Rapport with nature—Four years in the Air Force and the Symphony—First experience of Cosmic Consciousness—Coming home and building a house—The conservatory in Cleveland and the master teacher, Alice Chalifoux—San Francisco and spiritual mentors: Uncle Gavin and Alan Watts—A great reader of billets—The New Age begins—The concept of the highest destiny of music as healing—Evelyn Sullivan points me toward a healing career—My debut in New York, they lose my harp!—Miraculous meetings in New York—My work begins—Mass healing in Greensborough—Etheric healing technique—Creating a rainbow dome—Conversation with Divine Father as my Dad.

13. THE NATURE AND EFFECTS OF MUSIC 145
Music, a direct expression of the vibratory aspects of life—Nostalgia—The sphere of sound—Pulse and flow—The esoteric symbolism of all the elements of music—We are music—Translating letters into pitches—Pitches—Melody—Pulse or tempo—Meter, measures and bars—Rhythmic patterns—Tempo—Chords and harmony—Loudness—Tone Quality—Early associations with sound—All these aspects of a human being create a "symphony"—Music's hypnotic effect increases rapport with one's Higher Guidance.

14. REVEALING THE ANCIENT WISDOM OF THE ALPHABET, NAMES, AND WORDS 153
Name analysis—The revealing of the universal system—Analyzing words from Life—Good words and bad words—Examples—Letters as a sequence—Adjacent letters—Dissonance: the tritone—Resolutions—The half-step—Parents are guided when naming children—Nicknames.

15. STRENGTHENING OUR WEEKS AND RESTORING MEANING TO OUR DAYS 163
Do you know what the names for our days mean?—New names with meaning—Descriptions—The name "week" ("weak")—The power of what we say—A week "off"—A personal accomplishment week—Special Once-a-Month Days—The "Snowjob" Day—Breathing life into your days.

16. WHAT IS THIS THING CALLED LOVE? 173
What could we be meaning when we say "I love you"—Marriage for love, a Recent experiment—We need training for it—Seven positive varieties of possible meaning—Five negative varieties of possible meaning—Simple exercises to explore these meanings—Is it easier to fall in love than to separate?—A technique to prepare for a meeting.

17. EXPANDING THE DEFINITION OF LOVE 183
Mental love—The nature of the mind—Affirmation for harmony between your high self, your conscious mind, and your body consciousness—Soulic love—Past-life relationships and attractions—"Soul Mates" and "Twin Souls"—Emotional love—The 1x1 relationship—Negative emotions—Physical love—Spiritual love—Keys to communication—"Love ye one another."

18. KEYS TO UNIVERSAL LOVE: HUMAN TO HUMAN 197
   Lunch with a young man—Everyone is perfect, doing their divine dance—No need to change anyone—The right to absent yourself—Stay as long as you're loving then retreat to assess and learn—"Negative vibrations"—Peace and love, the rewards.

19. WHAT CAN WE LEARN FROM ALL THIS? 203
   Higher guidance essential to this book—I bless all religions—Processing one's past—The Law of Karma—We tend to be lazy—*The Urantia Book* and the Free Will Plan—The Fifth Epochal Revelation to our Planet—Satanism—Good and evil not balanced—The Time of Division—Science vs. religion (creation vs. evolution)—Life on a neighboring planet—We are created as eternaliters—Four major higher sources—You are loved and guided.

20. SUMMATION, NOW, AND LOOKING FORWARD 219
   Predicting the future and failed prophecies—The Egyptians and Mayans—2012 as a marker—Fears at the end of every century—The Second Coming—The Present Moment—Fear of death unfounded—Evidence—This planet is a school—Four extrasensory perceptions—War—Quotations from *The Urantia Book*—Visionaries: Edgar Cayce, Yolanda, Patricia Cota-Robles and others.

21. MORE QUOTES FROM VISIONARIES 229
   Grand Elder Don Alejandro—Barbara Marx Hubbard—Tom Kenyon (The Hathors)—Sri Amma and Sri Bhagavan—John Kimmey, Elder of the Hopis—Dr. Micheo Kaku—Peter Russell—When the Grandmothers Speak—Using The Net of Light—Eckhart Tolle *(The Power of Now)*—Books: The Sirians, Pleiadians, Egyptians, Arcturians, and Hathors—Sheldon Nidle, The Galactic Federation—How can we prepare?

APPENDIX I 237
APPENDIX II 253
GLOSSARY 257
BIBLIOGRAPHY 261
ABOUT THE AUTHOR 265

PART ONE

1

Prelude

Welcome, welcome, welcome to a feast of miracles. I have been preparing a banquet of revelations of healing, reports of illuminations, insights into our human and spiritual natures, new tools for life, and just-for-fun stories of my travels to many countries. Please pull up a throne to our round table and I will prepare something you would like to drink. I was just beginning a story about a mysterious visitor who arrived at my door recently. He provided the perfect opportunity for me to introduce this book to you.

A few days ago, I was looking out the window of my studio, studying some of the fruit trees that dot my 100-year-old apple farm. I was lost in wondering how I am ever going to organize all the miracles I would like to share with you, my readers, in this book.

Then there was a knock at the door. The man who appeared looked familiar in a strange sort of way. I felt as if I had known him somewhat years ago, but had not seen him since. Have you ever experienced this? So I was feeling this warm confusion when he said, "I understand you're writing another book. I enjoyed your last book *A Harp Full of Stars* more than I can tell you, and I just thought I would drop by and see if you might need encouragement or assistance." Even though I could not remember who he was, or his name, I felt that I trusted him, so I invited him in and offered him a chair.

My house was hot from the August sun even though I live on the Northern Pacific coast, two miles from the ocean, and when I opened the door to let him in I felt a cool breeze coming from the West, so I opened another door, creating an exhilarating cross-draft.

As soon as we were seated, he said, "After I read *A Harp Full of Stars* in 1989 my destiny took me all over the world and I lost touch with you. But since I had learned so much from that unique revelation, I often wondered what miraculous events you were experiencing and whether you were sharing more realizations about the nature of life and its connection with the higher laws. I was especially intrigued when a friend told me you were writing another book, since I had played and enjoyed an integral role in *Stars*."

Now, that statement really woke me up. I still could not place him, but I was feeling a deepening connection, bordering on love. Of course, it is true that everyone, and especially maverick innovators like me, respond to having their work appreciated. So I said, "My friend, what do you say we walk down to the beach and we can talk on the way?" He replied, "Oh, that would be wonderful. I've been curious about this coastline and it would give me time for the many questions I have." So off we went.

His first question was "So, how did you come to be writing another book?" I replied, "There seem to have been a number of factors. First of all, the miracles kept occurring, some of them somewhat familiar, but then there were also new types. Consequently, I was learning new life-principles. You see, I am a philosopher who, always in this life, has wanted to know more about the reality behind appearances. This constant curiosity and seeking has meant that some of the major issues I discussed in *A Harp Full of Stars*, such as new light on reincarnation, muscle-testing the subconscious, and communication between species, have gone right on evolving. There were also results of my more recent research into Higher Guidance that I wanted to share with everyone. There was the totally positive method that has been given me for helping a person process their past in this life. There were also the insights, over the past 40 years, regarding the principles of masculine and feminine outside of us and within us; and our basic nature and destiny."

Then for many years, at six A.M. every morning, I have practiced Tai Chi at my kitchen window, and for the past seven or more years I have had to stop to write down subjects, ideas, concepts, and miracles for a possible book. Still, working as hard as I do in my healing ministry, it is a daunting commitment to begin a book. In spite of the fact that I love to write and once I begin it flows quite well, especially if it is a subject I can co-create with my friends in spirit. Then the idea of taking a key to life that I know works, making many copies of it, and passing them out so others can use them, really fulfills me. It gives me the feeling I can help with the serious challenges besetting life on this planet at this time."

"Finally, on my last birthday I was 81. Contemplating that unbelievable figure, I realized that nine symbolizes "completion." I know I will be a young and vital 90—most people agree I look and act about 15 years younger than my age—and there are a number of priority projects I should finish before then, at the top of the list being this book. It galvanized me into action. In two weeks I had completed two chapters and was filling a notebook with ideas for other chapters. At my stage of life I am filled with deep gratitude for the manifold blessings I have experienced and I want to give it all back to my brothers and sisters and to life."

My new-old friend said, "This is all very exciting—but it raises more questions. First of all, how would you define a miracle?"

I said, "Now that is a crucial question. I am respectful of the practical laws of life on earth and the scientific approach to understanding them. In fact, my healing work has a scientific aspect, which I value. The system of symbolism for all the elements of music and the alphabet revealed by the sources is always checking on my clairvoyance. If I am seeing someone in a past-life and the scene is not reflected in the notes and patterns of the music, I could be wrong—but this has never happened. I love this harmonization in my work of what seem, to many, to be polar opposites. Let us not forget that wars have been fought over apparent disagreements between science and religion. To me, now, there is no conflict here; they are simply different, and valuable windows through which one can look at reality."

"Granting the veracity of physical laws, I am especially moved and exhilarated when something extraordinary occurs which implies, or even demonstrates, the action of "higher" laws. These could be principles of vibration, spiritual laws, the influence of invisible forces and beings, ascended masters, space beings, or angels. Fortunately, for my balance, and to support the clear thinking of my dear readers, I require either some documentation or the sheer weight of many occurrences for something approaching proof. The fact that scientific laws are reliable here on Earth and even extend out into space, to me, is considerable proof of Higher Intelligence."

"If people do not recognize the existence of the higher laws, they tend to dismiss a miracle by saying, "Oh, that's just a coincidence." The fact is that "coincidences" have been increasing in my life for many years, and in the lives of many of my friends. I wish I had written more of them down, even the little ones, because with miracles their size is not that important. The rich spectrum of miracles I will report should be convincing to the open-minded and at least give pause to the skeptical.

"This question leads to a much deeper and vaster question: and this is whether the universe is *alive* or *just an accident*. This book can shed some light on this question. Actually, and somewhat strange to be saying, if you acknowledge that the creation is *alive*, then there is no such thing as a miracle, since everything that occurs has antecedent causes, even though we might not be able to see them. Moreover, one of the most ancient and fundamental metaphysical laws is 'As above, so below—as within, so without.'"

"I've grown to love miracles—we'll still use the word—*because* they show the presence of laws of a 'higher' order and, apart from the miracles connected with my healing work, I'd like to remind my readers of some basic ones. For instance, no one knows what starts, sustains, or ends the beating of your heart and yet it continues for many, many years, approximately 31,104,000 times a year. It actually generates electricity through the interaction of two chemicals, making possible a long life of fun, learning experiences, and spiritual growth. Is that a miracle? Then consider the hum of your nervous system and the other awesome abilities of which your body is capable. Did you know that your liver has 500 functions? How about that intelligence—and that is one organ out of many? How about the incredible intelligence of the seed to grow into a certain tree? Seeds of grain have been found in the Egyptian tombs which have happily germinated after 5,000 years. The list could go on and on, and do not forget the wonders of the senses, the miracles of sex and procreation, and the ability to play a challenging musical instrument like the violin, the guitar, or the harp. By the way, the spiritual masters say deep gratitude for these gifts paves the way for more."

We walked along through the redwood forest and my new friend was deep in thought over what I had just shared with him. Then, as we broke into a clearing, I said, "A few years ago I became really curious as to how it is we actually learn from the information that comes to us. My vision opened and I saw the following process. Even including those of us who are trained in the scientific method, we could not live one day if we had to have demonstrable proof that each of our actions would be safe and successful. We rely on habits that have proven themselves. Moreover, how did we grow to trust these patterns of behavior? I think it goes something like this: A new fact comes in and we file it away with a date and perhaps with other ideas somewhat like it. Then it tends to recede in memory if it is not reinforced, but if anything comes in like it and supports it, it is pulled back closer to our consciousness. However, let us consider the case where we immediately meet this new idea with doubt and disapproval because we do not think it relates to anything we already know. It is as if it has a black mark across it, obscuring it, which will make it difficult for a new, similar idea to connect with it, strengthen it, and bring it back up out of the depths of memory. I was shown this connecting and shifting going on constantly in our minds. How often have we said, 'Now, that's impossible!' and then sometime later, when more information has come to light, wished we hadn't said that?

"So, how can we remedy this hasty judgment, which is holding up our enjoyment and utilization of an idea which could turn out to be of value? What I was shown was that if the idea does not receive support, it will gradually fade away so we don't need to reject it. Instead, we can train ourselves to receive gratefully everything that comes to us, without judging it. Remember it could be years before the reinforcement comes in. Is it not true that the only time we have to *assess* our knowledge is when we are going to *act* and then, hopefully, we select an idea that has received the support and reinforcement of related ideas, is a member of a group of thoughts, an idea that has been tested in our own life for its effectiveness? But sometimes don't we get bored and try something new just to satisfy our curiosity and for the excitement of it? Or is this only for the pioneering souls among us?

"With this attitude of withholding judgment, nothing we experience can be lost that might be of future value. Is not this how 'open-mindedness' actually operates? This model has certainly helped me. If you like, you could keep it in mind as you read some of the more unusual miracles reported in this book and file them away for future reference."

As we walked along, the trail curved and we could see the beach down a long ravine, the trail following the stream. White lilies dotted one side and on the other was a group of cypress trees sculpted by the offshore winds. We were excited by the low rumbling of the surf and the bracing sea air in our faces.

Then my companion said, "For some time I have wanted to know more about your background. You must have had some unique experiences and training to prepare you for this unusual career as a healer that could be inspiring for your readers."

I thought for a moment and then answered, "Well, first of all, to me everyone is unique, and there haven't been any doors that were opened to me that could not be opened to anyone whose Divine Plan, and desire, includes preparation for healing work. I can see that these 'miracles' could be encouraging to my readers, but when I begin to open up my early memory banks, it becomes clear that they deserve an entire chapter—there were so many of them. 1973 was the year I was opened to co-create music with higher dimensions. As I look back over the years prior to that (1960-1973), it was almost as if there was some kind of conductor saying, 'Notice this, don't notice that; hear this, ignore that.' This resulted in the building up of a consistent body of knowledge. There was still, often, the challenge to synthesize, that is, incorporate new knowledge. This usually meant finding a larger context, which would include concepts that, at first, seemed to differ. How much of this was my early natural desire to search for the truth behind appearances and how much was the guidance of the masters in spirit, I don't know, but I will be eternally grateful for this enlightening undergraduate degree."

"Then there was my gradual spiritual development. I began as a skeptic, with a sensitivity to nature. It was through experience and revelations from 'higher' beings, not through any organized religion, that my awareness and understanding of higher octaves of benevolent beings and the Supreme Being grew. Of course, it is possible to have these experiences through an organized church, but one runs the risk of getting caught up in dogma, what I call frozen revelation which has to be unraveled and sorted out later on. I was led to study accounts of personal illuminations—cosmic consciousness—experienced by the founders of our major religions and then to see this revealed truth gradually frozen into rules by their followers who had not been blessed by revelation and had often lost the essence of the master's teachings. (Footnote: See *Cosmic Consciousness* by Bucke in the Bibliography in the Appendix.)

"While I honor all religions since they contain truth, I can understand the current disenchantment with many of the organized religions. Their sins against people have come from the men—and sometimes women— in charge and should never be attributed to Deity. For example, Infinite Intelligence and Love never condones war. War is always a failure of negotiations. The fact is that in these difficult times people desperately need and want the truth. We are seeing all the hidden evil—"live" spelled backwards—coming out to be dealt with and we need Higher Principles to help us learn from this, heal it, and release it. Then we can move forward to a higher, more positive and loving, octave of life. In this book, you will find much to inspire you on your path toward recognizing your own version of the Light and the Love and expressing it."

The beach was strewn with wood, shaped and polished by the surf, and also a few trees, gifts from the larger river just up the coast during the recent storm. We found a tree with two branches opposite each other and sat down to rest. Whenever I am on a beach, I am aware of being on the dividing line between the land and the sea and have a choice of being a sea creature or a land creature—or both. As I tuned into the sound of the surf and the devic and angelic forces creating its rhythms and music, I remembered the *Sea Suite* that I composed for the harp in the 60's. I realized I was co-creating with the unseen forces of nature ten years before I began conscious channeling. This unique composition introduced 15 new, special effects on the harp and included sections of improvisation, precursors of creating music under higher guidance. After a few minutes, my companion said, "What else are you going to share with us in your book?

"First of all I'm asking my clients to report on their consciousness-changing experiences with the music: some short ones covering many types of responses, and some longer ones. Then my research into accessing the subconscious with muscle-testing, called 'kinesiology,' has developed a lot in the last 20 years. So there's a whole chapter devoted to a 'hands on' manual on how to do that. Next I'll offer the method I have been shown, and practiced with great success, for helping a client process, learn from, and release their past in this life and even past lives.

In addition, I would like to report on twenty-five years of talking to trees, plants, and animals. I think you will find these wonderful stories, suggesting 'the oneness of all life'. I have a special story by one of the experts in this field that I heard at a conference on "Interspecies Communication." Then, with the importance of relationships in these challenging times—I now call them supreme workshops—we are delving deeper into the nature of the feminine and the masculine. I will offer processes from my workshop, which explores this fascinating polarity outside of us and within each of us. This is one of the more hilarious of my seminars. But before all of this, just for fun, I will invite you readers to accompany my wife and me on a model journey around Europe, highlights of the 17 tours I have completed to 'centers of light' in those very interesting countries and cultures. Of course there are a few 'miracles' along the way.

"Other offerings include a detailed definition of love, and new, more understandable, names for the days of the week. I will also add affirmations I have found valuable, as well as a proven technique for instant healing of the Physical-Etheric body. There will be insights about The Source—or whatever name you like to use. Actually I will be using various names for this: Almighty, Everliving, and Everloving God, Infinite Intelligence, Eternal Love, The All That Is, Supreme Being, Love/Light, Everywhere Beingness, and more. In addition, I will present—again, because I presented it in my last book—a fresh, new, inspiring, logical, and singable name for our Creator. I should hasten to add that I approached this assignment with the greatest temerity, but my guides and masters gently and firmly talked me into it."

My friend said, "Now that sounds like a tasty and satisfying banquet of many gourmet courses. I can't speak for your readers, but I just can't wait."

And I said, "Thank you so much for your interest. If I am successful this book will reflect the totally positive view of our life on this planet that my Sources hold and will constitute a rich treasure chest of miracles and insights my readers should find inspiring, uplifting, healing, and valuable in their life journeys. My commitment is to recreate the large and small revelations of my life as faithfully and accurately as I possibly can, while maintaining a deep respect for my readers' fundamental Divinity. So, dear readers, before we embark I want you to know that I love you all as my brothers or sisters and the principles in this book are only suggestions. I honor your free-will choices. I know that only if you respond to something I say, and act on it, could it be life-changing. If it's made part of your consciousness, applied to life and found to be effective, then it becomes your bona fide possession and I have achieved my purpose: to promote your well-being and life on earth. If you don't respond to something I present, please just record it for possible reinforcement at a later date, and don't waste your precious energy worrying about it."

At that point, as I looked at my friend's face, I saw many faces pass over it, increasing to a blur, and I realized who he was. He was the composite of all my readers, who came to be with me when I wrote *A Harp Full of Stars* and was the perfect companion and questioner for that revelation. And I wondered if it might be possible that one or more of my master friends in spirit worked through this one.

I said, "Now I recognize you. Thank you so much for returning. Would you consider accompanying me through the writing of this book? I would be deeply grateful." And he replied, "I would be delighted. I anticipate with pleasure the revelations and higher principles that will emerge. There is such an accelerating need for this kind of positive reinforcement among the people of Earth at this time—it will support the Spiritual Renaissance. You know, it is not predictable what can come forth from a successful co-creation between a human and the spirit realms and beings—it can be exciting, awe-inspiring, wonderful and new." It was at this point that I remembered his name: Mykael.

My wife, Serafina, had invited my friend to dinner, so on the way back he asked me to tell him a little about her. And this gives me a chance to introduce her to you as, from time to time, she will be adding her inimitable, feminine insights to this odyssey. Serafina is truly a Renaissance woman. She left home early to begin her first career as a concert ballet dancer, eventually touring internationally. Then she spent 15 years as a classical Spanish and flamenco dancer and explored creating dramatic roles. Then she took up the folk harp so she could continue to play the flamenco music in her concerts. After we married, she wanted to study the concert harp with me. I declined, being not so sure that was a safe role for me to undertake as her husband. But with her insistence, I agreed, promising that I would drop that role at the end of each lesson. She wanted to learn the superior hand position and finger-action in which I was trained, the Salzedo Method, so she had to agree to not play any of her old pieces for a year. We ended up playing concerts together, one in Tokyo, and producing a CD together called *Paradise Bird*.

Her marriage to me brought with it a higher octave of spiritual awakening and study and one day she asked me to give her a new name. I hesitated with the responsibility, but she insisted. I asked for guidance and came up with Serafina, which means "angel." Through the years, I have become increasingly aware that part of her is from the angelic realm and sometimes I say, "I finally manifested my angel." Soon after that, she opened as an oracle for a group of angels and masters and she began channeling poetry and counseling for individuals. Also, for many years she has been diligently developing as a painter, bringing forth angelic images and scenes to raise consciousness and help the viewer attune to spirit guidance—her fifth or sixth career, depending on how you count them. And yes, she is fascinated with the arts of the Italian Renaissance. Looking more closely at her name today, I see that it actually means "to be (sera)" and "fine (fina)" And you could add to that, from the song "Que sera, sera"—"what will be, will be." Don't both of these meanings go along with "angel"?

Joel Andrews on tour with world-renowned healer, Jomanda

2

Odyssey to Europe

Before I report on the many miracles of my healing work with the harp, it has been suggested that you might enjoy hearing about some of my activities since my last book. Right away, it occurred to me to take you on a month-long model tour of Europe. This could be highlights taken from my diaries of sixteen tours—eight of them with my favorite companion, Serafina. Therefore, I am inviting you and Mykael to join us as we tour Belgium, Holland, France, Italy and Switzerland. I seem to hear you say, "Now that sounds very exciting and I have been planning some kind of vacation." I say, "I'm so glad you'll take me up on this invitation—it should be a unique and rewarding odyssey, with many miracles along the way. You have five days to pack as I've already made reservations for our flight to Brussels."

We have reserved a van, which will hold four of us and the harp. Gas is expensive in Europe so we fill up with diesel and we are off for Antwerp to pick up the harp. I found this harp many years ago and it was somewhat of a miracle. My harp is a Lyon & Healy with slightly increased spacing between the strings in the lower register, making it a challenge adjusting to a harp with regular spacing. The Antwerp harp is a "sister" of my harp, made in 1925 within 2 weeks of mine, in the same Chicago factory. So it has the same spacing between the strings. I only have to play on it a couple of hours and I am ready for a concert or a workshop. The owner uses the harp but only for one tour out of 17 was I not able to rent it. The tone of harps gets richer with age until they develop cracks and have to be rebuilt. The Antwerp harp has a wonderful tone quality but has had a large crack for years, for which I pray each tour.

As we continue, I remark to Serafina, "It certainly feels good to be in a more mature part of the world. Do you feel it?" She replies, "Oh, yes, and I love the accumulation of culture going back into history. Of course, in the background are the memories of wars and plagues and the human hardships that accompanied them. By the way, in terms of a person, how old would you say America is?" After some thought, I say, "Youthful: big and strong, full of enthusiasm, somewhat impetuous, and not too wise, but carrying a bright destiny of freedom and hope for the world."

A good night's rest, some practice on the harp, and we are off for central Holland. Our destination and first engagement is with Jomanda, "The Lady of the Light," in Tiel—right in the middle of Holland. She is, without doubt, one of the foremost healers in the world, so it was my privilege and honor to encourage her early in her career. She has recently converted an enormous sports arena in Tiel to accommodate the three to four thousand needy souls who come twice a week for healing.

She says the music I bring through enhances her work. She has 200 spirit doctors working through her and I suspect that they work with my own masters and angels to bring forth healing music through the harp. I have worked with her on almost every European tour. In the early years we traveled to most of the small towns in Holland, but now, since her many appearances on radio, television, and her healing sessions along the railway lines, a larger, central venue has become necessary.

Then you ask, "How did she get started?" And my response is, "Her father, who was a doctor, died just before she was born. She missed him more than she could admit at the time. She developed a career in ballet but as her sensitivities opened up, experienced more and more serious skin problems. Nothing helped until a well-known clairvoyant told her that her inner self was crying out for her father. This brought gradual relief and increasing rapport with her father and his associated physicians on the inner planes. In spite of disbelief, and sometimes ridicule in the press, her miraculous healing abilities developed into many forms and, along with this, her personal protection from negative forces."

We arrive in Tiel. A parking place has been reserved for us at the stage entrance and we unload and set the harp on stage. Long lines of people are entering, buying some of the water Jomanda has energized from the mountain of crates stacked up in the foyer. We take our reserved seats and at the appointed time the song that Jomanda was given to prepare people appears on the screen. It is simple but very moving, the music comes over the loudspeakers, and we all sing. As we finish, she descends a staircase dressed in a many-pleated Grecian gown. She is warm, but business-like, and begins by announcing how many people will go into trance—what she calls "narcosis." Heads begin to drop as she reminds us not to touch anyone in trance. They are under the control of the spirit doctors and, even though their actions sometimes appear bizarre, no one is ever hurt. Soon after this, a few people in trance, begin walking, even running, around the arena. We are told by Jomanda not to be concerned with what we observe—

that people are doing exactly what they need to be doing for maximum healing.

On the stage behind her are 30 massage tables and, as she invites people up from the audience, they are quickly filled. She is guided by the doctors to select those who are ready for this type of "horizontal" healing. Then she is guided to certain people in the audience by saying, "11th row, 15th seat, the lady in the pink sweater." Then she gives personal insights such as, "Your relations with your neighbor could get much worse if you don't resolve them with some love soon. This situation has its roots in a past-life where one of you ended up dying in prison. You both have come in to learn from it and heal it." All of a sudden, Jomanda says, "Everyone whose left knee is hurting may stand up" and 450 people arise. She turns to resume her work with individuals, only returning to the "knee people" 20 minutes later. During this time, she is working with those who brought photographs of family members who have passed on, loved ones, or pets.

Next, she announces that she will present her profile to the audience and anyone who looks closely may see the face of the person with whom they need resolution the most. After some minutes of this she comes up on stage and is guided to ask certain ones how they are doing. We can hear this conversation and she is explaining to us and the patient the progress of the healing.

Of course, all of this is absolutely fascinating—a revelation of what is really going on with us humans—but also a demonstration of how much, and intelligently, we are loved. Repeatedly our fundamental Divinity is revealed and the basic reason for all of our challenges is shown to be learning. All of this has taken some four hours and Jomanda announces that I will play to bring healing through music. I quickly check the tuning of the harp; say an affirmation, and put heart and soul into the music the higher beings give me.

After about 20 minutes, Jomanda returns and suggests that anyone who was involved in incest may stand up. She has been helping these souls for some months and 500 people, mostly women, stand up so the doctors can give them healing all at once. Then I notice a girl in the audience who I remember from three tours ago. She was involved in a very serious automobile accident but has been steadily improving. As I watch her, she goes into trance, slumps down to a sitting position on the floor and slides along, everyone clearing the chairs in front of her. After 50 feet, she arrives behind a man in a wheelchair who Serafina and I also recognize from previous gatherings. She stands, eyes still closed, and places her hands first on his head and then on his shoulders. On a subsequent tour, while I am playing, this man will rise up out of his wheelchair and walk.

Three hours later, she asks me to play again and by late afternoon, it is time for a meal. The four of us line up at the cafeteria and when we are seated, we have time to compare notes. You speak first, "What an extraordinary experience! I do not know what to make of it yet, but I saw incredible things, especially the feats of strength and the bodily contortions achieved by the patients on the stage. One man was lifting and balancing the whole massage table! How is that possible?" I reply, "I think the spirit doctors help them do whatever they need to do for their healing." Then you ask, "Are there other miracles she facilitates that we didn't see today?" Serafina says, "I have seen people receiving what look like chiropractic adjustments." And I add, "Oh, yes, and some of my friends have said she can take on different colors for different people, which are seen as meaningful by the observer, according to a system of symbolism. Also friends have reported that a piece of jewelry can be engraved with a pattern or word that is a significant healing message. Or it can fall apart, indicating that whatever they're concerned about, or holding onto, needs to be processed and released."

Then Mykael interjects, "Did you all catch it when the doctors were working on a women's husband who was not even present and then her mother who was in the hospital? Apparently time and space are no obstacles for the healers in spirit." And I say, "I can corroborate that from past sessions." And there are two other things I remember from the eight past tours I have worked with her. People often have scars from the inner plane operations. They are not painful and usually disappear much more quickly than "worldly" scars. Then, more recently, people are seeing numbers around her, which later become significant.

Then you ask what the circular pathway with the plants was all about and Serafina answers, "Isn't that for people who wish to see the past-life actions that are behind the current challenges with which they are working?" I reply, "Yes, that's right, Jomanda was guided to install it just before our last trip, two years ago." And Mykael says, "Haven't you called on the doctors apart from your musical creations: that is, for reasons of your health?" I answer, "Oh, yes, seven or eight times, for myself and for others. The most significant of these was when I went into the hospital for my hip replacement. This was after 50 years of lugging my harp around 12 countries. I was guided to an excellent physician, the operation went well, I had no pain, and my recovery was short compared to most patients. I was so grateful. Oh, I almost forgot, Jomanda passes out cards that have been charged with healing energy that usually last for about 6 months."

Then you ask, "Well, has Jomanda ever danced to your co-created music?" I reply, "Not in these larger gatherings but when we toured the small towns, she often did. She explained that seeing her dance helps to free up physical movement for those who need it, and it encourages everyone to celebrate and enjoy life. One thing I learned from this is that our higher guides and masters are willing to show us how to use everything we have learned for a higher purpose, in Jomanda's case, her early ballet training."

After supper, we take a walk outside the arena and Serafina asks me, "What about healing the animals?" I hasten to reply, "Oh, thanks for reminding me. A few years ago, it came to Jomanda that people's pets were taking on the problems of their owners, and vice-versa. After considerable alterations to the arena, and negotiations with the town authorities, this unique day took place. The animals were amazingly well-behaved. There was very little barking of dogs. It was almost as if they knew what was going on. But of course, they were probably also responding to the spirit doctor's guidance Much deep healing took place with the animals and their masters and one very valuable racehorse was rescued from a forced retirement.

After a lull in the conversation, Mykael says, "I know we're leaving for the south tomorrow. Is there anything else you might share with us that would fill out our picture of Jomanda and her work?"

"Well, after years of all kinds of healing miracles through radio, television, railway appearances, and sleeping four to six hours a night to answer personal letters, Jomanda's outreach expanded to the point where 6,000 needy souls attended the Great Hall in one day. At another location, she physically touched 13,000 in one long day! Finally, a group of doctors, feeling her competition for their patients, and, not understanding her work, thinking she was some kind of quack, launched a campaign to stop her. A trumped-up case was arranged where it appeared she had advised a cancer patient who, not going to a doctor, died. This was not true, but a court case ensued lasting some years, resulting in an injunction against her working in public for a year and the closing of the arena in Tiel. My heart, and the hearts of all those who had received miraculous healings, went out to her during this time of "crucifixion." Yet, it had an upside: she began traveling to many countries to help the underprivileged—especially children. I remember hearing she had 6,000 attendees at one meeting in Japan."

"Since then, I have collaborated three times with her and the spirit doctors at her smaller center in the south of Holland. Serafina reminds me that we arranged an evening for her in our hometown on the coast north of San Francisco, California. We drew 250, even though no one had heard of her before we started spreading the word. Then I also included her in a concert I presented in Victoria, Canada."

I will forever be grateful for the opportunity to work with Jomanda and serve her remarkable doctors, but also for all I've learned about my fellow humans, the art of healing, and the variety and accessibility of miracles. She has demonstrated these miracles for all to see and set a rare example of integrity, dedication, and humility. These qualities I am always trying to emulate.

There is evidence that one of her past lives was Saint Bernadette of Lourdes. Some years ago, she took a busload of her more experienced students to Lourdes. She was asked to clean out and heal that center of all the negative patterns the thousands of supplicants have dropped there through the centuries. I've had the honor of co-creating a similar cleansing of the power center of Glastonbury."

As we head south the next morning, still filled with awe at what we experienced the day before, I introduce to you and Mykael another miracle that unfolds gradually on this odyssey. This one involves Serafina co-creating a book of poems with her guides and masters.

We have to go back to the first night after we arrived in Brussels to tell you how it began. During the night, at the bed-and-breakfast by the woods, Serafina was awakened to write down the title, *Keys of Passage*, followed by a Table of Contents of 32 titles of poems. With some puzzlement, she showed them to me the next morning. I was impressed with the subjects covered so I encouraged her and then I said, "I wonder how long it will take to complete these poems—weeks? months?"

Coming through sometimes more than two a day, they will all be completed by the end of our month-long tour. One thing I find amazing, and you will remember this afterwards, is that she has difficulty with locks for the rest of the tour. I'll report two more miracles with these poems as they occur on our odyssey.

Next, I am slated to present a concert in Antwerp for the followers of a clairvoyant and spiritual teacher, Marie Diamond. She has scheduled the concert on the day people honor St. Michael and has secured a somewhat contemporary church sanctuary. She has suggested we take rooms at an old villa, a bed and breakfast east of Brussels called "The Scent of the Lord." We arrive early and, while the rooms are prepared, we explore the extensive gardens. Sauntering along well-planned pathways through verdant foliage is a welcome respite from the freeways. Some of us are wondering if the owners decided that the aroma of God must be flowers.

As it turns out the only room for Serafina and me is on the third floor, up narrow, winding stairs, impassable for the harp—and me with a unique program to prepare. The more angelic aspect of me, with complete trust, improvises under the guidance of higher beings but my human aspect is more comfortable having a rough idea of what I am going to play. So the only solution is to sit in meditation, ask for higher guidance, and imagine what I am going to play, something I have never done before. Spending most of the day in this fashion, I end up with a basic plan, hoping I can leave the rest to my friends in spirit. I do incorporate, after Intermission, the first five pages of a piece I have just composed that celebrates the element Earth, from my major suite, *The Five Elements*. It is called, *Lydian Madrigals for Gaia*.

The acoustics in the sanctuary are phenomenal for the harp and the concert goes quite well, except for another test for me: a string breaks about 20 minutes into the program. Even though a string hardly ever breaks during a concert, I had to train myself early in my concert career for this eventuality. I have to show no reaction to the inner shock to my nervous system, but also, since I am improvising, prepare myself for the absence of that note for the rest of the piece. I quickly say to myself, "All right, the rest of this composition can exploit all the other notes and that should make it especially rich." Similar events happen in life, don't they, and I think this principle has helped me adjust to my personal surprises. Someone made a recording of the concert and when I listened to it, I could hardly hear the "last gasp" of that string. No one mentioned it after the concert so I guess that, never having heard it before, the audience blanked it out. On the other hand, were they so wrapped up with the music that they assumed it was a sound in the sanctuary? A few days later I learned that a lady who attended the concert had been slated for back surgery but when she was examined by her doctor she no longer needed it. After the concert, over dinner, I say, "Tomorrow I'm giving one of my most interesting workshops, or what I prefer to call 'playshops,' and you're all invited. It is for those who want to work more deeply with the co-created music." Mykael responds with, "I've attended that workshop and I would love to experience it again but this is the only day I'll have a chance to see an old and dear friend in Ghent." You and Serafina say you will attend and we make our way to our beds.

Twenty participants show up for the playshop and I lie them down to prepare to receive the music. First I lead them in some relaxation techniques. Then they ask their bodies—all their bodies—to be super-sensitive to the sounds, so they can take them in, and they can do their work. I ask them to have a fantasy to the music and to remember it. I have been trained to help them understand the deeper symbolism of their fantasies, according to the system given me by the sources. These always turn out to be not only revelations about the past and the present but significant signposts suggesting the next optimum step on their spiritual path. It is uncanny: when I first hear the fantasy, I don't know what it means, but as the person repeats it image by image, it knits together until we all understand it. Of course, we all can learn from each other's fantasies.

We return the noble harp, which has become almost one of our companions, to its owner in Antwerp. She generously allows us to leave some of our luggage with her as we continue our odyssey south to Italy. A friend has recommended a beautiful, natural park southeast of Brussels and we arrive there just after lunch. It is one of those perfect days. The sun is shining, a relief after overcast Holland, and we appreciate strolling along the wide paths of the park through lush greenery under tall trees. Passing two small lakes, we come upon a man who is weaving old-fashioned baskets. Entranced by the inspired functionality of his work, Serafina buys a tray which we still use today, after ten years. This old-world craftsman told us that he harvests his own reeds.

It dawns on us that the park closes around five, and it is about that time, and we are still some 50 feet from the gate. We hear a loud honking behind us and, looking back, we discover that about 25 geese are rapidly closing in on us. We rush to the gate but find it locked. Remembering from a childhood experience that an aggressive goose can be dangerous, and multiplying that by 25, I am somewhat panicked. Fortunately, we find a gap in the fence about 15 feet to the left of the gate and escape just before the geese reach us. When we recover, I ask, "Do they train those birds? Or are they just claiming their after-hours jurisdiction of their habitat?"

The next morning we are on our way to Provence in southern France. Our goal is to reach Lyon, one of the centers of French cuisine for lunch, and then push on to the baths at Vals-Les-Bain. A soak in these hot, mineral-rich waters is the perfect antidote for the stresses of playing concerts, giving workshops, and driving. After the sweet balm of the baths we are ready for a bed-and-breakfast and a nap. Driving around the hills nearby, I notice a small sign that says "*cham-*

bres"—rooms. We cross a bridge over a deep gorge and a rushing river and discover a handsome mansion surrounded by bountiful, well-kept gardens and magnificent pines. We are met by the new owner who speaks just enough English—her husband speaks almost none. She ushers us into high-ceilinged rooms on the second floor, elegantly decorated, and overlooking the garden. We are all quite impressed with our good fortune, finding three rooms in this magical, old-world villa. She invites us, as soon as we are settled in and rested, down for a glass of wine.

In general, I have found the French to be guarded with Americans but we soon learn that she has just opened this bed-and-breakfast and is anxious to please. I offer to bring down a bottle of wine but she says no. Her husband goes to the kitchen, returning a few minutes later with a tray of white wine. It has a unique bouquet and flavor, and she explains that they have added a sweet infusion of the herb lemon verbena. It is a new and marvelous experience for us and, after two of these, all language and cultural barriers are dissolving and we are sharing like old friends. The husband is remembering some English, Mykael and I are coming up with more and more French, and our hostess with more and more English. They are recounting the history of the estate. The trees along the gorge are mulberries because the abandoned building there was a silk factory. They wove silk fabrics and produced high-fashion shoes for designer shops in Paris in the 1800s. After a light supper we retire late to our beds, four happy travelers—one or two of us probably dreaming of a life in southern France in the 1800s.

The next morning, after a special French country breakfast and a walk in the garden, we are making our heartfelt farewells, when our host and hostess present us with a CD. It is a concert they just enjoyed, featuring the orchestral music of the composer Gustav Mahler. This was especially satisfying as we consider ourselves citizens of the world; but we are seldom accepted as such so quickly, especially in France. The whole time at this charming bed-and-breakfast was unforgettable.

We head out for the little town of Apt, which is about two hours north of Marseilles. We are invited for dinner by a healer friend of ours, Yvette de Gueltzl or, as she prefers to be called, "Kyllikki." The landscape becomes drier, reminding Serafina and me of southern California, our birthplace. We see the special light that illuminates the canvases of the Provence painters, van Gogh, Cezanne, Renoir, and the others, and then we see the sunflowers and the tall, slender green poplars we remember from these paintings. Mykael asks, "Could we visit

Grasse? As you know, it is one of the perfume capitols of the world. I am making a study of the healing properties of aromas and I would love to have at least a brief look at how they extract the essences from the flowers and herbs. Would that interest the rest of you?" After everyone nods, I reply, "I don't see why not; that's right on our way to the coast."

We enter Yvette's valley and very soon see, and smell, the fields of lavender. What a magical scent it is. Finally, around three, we cross a creek and pass the small oak tree that gives her estate its name, "Petite Blacque." Then her group of one-and two-story buildings come into view. They follow the contour of the hill and are constructed from the local, pale-gold sandstone. After hugs and greetings, she invites us to have a swim in her new swimming pool. Later she offers us champagne with a nip of Pim's Cup, a liqueur, added and announces that the local chanterelle mushrooms are in season and she will take us mushroom hunting in the morning. She serves us chanterelles as part of the dinner and we report on our day with Jomanda. After a tasty country dinner, we dance to Latin music, as is Kyllikki's tradition. After awhile I sit down to catch my breath and I see Serafina pass by, executing fancy Tango steps. Later she explains that her partner is a well-known tango teacher and that slight variations in the pressure of his fingers led her across the floor. Of course, Serafina has years of experience in ballet and flamenco dance.

At breakfast, Yvette tells us that there is, that day, a huge craft fair in the center of Apt. So, after mushroom gathering, we pack up and attend this colorful, festive fair. We do not have much room in our luggage but the salad utensils of 300-year-old olivewood and the tablecloths and napkins in Provence patterns are irresistible. Heading southeast, we pause in Grasse just long enough to tour a perfume factory. This proves to be fascinating, especially for Mykael, who is pleased that they make an effort to use natural methods to preserve the intrinsic vibrations of the flowers and herbs. In the store outside the factory, we purchase bags of "Herbs de Provence" which will spice up our cooking for months and remind us of this fragrant land.

As we leave Grasse, we are enveloped in a green cloud of the rich "Herbs of Provence"—even though we have stashed them away in our luggage. Our conversation is equally rich as we compare our personal impressions of France. Eventually we are sharing our growing anticipation for Italy and Assisi.

Joel and Serafina Andrews on tour in Belgium, France, and Italy. Taken in a Flower Market in Rouen, France.

3

European Odyssey Continues

After a night in colorful and artistically decorated Florence, we arrive in Assisi, the home of St. Francis. First we visit the three churches—one on top of another—built to honor this humble and dedicated saint. In the 12th century he left the comfort of his wealthy, fabric-merchant father and built a chapel, stone by stone, with a few of his loyal followers. He set an example of simple faith that founded a Catholic order that has lasted until this day. It is said that his peace and love attracted animals and birds to flock around him.

After admiring the art in these sanctuaries, we visit the huge basilica built in his name. In the center, where the arms of the cross intersect, is placed Francis' original chapel. History holds that when an earthquake all but leveled the enormous stone basilica, the chapel remained standing.

Now, do you remember that Serafina has been inspired to write poems every day of our tour for *Keys of Passage*? And that she has been having difficulty with keys and locks throughout our trip? After a nice meditation in Francis' chapel, we emerge into the basilica to find, descending the walls from the dome, 15-foot angels, carrying four-foot keys of gold. What a sign! Especially as Serafina has had doubts about the future of *Keys of Passage*: whether it would be good enough to be published and how it would be published.

As we recover from this miracle, I offer, "Well, you know that the Ascended Master, Kuthumi, who opened me as a channel for healing with the harp, and has given me much music, appeared on Earth as Francis. Perhaps he is watching over your project."

Later, at dinner, you ask, "Who were some of the other masters who took bodies?" Mykael answers first, saying, "I believe that Serapis Bey appeared as Akhnaten, the pharaoh who tried to turn his people away from the worship of many gods to one God." And I add, "That's what the records of the Ascended Masters indicate. I have also had the great honor of visiting Serapis Bey at his Temple of the Ascension on the inner planes under the sands at Luxor, Egypt. Once I brought through music from him. It was like hosannas of praise being sung by nine choirs of angels. The style was so like the master composer Bach that I finally had to corroborate my suspicion that this towering genius must have been overshadowed by this ascended master—and sure enough it was Serapis Bey." As I write this I am producing this elegant music on CD. It is called *Seraphic Aurora*, and it also contains *The Partita II in D minor* by Bach, which reaches its climax with the celebrated *Chaconne in D minor*.

I remember also to tell you all the story of an ascended master's embodiment as "Le Compte de St. Germaine" who appeared in body for 200 years, advising the kings and queens of Europe. He was active in the Rosicrucian Order, helping to prepare the way for the founding of America. It is said that The Declaration of Independence was being passionately discussed by the signers, most of whom were Masons and Rosicrucians who were dedicated to the Light. Just when an issue was being hotly disputed, a tall gentleman rose in the balcony and delivered a moving speech. This led to an almost unanimous vote and the signing of the revolutionary document that set forth the principles of freedom, representation, and honoring of the people that founded America. Shortly afterwards, realizing that it had been a closed session with all the doors locked, some of the founders asked, "Who *was* that man? It was St. Germaine. These three: Kuthumi, Serapis Bey and St. Germaine are members of the seven major "Chohans of the Rays": II, IV, and VII, respectively.

The day before we leave Assisi, we visit the retreat of Francis' female counterpart, Claire. I wander into a small chapel and there is Jesus nailed to the cross—but smiling. I am intrigued by this because I find it depressing always seeing him immortalized in anguish when we know he transcended and ascended. *The Urantia Book*, one of my most trusted sources, explains who he really was and is: "The Creator Son" in charge of our local universe, along with his consort, "The Creative Mother Spirit." As a Descending Order of Being, he earns his complete sovereignty over our universe by living the life of seven beings of his own creation, on seven different planets, the life of Jesus being the seventh and final of these bestowals. They are all described in *The Urantia Book*.

The crucifixion, for him, was the equivalent of our Ascension. Since he is created perfect, he evolves through service. So, as I sat there alone, in meditation, I understood his smile: being "nailed" to the cross symbolizes his destiny and triumphant surrender to the material world. And is not this world a creation of The Supreme Being? I then understood that this fully experiencing of our level of consciousness, and our physical life, gives us the faith that we can come to him, knowing that he has the compassion for our situation that comes from direct experience. Therefore, his smile suggests that we, too, can transcend the material world. I realized that his life was a supreme example of how to deal with our challenges.

At our last dinner in Assisi, as we share our amazing experiences, we're also feeling gratitude for our comfortable accommodations at the Ananda Center, a branch of the Kryananda Retreat in the Sierras of California. I remember playing concerts in their 50-foot dome and being given music by a sacred cedar named Ematana (see Chapter VII for story). We are filled with the Light of miracles as we head west for the ancient ruins of Pompeii and the legendary island of Capri. The second century town of Pompeii, near Naples, is incredibly well preserved as it was covered by volcanic ash from Mt. Vesuvius until fairly recently. It gives us a welcome chance to stretch our legs, after driving across Italy from the east coast to the west coast. The art on the walls appears almost as if it was painted yesterday, bringing to life the culture and habits of these early Romans. Our hotel tonight is on the cliffs overlooking the sea and the town of Sorrento—romantic.

The next morning we catch the boat for Capri. No cars are allowed on the island—a relief after the pandemonium of traffic around Naples. An almost vertical railway takes us up 60 feet and deposits us at the town square. The first sight we see is a church named "Serafina." What a special welcome. The isle of Capri is a jewel and we first explore one of the villas of the Caesars.

Then we enter a large Benedictine retreat center and soon discover a spacious sanctuary. There is not a soul here so we have it all to ourselves. Later we learn that this is no longer an active retreat. You and Serafina walk around, exploring the bas-relief that decorates the walls. It matches the muted, beige-gold of the walls, made from the local stone. I want to experience this space through sound, by chanting, so I ask Mykael, who has just closed his eyes in meditation, if that would disturb him. He nods a "no" so I begin to tone on the lowest note with which I can produce a healthy resonance and gradually ascend the scale. Usually one note will be louder than the others and this is the note of the room—the shape and materials of the room reinforcing that pitch. In the sanctuary, this note is especially loud and so I suspect that it was designed for its sound properties.

I begin to chant overtones and the space comes alive. I will explain overtones—The Law of Resonance in nature—soon, but I should tell you what happens next. I notice that behind where the priest would have stood is a roughly semi-circular concavity, which I suspect amplified his voice. So I ask Serafina, who by now is standing about two-thirds the way back, to compare my volume here with what it was when I chanted halfway back. She says, "It's definitely louder. That hollow behind you must be amplifying your voice." It is even louder when I turn around and chant *into* the cavity. Then I remember that a priest often chants as he faces the altar. This is why the church architects, lacking microphones and speakers, had to become masters of acoustics. I can also be heard perfectly at the rear of this block-long sanctuary. I am so inspired by this resonation that I chant overtones for 25 minutes and you three say you feel the peace, grounding, and expansion of consciousness. Later I remember that I have had former-life experiences as a priest and that perhaps I was reliving one here.

As we sit in the charged space, you ask, "What is the Overtone Series?" I answer, "It is the Law of Resonance which everything that vibrates follows. Picture, if you will, a low string on the harp. When I play it, its entire length vibrates, producing what is called the 'fundamental' note. *Simultaneously* and *spontaneously* it divides into two halves, each one producing the pitch an octave higher. Then three pieces—the fifth, four pieces— two octaves up, five pieces—the third, continuing on to infinity. It is a miracle. And since *everything* is vibrating at some rate, this law is manifesting throughout the natural world. Some astronomers are even finding these ratios among the planets as they are positioned around the sun."

In case you'd like to hear the first few notes of this chord, and you have a keyboard handy, start with a low C, then play the C an octave higher, the G above that, then ascending, C, E, G, Bb, C, D, E, F#, G. Keep in mind that the "Tempered Scale" on the piano was altered from the Overtone Series in the late 1600s, around the time of Bach. So the E, Bb, and F# should be lower. Devotees of returning to the true scale of nature call the "Well-Tempered Scale" the "Ill-Tampered Scale." I have been occasionally tuning my harp to the Harmonic Scales, over various fundamentals, for 30 years. I have to select one fundamental, which I do, knowing the intrinsic symbolism of each note. It takes longer to tune, but listeners often say, "Oh, that takes me home," which in a sense, it does. Of course, some wonderful music has been composed in the tempered scale, but nowadays are we not seeing a return to everything that is natural? I think that, as we grow in our sensitivities, there are some of us who are being somewhat debilitated by the tempered scale. I know that when I tune my harp to an overtone series and then tune back to the tempered scale, I am very aware of its inherent dissonance.

At this point Mykael says, "Perhaps you should explain the difference between these two scales, if you can avoid getting too esoteric." I say, "I'll try. On the keyboard the scale consists of 12 equal half-steps, unlike overtones, making it possible to transfer any pattern to different parts of the scale and from key to key; that is, scales starting from certain notes. This makes possible many patterns of variation. In contrast, each harmonic scale is autonomous, unique unto itself, so you would need an enormous instrument to embody a number of them. When I asked my master guides why the Tempered Scale came in, the answer was: 'to prepare people's minds for the scientific age. Remember, it came out of men's minds.' The pioneer proponent of the Overtone Series, in the 60's, was Harry Partch. He wrote a book called *Genesis of a Music*, built instruments, tuned them, composed the music, trained musicians, made recordings, and sold them. He was a one-man music."

With the rampant spread of many varieties of pollution—a form of dissonance—and the dying of many species, it is becoming increasingly crucial to honor the Divine Feminine and extend our gratitude through caring for Mother Earth. Our need to bring harmony into our lives has become desperate as we realize that our survival depends on the survival of the Earth. In music, this means returning to the Harmonic Series. I have waited for 25 years for the go ahead to play an entire concert in the natural scale and was recently awakened at 2:30 in the morning by my higher guidance announcing, "It is time." I just played the first concert. It required two harps, tuned beforehand, then a ten-minute intermission to retune one of them.

Serafina says, "Haven't I heard you say most of Asia tunes to scales based on the Overtone Series?" I respond with, "Oh, yes, and the major cathedrals of Europe would have long ago collapsed if the masons who designed and built them had not added the buttresses to meet the walls at harmonic node points. These are places of relative stillness: one-half, one-third, one-quarter, one-fifth, on up the wall. Remember our division of the harp string? Even the composers of the last 300 years show an instinctive honoring of the Harmonic Series patterns in their tempered-tuning music. It is not that difficult to learn how to sing overtones, I teach it in my workshops, and it is very healing, bringing harmony to your various bodies."

I hope that this has not been too technical for you, and that you are still with us. Please bear with me as I serve the musicians among us and those clients who have ordered individualized CDs in an Overtone Series tuning. They choose a fundamental out of the 12 notes on the piano that they feel will speak to their condition. I have some inspiring letters from these clients.

We're already feeling pangs of nostalgia as our boat pulls away from the dock and unforgettable Capri fades into the Mediterranean.

When one of us begins to sing the famous song, *T'was on the Isle of Capri that I Met Her*, we all join in. It is a sentimental song, but it fits our mood. As we land at Sorrento, we are realizing we must head for Antwerp to pick up our luggage and then to Brussels for our flight home. But I remind everyone that I have planned a few interesting stops along the way.

We cannot resist two nights in the unique floating city of Venice. In actuality, the city rests on huge trees, felled in Yugoslavia and sunk in the lagoon. The first night we hear a concert of Vivaldi and Bach by the world-famous Virtuoso Strings. The second evening is a chamber concert in a palace by two veteran opera stars, singing arias from the best-loved Italian operas. They are accompanied by stringed instruments and, believe it or not, a harp and a ballet dancer—just for myself and Serafina? They are all arrayed in colorful costumes and masks from their world-famous Spring Carnival Festival.

The second evening I have yet another unexpected miracle. As we walk along the Grand Canal, a voice behind me mentions San Francisco. I turn and say, "I live near San Francisco." The woman to whom I'm talking turns out to have been a harp student of mine in the 60's. She says she is still playing her harp and then adds that she would like to learn how to improvise. I say, "I've just devoted 30 years to developing that art and I would love to help you." All of us are dumbfounded, realizing that the odds against this happening are phenomenal.

We take the tunnel through the Alps and stop for lunch in Basel on the border of Germany and France. The restaurant is perched on a parapet overlooking the Rhine River. A small group of musicians is playing, first some Swiss tunes, then Dixieland, and then a Beatles Song. But then we remember that Switzerland is known for its international outreach. Driving through the gently rolling countryside of Alsace Lorraine we stop at two of the many vineyards to sample the unique Alsatian wine.

Presently we come upon a sign with a huge stork on it and we exit the highway to visit a stork sanctuary. We have been seeing a few of these large, white birds flying south and even some of their nests on the top of chimneys. We park and walk to the entrance, but find that most of the storks have migrated south to Africa for the winter and the sanctuary is closed. As we walk back to the van, Serafina notices, on the other side of the parking lot, a long, low building with a seven-foot high butterfly perched on its roof. Filled with curiosity we go to the entrance and find that they will be open for one more hour before they close for the year.

We enter a magical world of *papillons*. This humid, tropical environment is home to probably 50 varieties of butterflies, of a wide spectrum of exotic colors, some of them nine inches across. As we explore we observe all stages of their evolution. What an unusual treat—and somewhat of a miracle.

As we leave Alsace, we veer west to avoid the industrial district of Mannheim. Then continuing northwest we skirt Brussels and you remark, "Haven't we just completed a grand circle?" I say, "Yes, and in 45 minutes we'll be in Antwerp to pick up our luggage, with just a few hours to catch our flight home." There is one more miracle to go.

Elizabeth is on a trip to England but she has given us her father's phone number and he is waiting for us at her apartment when we get there. He reports that when he first arrived and opened her door the cat ran out and, as he reached to catch her, the door closed and is refusing to open with any of his keys. With the urgency of the situation, he has called a locksmith who, unsuccessfully, is trying to drill out the lock. Our clock is ticking and you say, "Are we going to have to board the plane without our luggage?" After an awkward pause, Mykael says, "Serafina, haven't you been having trouble with keys and locks on this trip? Do you think that this stubborn lock could possibly be related to that?" She thinks for a moment, and then replies, "Well I have finished all 32 poems of '*Keys of Passage*' and I'm just realizing that this could be a nudge to commit to publishing them —which I certainly will." Immediately, the drill goes "zzzt" through the lock. We retrieve our bags and head out for the air terminal to catch our flight home to California. On the way, we are reminiscing about the "once-in-a-lifetime" experiences of this odyssey and giving each other heartfelt thanks for sharing them. Then, about 15 minutes before we reach the terminal, after a few moments of contemplation, you say, "You know, I don't feel quite ready to fly home. I think I'll go on to the next chapter." And I say, "Come to think of it, that's where we're headed. Thanks so much for reminding us."

Lest you suspect that any of these experiences are invented, I hasten to reassure you that every one actually took place on tour. I will admit that they are selected from a number of tours. My 17 tours of Europe, Asia, Canada, the U.S., and the Caribbean have involved Serafina and me in many more such adventures and perhaps, one day, we'll write an entire book about them.

Joel and Serafina Andrews in concert.

4

Responses from Clients

In the following pages have added subject headings to help you find a specific testimony.

Let us turn now to the unique kind of music I have been co-creating with beings and forces in spirit since my last book and the remarkable healing effects it has had on my clients. I can hardly do better than step aside and ask them to relate to you their experiences. I have saved hundreds of letters of thanks from my clients and I am so grateful to have them so I can share them with you. They cover a wide variety of responses from simple to complex, mundane to spiritual, physical to deeply psychological, the healing of little irritations, even the resolution of long-held family grievances. Some of these, according to the clients, go back into past lives. Some are obviously weeping as they write, they are so moved with gratitude. Some of the thanks are directed to me and, of course, I do my part in bringing the music through for them, but a larger percentage is really due the shining presences, so brimming with love and wisdom, who develop the music and give it me, and then guide me in its interpretation.

My sources have helped me develop four methods of receiving their music: clairaudience, hearing with the inner ear; clairvoyance, seeing with inner vision; clairsentience, receiving sensations; and telepathy, ideas and concepts received by the mind. Whichever is the easiest and the clearest is used.

I should describe my process in co-creating this music. I have carefully tuned the harp and set the microphones and recorder. Next, I say an affirmation to clear myself of my own "stuff," my personal thoughts and feelings. Then I meditate for five minutes, coming to a deep state of peace and openness, start the recorder, and say the affirmation, offering myself for one of the many healing purposes described in this chapter. Then I go into a light trance. I hear music with the inner ear and play it on the harp. Once I begin I'm hearing the music intuitively and from the harp simultaneously. After I've finished the music and turned off the recorder, I meditate for a few moments to remember what I have seen and I sometimes receive important words for the client. Then I set up the recorder so I can record the Interpretation with the music in the background. After I give thanks, I make two CD copies of the session for the client. Here is one of the salient features of these responses. Even though they were written by people with a wide variety of educational experiences and backgrounds, they show, at times, a very creative choice of words, bordering on poetry, which you will see and, I hope, enjoy. I attribute this to the fact that they are still in a state of euphoria as they write. Of course, some have just had life-changing epiphanies. See what you think.

I have gone through these letters with the utmost enjoyment and satisfaction, and divided them into two main categories: the shorter ones for this chapter, and the longer ones, really mini-stories, for the next chapter. Then I have separated the short ones into the subjects that they cover, so you can appreciate the rich variety within each type of healing, but also so a reader who needs a certain type of healing can find a recommendation for a CD that could help. Then I have added some comments, drawing on what I have learned through the years about these revelations.

So now I introduce my clients to you so you can enjoy their experiences, not only as examples of healing but also as inspired steps along the path of spiritual awakening. I have edited these statements as little as possible, only for spelling and clarification, and I assure you I have added nothing to them. I have added some commentary, out of years of experience, to help you understand and expand the message. With the exception of four or five from *A Harp Full of Stars*, which I have included just to fill out the spectrum of applications, these have all come from the last 20 years, since that book. I will begin with some responses to my recordings.

REVIEWS OF CDS PRODUCED FOR USE BY ANYONE♦

The first five comments are by Susana Andrews, from her column in a magazine.

> "The tones of ***Iridescence*** are God/dessly exquisite. So beautiful, this music soothes and smoothes, creating an integrated feeling of seamless centering and harmony. Resistance evaporates, the tonic tones literally penetrating as a gentle mist—opening, liquefying, caressing, lyricizing, expanding, loving—creating ebullient lightness of being." — S. A.

> "***Splendor of Light*** is dramatic, compelling, and commanding. It quickens, expanding almost to bursting, creating tidal explosions and intricate, interlacing waves of pure, flowing energy, leading to

---

♦ For a listing and descriptions of my recordings please see my website: www.harpofgold.com

an evocation of angelic voicing. It creates a tugging, teasing, trilling, thrilling interplay of sound and light of an almost unbearable profusion and intensity! The drama of rapid sequence movement from octave to octave, from deep, resonant intonation to exquisite lightness of upper register tonality, implies a fuller orchestration of luminous overtones." —S. A.

"*The Violet Flame* is tender, its tones pure, precise, specific, intricate and graduated. At times purposefully tentative, hovering just long enough to be incisive, this music is as playful as a flame dancing—designing, ebbing, flickering, almost disappearing, then alighting anew in yet another molecular sequencing. *Violet Joy* is softly seeking, sensitive flourishing, formal formlessness, finding, feeling, filling—elegantly evanescing, all-encompassing rivulets and rills, unreserving. After teasing and infinitesimally tickling us, bringing us joy, the compassionate, lovely, luminous, living "Violet Flame" tip-toes away, leaving us transformed, revitalized and renewed."—S. A.

"The Violet Flame, the Law of Grace, may at any time be called forth. When an individual, through the magnetic power of the Heart Center, makes conscious attunement with The Violet Flame, there is an immediate increase in the vibratory rate of the inner atomic structure. The Light in the core of the atom itself intensifies its concentration to a point of vibrant radiation. This potent and brilliant radiation dissolves and transmutes all dense energy and all limiting conditions surrounding the atom, liberating any imprisoned elemental life forces, raising the purified consciousness to a profound realization of its true nature." — S. A.

"*Paradise Bird* with Serafina Andrews, harp, Peter Velasquez, kalimba and vocals, and Joel, harp and whistling, is a joyous Latin celebration! The songs and story of Perico, the Paradise Bird, will enchant and delight young and old, will set your feet to dancing to playful tunes and sensuous rhythms. Then, moving into the deep contemplation of *Chamber of the Heart* and on, *Ambhori* expresses the sweet rapture of lovers on being re-united after a long separation. In *Andalusian Fantasy*, an expressive collaboration by Joel and Serafina, your heart will be set singing with exuberant love, and your spirit soaring into sun-filled realms! This is a CD of light-hearted fun and fanciful flights of free imagination, sure to delight any child and the child within us all."—S. A.

General Comment on the Recordings of Joel Andrews:

"As you, the listener, hear these resonances gradually receding from each richly radiant harmony, you will feel a sigh of release, bringing deep fulfillment to the core of your being. If allowed, the lush opalescence of these many-hued tone poems will thrill you and raise your spirits to unimaginable levels of spiritual ecstasy, freeing your creativity. Following the steady pulse of this comforting music can lead you to profound peace and the experience of Divine Love."—S. A.

CHURCH

"At times words become inadequate vehicles of expression and this is such a time. How do we thank a beautiful spirit for bringing angels and blessings into our presence? Yet this is what you did for The Church of Inner Light on our Dedication Day. As no amount of groping will bring the right words to mind, we just say thank God that He loves us enough to bless us with your presence and the presence of the Ones you brought with you. God bless and keep you."—Reverend P.P.

CONCERTS

"At your concert (in a dome by the sea in Florida) I immediately found tears running down my face, spilling from a heart yearning to be back in balance. Later I felt the lifting, skull-shining brightness so familiar, but missing for so long. This, before I realized that it was more than a mere harp concert. I had no idea about you—I was there simply to hear a harp played in the magic dome by the sea. What a blessing you turned out to be! Thank you".—E.C.

It has happened quite often, where a person is guided, without knowing why, to attend a concert, which they later find to be uplifting. Was this their guides and masters? Their guardian seraphim? Their High Self?

"Thank you from my heart for the music at the end of the concert. I would like to share two experiences with you. First, by the end of the music I felt as if I were a pyramid of concentric circles. Second, somewhere in the middle, after you struck certain notes, I had a very clear feeling that I was meeting my grandmother again. I loved my grandmother deeply, but she died when I was eleven and it affected me very strongly. When people started leaving at the end of the concert, I was still very much far away in the music when an elderly woman in her early seventies came over and put her arms around me, held me, and said she had been watching me. She said she loved me and had really "come into" me. This was overwhelming for me and we hugged with me thanking and blessing her. Then, as there were no words, we both started humming as you do during the music. Then we parted. I do not know who she was or if I will ever see her again. I sat for a few moments, trying to let my rational understanding mind catch up. Then I remembered the part in the music that called up my grandmother and I cried.

"I do not know exactly what happened. When I was "out there" with the music, did I meet and touch the elderly woman, "out there" also? And then the only way I could understand it was to think of my grandmother? Or did my grandmother hold me again through this lovely woman? I do not suppose it matters exactly how it happened, but somewhere in there it struck me that this is what "Christ" means—this coming together in love, openness, and oneness. For the rest of my life I want this to happen again and again —nothing else really matters. So to you and your guides, teachers, friends, and loves, thank you and God Bless you."—R.

A College Lecture-Demonstration

"This was a great report. I learned so much and some of my questions about life, death and fate were answered—very interesting—and I would like to learn more. I have experienced examples of what Mr. Andrews has given. It made me aware of myself. I want to listen more to my angels.".—D.B. (age 19)

Concert-Lecture

"In gratitude, I write you for all you do and in thanks for all you touch. I wish to share some of my experience of your channeling, which has brought healing to me—and to us all. I am a maker of stained-glass windows and also play the violin. I've always felt a seriousness and joy with the windows, working with God's Light and letting the colors sing. I feel the possibility of healing energy by expressing people's individual sense of joy through glass and light. Then came my first church; everything perfect, and I freaked! But voices were telling me what to draw, as I prayed and resisted, feeling a previous life as a nun. I almost blew it. Then a patron sent me to Europe to study contemporary glass. Despite discouragement from everyone, and my own wondering why, I took my violin.

"Even after I returned, I hadn't accepted the significance of taking my violin until a counselor told me you were to play that night and again in a nearby town. After hearing you talk and play, I reflected on my experiences playing the violin in Europe. I was amazed as I remembered standing on the roof of a 14-story hotel asking for sounds to come for peace in the hotel and the city, then wondering what sounds might come for Barcelona and other towns I visited. And I found this poem in my trip journal:

Play me something sweet

Play me something lovely

Play me something for the joy of my unknown company.

"And I realized this music was a center for me on the trip when there was not much else and I discovered that music was a food for me. Yet, when I returned, I didn't remember this, dismissing myself as crazy. Then, at your concert, I saw movement above your harp, and I thought I was hallucinating an angel and my mouth dropped open when you mentioned that many others had seen her there also. I wore a skullcap of energy home, thinking it would keep me warm somehow, riding in my freezing truck, and then minutes later the broken heater began to work!

"The following day I played my violin and sure enough the design on my drawing board came to mind and I saw an image from the man who was to receive the window—something of his experience. This was totally new and a glimmer of possibility for me to use my violin to bring through designs. I realized I could even record what I play in meditation to use as background when I draw.

"I'm still walking with fear, but much closer to being without it, since experiencing your music. Not only did it show me my negativity, but also by the end of each concert it was gone and I was relaxed, full of love, and bubbling with expression. Thank you."
—J.W.

What an inspiring testimony to the importance of listening to the "still small voice" over the negative voices from our past that would keep us from our highest destiny. And here we see almost instant rewards that at times seem miraculous, like the broken heater working and seeing the angel over my harp. You can almost see her guides and masters trying to get through to her, but of course, they must respect our free will, which they do with almost divine patience, respect, and love. What a privilege and pleasure for me to be used to inspire another musician and artist to co-create with the celestial artisans. I have come to know, for myself, what primary food music can be. Her music inspiring her images is what they call "synesthesia," or translation between the arts that are connected to our different senses. This implies basic, universal underlying patterns which connect everything and which connect us with realms of spirit. I will speak later about the congruence between my clairvoyant impressions and the system the masters are using for the symbolism of all the elements of music, a congruence of which I am not consciously aware when I am co-creating the music.

> "I am hesitant to begin this, not knowing how to make myself clear. I have never asked a stranger for help before so part of me feels foolish for bothering you, but here I am writing it, not merely thinking about it, and this convinces me that it's correct. A friend just attended your concert and then shared your recording with me. I have listened to it many times in varying situations and always am haunted by the feeling, no, the knowing, that I have played this music before—two themes in particular, what I call the second on each side of the tape. It is difficult to explain the strength of this knowing as the answer seems to be just beyond my conscious memory, yet no rational, as opposed to intuitional, approach calls up the memory.
>
> "I have used the cassette in meditation and, aside from the other beautiful healing effects, I still have not been able to call up the memory. So I've been given a challenge to resolve by seeking out what lies behind this incredible knowing. I have studied piano and have a familiarity with all kinds of music but this is a first. Can you help me understand it? Does this kind of experience happen very often with your music? In any case, thank you for such incredible music."—L.W.

Only a few others have reported similar responses, but each has its uniqueness. One man sitting in the balcony at my concert experienced actually playing the music, sitting at the harp where I was sitting. One factor here is that after my 30-year career as a professional harpist playing many styles of music, my sources developed an amalgamated, universal style so that as many people as possible could relate to it and this probably helped L.W.'s experience. Secondly, it is possible that in a past-life scenario she was co-creating music with my sources. If she has had experiences where healing resulted from her music, this would tend to be corroborated. Third, as she listens to my recording my sources bring memories to her. In addition, there may be other explanations as well since we are talking about consciousness, universal and individual, and its kaleidoscopic variations. Music is certainly one of the most universal languages.

Music For A Relationship

"We have so enjoyed our individual and relationship music and interpretations. Thank you, thank you, for you and your gifts. Your influence and love have been wonderfully strong and deep. Ken and I just celebrated our 10th wedding anniversary, even though we were physically separated—he was away on a job. During our 'ceremony time' I lit a candle, played our 'soul music,' and danced."—S.

Music in general, and co-created music especially, can certainly help us transcend time and space, especially if Ken was listening at the same time.

Music For Transmuting Negativity

"Wow—what truly divine music! *The Violet Flame* is so beautiful. I can't wait to receive my next CD. I've never experienced anything like it. Thanks. I will want to distribute. Also, thanks to your staff for the speedy response—the angels must have flown the CD here themselves!" —L.

She is very perceptive. How could she know that a tape or CD has never been lost in 30 years and over 4,000 mailings. I often say, on my way to the post office, "O.K., masters and angels, this is your work, so I leave it to you to deliver it to this client." I have never had to do one over, or replace a general CD, one produced for everyone. Is this not a major miracle?

"I so enjoyed sharing energy with you and your wife after the concert at the Unity church. The angelic presence is very strong with your wife.

"My first experience with your music was *The Violet Flame*. My grandmother had just died and I was entrenched in a very negative job with negative people. As I first listened to the music, I felt my heaviness lifting and it allowed me the space to experience my grief and to release the anger over my job and be complete with both of these. Then I bought *Ave Maria* at your seminar. It is absolutely wonderful! I can feel my heartstrings responding and a feeling of calm pleasure comes over me. I know, within myself, your music is the key for which I have been looking. Love and Light always."—R.M.S.

So much untold, on-going misery, anti-life behavior, and ineffective living are caused when we don't process, learn from, and release the challenges life brings us. More often than not, we do not do this processing because we are "brought down" by the negativity that surrounds us. Here this unique music brought peace and connection with higher inspiration to catalyze a swift and complete healing. And this without the need or expense of a lengthy series of sessions with a psychiatrist. Of course, this could be an option in the future. Another principle that comes to mind here is that many factors can be helpful, but in the end we need to complete the work ourselves.

CREATIVITY WITH CHILDREN

"I thank the angels for Joel Andrews. The healing music channeled through him and his harp has deeply affected me and also the children I play with in my private practice. I experience a profound sense of peace and joy each time I listen to the music channeled for my personal healing. Surprisingly, it helps me step over "issues" which were previously stumbling blocks in my life and which gave me feelings of disequilibrium. Each time I listen, I am taken to my center point, which is most useful when I am out of balance with what is happening in my life.

"The children ask me to play their music. They say, "It helps me to move." These are children who have a behavioral and/or learning problem and cannot readily get their bodies to perform as they would like. One child said it helps him concentrate while he's doing his homework. It makes him feel calm and happy. The special educators who have heard your music for *Creativity with Children* have repeatedly asked to buy it for classroom use.

"We are all so grateful for Joel Andrews and his willingness to channel the music for our healing."—S.S.

MY BOOK: *A HARP FULL OF STARS*

"I want to tell you how excitedly I am reading your book and how much your music means to me. The quality of your performance at Golden Gate and the CD you gave us (*Iridescence*) are so pure and touching and marvelous! When I read your book and play the CD, I go into the wonderland of your thoughts—it's like finding a dear friend!

"I was astounded when I came to the section on the symbolism in names as I am in the process of changing mine. It is so encouraging and it removes some thoughts that I might be misdirected in doing this. I am so thankful for your years of study, pursuits on the path and mastery. I love your book. How courageous of you to write so openly!—G.S.

I do not remember anyone reporting reading my book while listening to the music. Of course, since they are both co-created with the masters, the music would raise the reader's consciousness, putting them in touch with their High Self, so that they could resonate and understand more readily the higher messages in the book. She is wise to be cautious in changing her name since, as I explain in the book, when you write your name, say it, hear it called and say "yes," and identify yourself inwardly with it, you attract the vibrations of each letter into your life.

The symbolism for the alphabet was revealed to me by the masters as an ancient science, going back centuries to Sanskrit, even Lemuria, and corroborated by my over 1600 analyses of names. I have even helped corporations select names for new ventures. I begin each session of co-created music by playing the name translated into pitches. This shows the masters in charge of the records that permission has been granted and is also the file name on the records, calling them forth. In the trade, they are called the "akashic records," "akasha" being the East Indian name for the substance upon which everything is stored that has taken place on Earth, including files on individuals. It was a great adventure and privilege for me to visit one of the five largest archives of these records where I was served by a holy "librarian" in charge and shown information that proved to be most valuable.

> "This book is the intimate life story of how, after years of harp playing, one man took a turn into eternity as he opened as a channel for the shimmering song of The Light."—L.M.

> "Joel reveals clarity of intention time and time again throughout this book. There is no better example of this than his sharing with us his practice of invoking and honoring Source through affirmation before each and every attunement or concert. And that he continues to do so. Inasmuch as each of our lives is a living legend, the potential experience within the pages of this book implies a profound step toward the sound and abiding presence of Love."—S.A.

When she says each of our lives is a living legend she is revealing the true meaning of the harp being "full of stars." We are all the hero or heroine of our life drama. The above quote is taken from a much longer, and sensitively written article about *A Harp Full of Stars*.

Manifesting A Love Partner

> "I wanted to send you greetings and tell you a short tale. At your concert, when you asked us to think on what we wanted for healing, I thought it was time for me to put energy into a relationship. By intermission a man I have known for years only as a friend was

sitting next to me and we have been in relationship ever since. Who knows where it will go but it has been a lovely experience full of personal growth. I simply wanted to share this with you. Also thank you for your loving support after your 'reading.'"—L.M.

This was twenty-five years ago and already things were speeding up on Earth! On the other hand L.M.'s almost instant manifestation of a partner could very well have been aided by the musical ambience created by the masters. Of course, we must not forget that she called it forth and opened herself to it.

CORROBORATION BY ANOTHER INTUITIVE

"I received my attunement some years ago, but I must tell you now that it is wonderful! I sometimes listen to it every day and the messages in it. It helps me very well to find my spiritual balance and it makes me very sure about the future. A lot of things in other lives came to me before and it's a great help to hear that they were O.K. and correct. It helps me to go further on my own way. Last year a medium told me the same as you did before (I hadn't told him about your work). Love and God's blessings."—E.B.B. (Dutch)

I love the Dutch people. Holland was the first country in Europe I toured and I have returned there 16 times. There is a special connection between Holland and America. They speak quite good English, but you will notice here a little "quaintness" of writing style. English is certainly the most universally spoken language, but it is not an easy language to learn.

AN APPEARANCE OF A GUARDIAN SERAPHIM

"Thank you for the *Seraphic Attunement* CD. It is really beautiful and some passages are like my *Soul-Path Re-Alignment*. I write you now about what happened late the other evening. I was listening to the "Seraphic Attunement" and I was thinking of the angels, especially my guardian angel, and I asked to see him. A few moments later, in that meditative state, I opened my eyes and right before me I saw a beautiful young man with short golden hair (it seemed like that). He was maybe 20-25 years old and he smiled very kindly at me. He was not dressed in a white robe, as I would expect of an angel, but like one of us. He looked at me very gently and then suddenly disappeared. My thought was "What a pity I couldn't talk to him and ask his name." I wish you both much inspiration and love for your further healing work. May the Light of God bless you two and I send my love to you both."—N.P.

You might assume that she imagined her angel (a projection) except for how he was dressed. This is what intuitives call "evidential," suggesting some kind of proof. What is more important than the picture one sees is the feeling one receives and its symbolic meaning—in this case the angel's youthful beauty, his golden hair—gold symbolizing wisdom—his smile of kindness, and his gentle look. We all have a tendency, especially at this time on Earth, to want to know the details, like his name. I hope this did not deter N.P. from fully receiving her angel's message. When she wants to know his name so she can call him forth later, this is putting energy in the future at the possible expense of the eternal present. She had already proven that she could manifest him. Is it possible that when her guardian seraphim realized that she wanted to *talk* about it, he made his exit? If I am exaggerating, it is only to share realizations that might be valuable to my dear readers. I do not wish, in any way, to diminish the beauty and value of this woman's vision.

Another valuable technique I would like to offer you is that when anything appears to you, it is wise to challenge it in the name of whatever you hold to be the highest. I use "The Living Christ," but there are many other names that carry the same power, love, and wisdom. I say, "If you come for my highest good, I welcome you and your gifts. If not, be gone at once in the Name and Power of the Living Christ." If they are not for your highest welfare, they will go "poof" and disappear, as they cannot resist what you have invoked. I have found this quite effective on countless occasions.

Ascended Masters

"After asking inwardly for guidance in a difficult situation in my life, I was definitely led to the three "Initiate" books (anonymous author). These books made quite an impression on me, have been quite helpful, and have reassured me of some of my previous beliefs. In these books, the master "Koot-Humi" is frequently mentioned and the name kept ringing a bell somewhere in my mind. In the last book, the author speaks of work to be accomplished in the future through "musical sound," but I connected it with your work only faintly.

"Then I had a persistent urge to pull out your CDs again, and as I was listening to *Locrian Invocation* and looking at the face (Kuthumi) on the cover, I saw the name "Kuthumi." It was like an electric jolt and I was sure the two were one. Since then I was guided to a book entitled *Kuthumi—Studies in the Human Aura* (Mark L. Prophet). On the back cover, it says that Kuthumi is also known as Koot-Humi. It seems amazing to me to have listened to your CDs, and benefited from them, and then to be directed to books dictated by the same master written 40-70 years ago which speak of healing music that will be available in the future—all of which I was led to without knowing of the connection between them! I was indeed given the help I asked for— in such a delicate and subtle way that I might have easily overlooked it. So thank you for your music—it has increased the light for me."—J.B.

Guidance from our higher selves, or our masters and angels, is rarely a strong message since they treat us with such respect for our free will. It is more like a suggestive nudge, but here we see the results of her listening to the "still small voice." The "electric jolt" was her shock of recognition. My instruction has been that The Creator of All That Is values and loves his/her creatures so much that dire consequences have been set up for beings like masters and angels tampering with our free will. Later I will expand on the Free Will Plan under which we evolve. It is worth noticing that it is called the *still* small voice, implying that we have to put aside the worldly chatter of our conscious minds in order to hear it. Is it possible that much of the suffering in the present day world is due to the many forms of hyperactivity: stimulants, advertising, propaganda, telephones, television, computers, and cell phones? One of my missions for the last 20 years has been to get people to slow down for quality and culture.

A Channeling From An Ascended Master

"Music. It is healing quality. It is vibration. It is an energy to be used in this way. You have a harpist, I believe and understand him to be Joel Andrews. He is of those who are receiving the energy. He is receiving it through the Master Kuthumi, on whose ray (Second) he happens to be. He is also on the Fourth Ray (Serapis Bey). Bless this man, for he is serving his purpose and he will do it nobly."—Jo Lala Kahn (1975)

This was just three years after Kuthumi opened me as a channel. It came from a source with a reputation for reliability and was most encouraging. I had turned away from my career as a professional harpist and embarked on a path trod by only three or four musicians of whom I had ever heard—and my path was somewhat different from theirs, embodying past lives in the music and the symbolism for the elements of the music. The friend who sent me this channeling closed her letter with "Doesn't this make it worth all the effort? You are super-blessed at every turn!" This was so welcome to me at a time when I often wondered if somehow I had gone too far "out on a limb."

Effects, Through Crystals, And The DNA

"When I heard you play in a concert around 1980, I was filled with the voices of love! Since then my search for ultimate truth has led me, through philosophers, masters, and cabbalists, to many modalities of healing. In 1988, I was introduced to the crystals work of Marcel Vogel. Now, when I work, I see the chains of DNA and I use a crystal, as you know it. I am only the assistant, the arrow—my Creator is the archer.

"Just when I was feeling I was at a plateau in my work I was given your CD *Seven Wheels of Light* (1-hour healing for the chakras) and I noticed on the cover your work with Marcel Vogel. When I use your music with the crystal, I can see the notes pass through it and how the musical patterns actually heal the human DNA. Each note and pattern targets a specific DNA that needs restructuring—physically mending the genetic coding—and all according to the individual's original purpose. It is spectacular! The value of your music in my work is remarkable and I feel so high and blessed with this gift. I am sending gratitude to you and the community of masters far more potent than I for taking me to this ultimate level."—L.R.

When I'm channeling music I'm so totally devoted to translating what I'm hearing to the harp that I don't see the masters, angels, or space beings giving me the music. I also don't see how the music is affecting the clients or audiences. If I saw these things I would be too distracted to play. So L.R.'s highly-developed perceptions are welcome revelations to me about what I'm doing. Once, after playing a concert in Japan, a group of scientists there sent me a letter saying that they had worked out a method of translating musical notes and patterns into DNA language and they had found many DNA sequences in my music—another corroboration from an entirely different source.

At this point, my friend, who had been listening attentively to these responses, said, "Amazing. I was very moved by these personal 'confessions'. What intimate and incredible disclosures and, you know, I don't think there are very many of these in print. They really show the profound effects that are possible with this kind of co-created music. You have truly put your readers in touch with your clients. How do you feel about it?"

I answered, "First of all, I trust my readers will find these testimonies enlightening, or confirming their suspicions, or at least interesting enough to open up new vistas for them. I can't tell you how supporting these testimonials have been for me over the years. I am deeply and eternally grateful that these sweet souls answered their inner nudges to write me and I hope some of them read this book and recognize their quotations. They significantly helped to keep me going at times when I would feel alone and wondering whether the sacrifices I was making to do this pioneering work were worthwhile. But these times of doubt have been rare. Most of the time playing the music and feeling the healing energies coming through me has been sustaining, not to mention the feeling that I'm doing what I'm supposed to be doing, and making a living at it. At this point I'm convinced that each one of us has a unique, most satisfying work to be doing, and it feels good to be an example of this potential."

"What do you say we take a walk down to the beach? I have a secret cove I'd like to show you and you can tell me more about your work on the way."

Joel Andrews on tour playing for a peace conference

5

Deeper Testimonials of Healing

At this point, my companion said, "I am so impressed with the testimonials from your clients. They are so heartfelt, especially the life-changing epiphanies. They cover such a wide spectrum of healing. Is it possible to explain this?"

I answered, "The simple explanation is that, first of all, music by its nature as a kind of shorthand for life provides general healing qualities such as continuity, peace, a vacation from one's daily routine, stimulation through drama, and surprise, to break up and dissolve negative patterns. These are in an abstracted form of pure vibration. Then the client's higher intelligence uses them in many personal ways, superimposing them on patterns that are not working so well, to modify them. Another aspect of this abstract language is the system of symbolism used by the masters for each element of the music, which is standard for everyone, but individually adapted. Beyond this, the music is used as a carrier wave, by the masters working through me, for more subtle energies and patterns of healing, specific to each client. These are some of the factors that produce the individual variations."

My friend said, "I find this variety fascinating, because it is one of the facets of your work which I find suggestive of a kind of proof of its validity—apart from how it is accomplished." And I said, "Perhaps I should share with you some of the longer, and more detailed responses I've received. And again, you might enjoy noticing how their writing style is inspired by their experience of the music and a few are poignantly poetic."

Physical Healing

"Dear Mr. Andrews, I touch you in love, heart to heart, mind to mind, and spirits merging and dancing with joy. What pure delight you have given me with and through this music. Its beauty fills my room and my being as I fall asleep at night and again as I awaken—and even sometimes in between. It arrived when many in the house were ill and I had also decided to do the same. I feel it made a remarkable difference in that temporary condition since I recovered after three days while others have gone much longer. I also feel it has initiated a deeper healing process that will be ongoing until it is complete. It is my intention to focus on maximum health and well-being for the physical body until it is done. I feel that the influences on the CD are encouraging this and will help. Even in these days I'm being told how much better I look—how much younger and alive I seem to those around me. My thanks and my gratitude go out to you and to the Blessed, Beloved Ones who work with you on all planes of being.".—S.

Notable here is this woman's acknowledgment of her own part in allowing her condition. I have found in my counseling that if a client can accept her power to *create* the condition—through thoughts, emotions, and unprocessed patterns from the past—she can feel empowered to *uncreate* it.

The following is an update by a healee I reported in my last book. The serious skin condition on her hands was deeply affecting her life and her relationship. Her recovery was dramatic at first, but still continues. One never can predict how long a healing is going to take since there is always past-life karma, processing, learning, and releasing to be done.

> "My hands are better than ever right now, even though we have had some hot days. They always improve and never regress. I am *so* thankful! That healing was a turning point in my life and I've come a long way since then. Life has meaning to me and I am gaining an understanding of death, or of the continuation afterwards. It all makes me feel happier."—B.

> "I thought you might be interested in my reactions to my music: With the opening chords, I had tears and saw a purple-violet pyramid with changing forms like jumping and undulating flames, these exquisite patterns producing more tears. Next came a sensation on my skull behind my right ear—a 2-inch band moving up my head and stopping at the very top. It was like a tight band of pressure moving up and out. The color has now changed from purple to violet and is forming what look like colored hills.

> "I'm feeling adjustments from the base of my neck (or atlas) area—four adjustments, almost simultaneously and ever so gentle. At one point in the music there seems to be a stream of force going uphill and over, like circling a globe (my head?). It resembles water being pulled uphill and it seemed grey or dove in color and very smooth and gentle in its rhythm. The color has come back, but the violet and pale purples have changed to pink and violet, always changing and appearing as a long range of mountains. Now a background starts moving in: a rather solid, but warm, golden-brown, becoming lighter until it is like a golden atmosphere. This

is on my left as I face the mountains and the violet-pink is on my right—very, very subtle and beautiful as the gold comes in."—M.L.

This is one of the few I have received that was written *as* she was experiencing the music. Is there any doubt that these patterns were accomplishing healing for her? Colors are always meaningful in their esoteric symbolism, a fairly simple system in which I have been trained and which you could learn. Violet is transmutation, clairvoyance, and the sixth chakra, Third Eye, Divine Mother.

"I recently purchased *The Violet Flame* and I love it! Side II, *Violet Joy* relaxes and cheers me up whenever I listen to it, but Side I gives me a totally different effect. I have a very strange sensation—pressure—in my temples, mostly on the right side, and slightly toward my forehead. Also, there's a tingling at the top of my head. The first time I listened to it, the sensation was more intense, more like a "rod" being driven into my right temple and coming out the other side, followed by an explosion of light inside my eyelids.

"I'm wondering if this could have something to do with the third eye. I haven't been trying to open it, but I am somewhat familiar with it. The books I've been able to find on the subject do not describe any sensations that coincide with the process, but I'm wondering, because of an inner vision I had a couple of nights ago prior to sleep. I was looking at a rather large eye directly ahead of me. It was floating in smoke with different colors floating through: purple going to reds, oranges, and yellows, finishing with green and electric blue. I also experienced the same pressure in my temples during this pre-sleep vision as I do when I listen to your *Violet Flame*. I would very much appreciate your thoughts on this."—J. B.

First of all, the master clairvoyant Edgar Cayce said we should never *try* to open a chakra—that they open of their own accord, when the time is right. I know that psychedelic drugs can open them prematurely, leading to psychological problems. The Third Eye usually opens when the kundalini rises through the chakras, which is implied by her sequence of colors. Therefore, it is possible she was drawn to the music to help insure the safety of her opening. Blue, in general, symbolizes the Will of God and electric blue is the color often associated with the Christ. We should also notice here that although she described a "rod going through her temples" and an "explosion of light," she didn't experience pain.

Her experience is consistent with other reports I have heard of opening the Third Eye, the Sixth Chakra. Following this opening a person's clairvoyance—psychic perception—might increase, which would not necessarily indicate that they need to be institutionalized. There are patients in mental hospitals who are simply adjusting to this kind of opening. They can be hearing the voices of their higher guides and masters. Shock treatments for these advanced souls are, to my mind, uninformed, insensitive, and cruel.

"I do want you to know a way I've been using my music, which has been very effective. It provided essential balance during the first few months and I played it daily. By placing the recorder on my solar plexus, with my fingertips interlaced on the speaker, I could *feel* the music and not be caught up in trying to intellectually understand it. I had never experienced feeling music: the vibrations actually moving within me to cleanse, heal, and comfort. Thank you for being such a fantastic channel!"—E K.

Does not this unique use of the music, so close to the body, within the aura, suggest the *safety* of the vibrations, which are adapted so perfectly to an individual by the masters?

"I do not know what a healing is supposed to feel like but I experienced many physical sensations while meditating *during the time you were doing my channeling.* I felt a crawling, tingling sensation in various parts of my body and a flow of current through my temples. I felt a strong pressure and a pulling sensation in my Third Eye, resulting in a slight headache—a dizziness, as though my head were swimming. At times, a saw a white light through my 3rd Eye that would come and go accompanied by a low rumble much like bass chords on a pipe organ. Harp sounds also flowed through my mind, but I think this may have been my imagination." – H.W.

Remembering that this client was in another location from where I was channeling, is it not significant that she was feeling almost the same sensations as the previous two in-person reports? This woman asked two questions which might be of general interest, since they are asked quite often.

First: "Why don't I remember my past lives?" Apart from the obvious "Because you have not practiced this art," I offer, from my experience, that you embody all your past lives and see and experience the world through their eyes, as well as your higher vision. But you don't remember your more challenging lives until you've developed enough understanding, love and forgiveness to learn from the anti-life actions you've committed and release them. Of course, all your positive life experiences are ever-present, helping you celebrate life and enjoy who you are.

Second: "If I developed my capacity to love in my two previous lifetimes, why is it that this lifetime has been so stormy?" I've found it a very common pattern that after a lifetime of deep love, while that love is there to draw on, situations often come up to test it. In addition, one is often attracted to another who is not so experienced, or has a block in love, so *they* can learn how to love. Then the first person has the opportunity to be a good teacher by example. *A Course in Miracles* says teachers are students and students are teachers. There could be many reasons why a life seems stormy, but the wise ones are always impressing on me: everything that happens is for learning and spiritual growth.

The following is another *in absentia* report:

"Thank you very much for the channeling-attunement. During the session, 6:00-7:00 P.M. my time, I experienced a wonderful pulsating sound in my right ear. This was not the usual Om-Dhvani-Pranava sound of nature that I usually hear, nor was it the hydrostatic blood flow sound. It was like a gentle breath, in and out. In time, after being unable to hold my concentration for more than 25 minutes, my thoughts turned to the problems involved with a love relationship and concluded the session. The music has brought great joy and strength to my being, manifesting on the physical plane now, to work out my karma and realize my soul potencies."—R.L.H.

How perceptive of this obviously experienced meditator to be able to distinguish between the sound current, OM, the sound the circulation of his blood makes, and the new pulsations his music created.

PERSONAL PAST-LIFE MUSIC AND SOUL-PATH RE-ALIGNMENTS

There is something I should explain about the past life attunements that I do. While there is much evidence, and books written about, past lives, there are many who doubt their veracity, don't value them, and so aren't interested in them. In the *Soul-Path Re-Alignments* I do, the relevance and importance of a former life is not its details—*who* you were, *where* and *when* it took place—but the *quality* of your life. And this includes your challenges and how you grew with them, your *development in consciousness*—in other words, its *symbolism*. So they are vibrational portraits of a number of important *aspects* of you. This is why they help people know who they are, understand their present challenges better, and know what they're drawing on from the past. This is why clients find that these musical "biographies" are helpful through the years. It has even happened where a client will write me—and this can happen with any of the various personal CDs I create—saying that they just heard *new notes* in their music! My answer is usually that anything is possible but, probably, those notes were always there and, with their life changes, they've come to a point now where they need to hear them.

> "It is my opinion that Joel Andrews has become one of the clearest channels of healing sound vibration, for the benefit of God, man, and man's environment. Because of his sincere, conscious desire for healing all, he truly and humbly releases himself and his talents to the service of that healing.
>
> "Personally, I have found my own soul's music placed safely in Mr. Andrews' harp and hands, for the edification and healing of my mind, bringing into awareness a greater harmony, wisdom, and understanding in living my daily life. On the physical level, there has been release of muscular and nerve tensions throughout the body under the sounds of my own music.
>
> "Joel, while not knowing just what form the music will take, simply plays in full faith that healing will be done—and it is."—Marlene Weiner, Metaphysical Consultant

After writing me the above, Marlene set up personal sessions for her friends in New York. This was at the outset of my healing work and I remember there was such excitement that I did three, two-hour sessions a day for a week, hardly taking time to eat.

> "Standing alone, it is beautiful music, but in addition, the music strikes a very deep, responsive chord within me. I realize that here, in fact, is my own soul music. I play it very often and it never fails to elicit a feeling of serenity and peace from my soul level. Similarly, the interpretation of the music means a great deal to me; it is as if something deep within me surges with the knowledge that here, indeed, is what I am all about, and I feel I truly know where I'm coming from.
>
> "I wish it were possible to put into words how happy I am to have this healing music and what a blessing it is in my life. Thank you, Joel, for sharing your remarkable and lovely gift with me."—D.H.E.
>
> "I am enjoying getting to know the music and myself through it. I am using it to help me put joy into simple activities and to help me

remember things from my childhood. I feel that meeting you and receiving the gift of this music has connected me very strongly with the sources of my energy, after I had begun to feel I had lost touch. I had so many doubts and had lost almost all sense of purpose—really had been wondering why I was here on Earth. I was expecting to slowly wither away soon, for lack of dedication and direction. I think this wonderful gift of grounding and centering, and charging my heart with love and mercy again will heal my body, and give me balance so I can continue on the path to help others. I'll keep turning to the music for this help and, of course, to mother Earth. I've always known she was behind all my strength, love, and learning, but often I have forgotten to go back to her and even worn myself out trying to go it alone.

"Last night, with someone with whom I am very close, I listened and had him touch me with the music. It affected us both very deeply. I was able to face a lot of the pain that I carry from the third life on the CD: I understood much about what happened, and gained a vague sense of a purpose in it all. I knew that the one I loved had to go at that point, but I gained a sense of that soul's presence, somewhere not totally out of reach. It gave me peace and hope so now I can see more of the joy and beauty in that phase of the music and I'm less overwhelmed by the sadness." – Anon.

To me, this account reads like the climax of a novel or film about romantic love. Surely, one of the most poignant healings we have is the resolution of apparent separation from those with whom we have shared a deep love. These *Soul-Path Re-Alignments* show that there is no lasting separation, once a relationship is begun. Often a client becomes aware of souls in this incarnation who they have known in the past, even if the relationship has evolved and changed. It is as if this incarnation is one chapter out of the book of a relationship. So we cannot, necessarily, expect to share or resolve everything with someone in one life.

"Words couldn't possibly express the joy and beauty, in the heavenly music of your concert at the Atlanta Conference. We all thank you from the bottom of our hearts for coming and sharing your extraordinary talents.

"As for the individual *Attunement* which you gave me, I can only say that *never* have I been transported to a higher plane of harmony, peace, calm, joy, and at-one-ment with the heavenly spheres. I've had 500 "readings" and this was the best of them all! It seemed that every fiber and cell in my body responded to the notes which you said were mine.

"I felt completely balanced and at peace, yet keenly alive. It was a masterful, powerful experience that can never be forgotten. I am extremely grateful."—C.T.B.

"I just finished listening to my CD. Since I saw you in Springfield, I was laid off in a very bizarre manner and I've been trying to deal with my anger. However, listening to the music has left me calm and feeling that this recent negative experience was really a *freeing* one—unique for me as I'm a true pragmatist! I have the feeling that over the next few months my life will become clearer, as what you said about me in my 60's fits with a set of dreams I had last September. Thank you for sharing your God-given gifts."—L.K.

Is it not true? How often we are shocked and threatened by a sudden change like "losing" a job, or a loved one. Then, after a time, we find that we have been freed to explore a more interesting and often higher path. Concerning the "bizarre manner": this client and her boss have separate karmas, even though they have temporarily intersected. It greatly simplifies things if we attend only to our own challenge, leaving the other one to deal with the consequences of their actions.

"I was very moved when you played your harp in the church and I interpreted it as a remembering at the soul level. I enjoyed my *Attunement* and will use it for my healing. Your interpretation of my present incarnation was right on, for I have always had a great love for both art and music. I studied art at the Art Institute of Chicago but my choice became music and I received a Bachelor's in Music Education. I am a pianist and taught in the schools for 7 years. When I first heard the second past life (an artist in Italy), tears came to my eyes, and I took that as a validation of truth. I am now in training to go into the healing arts and a spiritual minister advised me to play the harp. She says my music will heal souls. Now I know my Higher Self is guiding me to the right music and I've been told that when in spirit I worked with the angels of music. Can you help me find a harp and get started? Bless you for your holy and needed ministry."—K.G.

If she worked with the angels, they probably guided her to the angelic music coming through me. Also, her Higher Guidance could help her more easily if she began improvising. A comment on client's tears: they are very rarely sadness, but most often the reaction to being put in touch with who they really are. We all get "off track" at times, distracted from our chosen pathway toward the realization of our highest dreams, the manifestation of our divinity and spirituality on all levels of our being. This remembering can be very moving.

"I want to tell you about the events surrounding the life reading you did for me. You told me about a life I had traveling from Britain to Spain to study Flamenco dancing. It wasn't until later that I made a connection with my teens. My grandmother bought me a guitar and, with two friends, I formed a folk group. After just a few months we all became totally involved in studying flamenco guitar, and this interest lasted for a year! I still have a deep relationship with those complex rhythms and the vibrancy of that style.

"Most unexpected, however, is what happened after I left your house. As I got into my car to keep an appointment for an interview, you looked at me rather quizzically and asked if I was okay to drive. I thought that was odd and said that, of course, I was. I wasn't five miles down the road when I realized I should not have been driving! I recalled that you "moved some energy" at the end of our session. Boy, did you ever! I admit to being a bit of a skeptic—but not now! I was feeling high, like I was being worked on by my guides. The last thing I wanted, right then, was to be doing some earthly (and dangerous) task like driving a car in traffic! I persevered, however, but I never made it to the interview, which ended up working out for the best. I listen to my music quite frequently and it always leaves me feeling peaceful and centered. Thank you for sharing your gifts."—H.E.

After I finish a channeling, I never feel tired, but uplifted. The semi-trance state usually lasts for 15 or 20 minutes, so it is advisable to wait if I need to do something like drive. For some years now, I close my upper chakras—they all open for a channeling— and this reduces the re-entry time. I am so glad I was guided to ask him if he was okay to drive.

"This *Attunement* verified things I have seen in dream or vision, and it also dovetailed with things another well-known clairvoyant told me. While it seems natural to put these things in the past, they also seem to transcend time, having a "present" aspect relating to a meditation practice I've been doing, and even predict the possible future. Then also, they seem to be unfolding on all three levels: spiritual, mental, and physical and even in my dream life. One night I suddenly woke up thinking that someone had turned on all the lights and found the room to be dark except for a small sanctuary candle! I eventually realized the "turn-on" had been interior and then remembered other step-ups of energy over the past month.

"Since using my music, I find that when I do something I shouldn't I get immediate feed-back, usually some accident to the body, or something I really want to do is put off. Yet I hate to think what it would be like without my meditation time with the CD. Things seem to bubble up as I'm ready for them, or need them, and I'm receiving more subtle feedback from prayer and meditation than ever before. I have finally realized some much-needed spiritual lessons and it is appalling how elementary some of them are; but if I don't pick up on them when they first come to my attention, I wind up experiencing them the hard way! From the music, I have realized I had been painting too dark a picture of myself, and sometimes of others, as well. So I am now much more aware that my mind has to be the loving servant of my spirit.

"Part of these illuminations were the visual masterpieces to which I was treated when my puppy ("little four foot") woke me up in the middle of the night. Once outside the house, I saw my first UFO. I watched it for several minutes and then it just disappeared! We've been having a gorgeous full moon and twice in a fantastic setting: a green and purple ring around it, then a huge circle of cloudy sky, circumscribed by a ring of white, taking up most of the sky, then, outside of that, the stars. It was the most stunning sky I have ever seen! And here it was 4:30 A.M. and I didn't dare call anyone!

"When I asked what these wonders meant the feeling was that they signify a coming influx of great spiritual energy for the planet and that it is more and more imperative that we live the Way as we should and that time is running out for the "leave it to tomorrow" approach to life.

"Above all, or perhaps fundamental to all these responses, the CD relaxes, draws out my tensions and negativity, and rejuvenates and heals. I think that it is the love and concern on your part, as well as the masters in spirit, that make this special music such a healing experience. There have been answers to prayer that have been fantastic, and far beyond what the workings of my mind could have accomplished. I think the music really gives direction to my life and a greater ability to be aware of the good things. This has been very precious to me, something for which the words "thank you" are not enough. In His Love and mine."—L.L.

A number of things are worthy of special attention in this richly detailed testimony. In the first paragraph: the corroboration of the reading by dreams and by another clairvoyant, and the transdimensional aspect: past, present and future implications as well as physical, spiritual, and mental applications. Then the sudden bursts if "light" together with the magnificent visual displays at night, suggest that the reading coincided, and perhaps even triggered, what is called a "cosmic consciousness" experience—a major illumination.

This is reinforced by her revelations, in paragraph four, about what is going on in the world and her statement about time running out for the "leave it to tomorrow" approach. It is only since around 2000 that there has been the widespread feeling among our visionaries that the Aquarian Age is *here* and the time is *now*. So her statements fall into the category of predictions of the future—prophecy. Related to this is her awareness that her negative thoughts and actions are manifesting quicker—accelerated karma—another characteristic of the last 10 years.

Yet another insight that has become widespread recently is the necessity for us to respect, feel good about, and love ourselves, for optimum personal growth and value to the human family and its rich, higher destiny.

Then add the perceptive appreciations in the last paragraph and realize that the responses above are high points selected from her three-and-a-half page, typewritten letter.

"I'd like to begin this writing, knowing that it is the Mother-Father God speaking through me, with a beautiful quote from your book *A Harp Full of Stars*: "Music is God's best gift to man, the only art of heaven given to Earth, the only art of Earth we take to heaven" (Charles W. Landon). That says it all for me—how I feel about music. (She is an organist with a Master's Degree.)

"Nothing seemed to be going right in my life and I finally asked you for a *Soul-Path Re-Alignment*, but it was several weeks before I had the courage to listen to it. I think I feared that I had been a terrible person and did not want to know about it. The mind can put one through a form of "hell"! Then I attended my son's wedding in Germany. It was an extremely difficult time, magnified by going with my former husband and spending two weeks with him. It was a devastating experience! Weeks later, when I finally listened to my music I divided it into four sessions, one for each past-life and then the present life. It was so beautiful, so loving and caring, and the Interpretation was incredible! I cried through each part, deep, wet tears from the soul level. Why I was so afraid I'll never know and, looking back, had I listened right away, it would have helped me in Germany.

"Your *Interpretation* has helped me a great deal. It provided many reasons why I have done what I have in this life. It is amazing, totally amazing, how much sense it all makes when the Interpretation enters in. So my understanding of myself, and also other people, has increased. As a result, my self-confidence has improved, my musicianship, and I am a better person. Thank you for this wonderful gift. Bless you, bless you, bless you, in the Light!"—B.S.

If people only knew the power of their thoughts, fears in this case, to manifest conditions and events in their lives, they would learn the art of catching negative thoughts and cancelling them or replacing them with positive ones. Many of the ideas we carry are not really ours anyway but ones we have picked up from others, beginning in early childhood. Not that it's easy, but with practice, this is an art we can learn. You would find it of inestimable value, especially if it develops the art of positive affirmation of how you would like your life to be. What a privilege it was: to have helped this client understand, and feel better about, herself.

"This music deeply touches me, opens me, and reveals me, as I prepare for the coming of this child, this long and arduous surrender to this awesome unfoldment of Divine Love on Earth. And though, at times, my mind has grasped the magnitude of this endeavor, and my heart tasted momentarily its glory, my human consciousness has never quite accepted its reality, nor felt itself worthy. Though the mind and its thoughts may deceive, music is more susceptible to Truth, and when I listen to this music, Joel, I can no longer doubt the joy and the blessing that this soul brings. For you to have heard the song that opened my heart, what seems so long ago, I am a puddle of tears. Dear friend, you have given me the gift most precious and intimate of all—the memory of the song my heart has always sung, but I could hardly hear, hardly believe.

"I knew the CD was on its way—I could feel it—and it came at just the very right moment. Your gift is your "givingness." As I listen to this music it seems not so much that the notes are important, but the silences that are happening between them. Therein, Truth lurks.

"I have one small question. In the CD you did for me seven years ago, there is a challenging transition, in the present life section of the music, from past energies to a new vibration occurring around this time in my life, and the difficulty is embellished. But there is a similar section in this new tape, which resolves the situation beautifully! Any comments?"—D.S.

Isn't this poetically written for an architect? The style is also reminiscent of the transcendentalists Emerson, Hawthorne, and Thoreau who also lived in New England (D.S. lives in Vermont.) Again, we have here the power of his personalized music to uplift his confidence in himself at a crucial time in his life, the arrival of his first-born child. And does it not tend to prove the higher intelligence behind the co-created music that a theme is developed seven years later? I can guarantee that I do not ever listen to a client's previous music before channeling new music for them. In my 40-year, deep quest into the true nature of music, I have also been guided that, while the frequency of each note has its importance, it is really the spaces between the notes that create the *journey* which music is for us and its capability of symbolizing our own life journey.

"The South is behind me, I am again in the North, and I think that the angular, chordal section in my *Soul-Path Re-Alignment* music is the 14 years I spent in a modern-day Essene community. Where the music breaks free of the block harmony and becomes running eighth notes, cascading and shimmering, is my moving to New York. And I'm sure this represents my leaving behind my feelings of having been a failure and opening myself up to the very real possibility that I am succeeding—that the stone wall I constantly saw myself up against, in meditation visions, is actually gone!

"Now my High Self's desire for completeness is taking me over and this beautiful channeled music has helped the process. In your Interpretation, you confirmed much of what I have intuitively known for years about my past-life background. Now things I did around puberty, strong attractions I have to certain countries, cultures, and art forms, make sense." —J.A.

Here we see some of the actual connection, or congruence, between the musical patterns and their symbolism for the client—she is a musician, a harpist. Again we have the release of long-held, debilitating patterns from the past, the freeing of self-esteem, and the opening up of a higher, more successful future.

"Listening to the tape I sleep a lot sounder, don't wake up an hour before the alarm, or have to get up so often to go to the bath-

> room—a direct medical effect. I find I am more in harmony with myself and loose my temper less. I've also noticed that the musical program of the tape parallels how I learn things.
>
> "About the 11th and 13th chords you say are so spiritually uplifting, my theory is that they suggest the Overtone Series and that the mind's ear completes the chord after the notes leave off, carrying it to higher and higher tones." —T.F.

He's a musician and is very perceptive about the Overtone Series, which is the Law of Resonance to be found throughout nature: Everything that vibrates spontaneously divides up into segments, 1/2, 1/3, 1/4, 1/5, and so on, each segment sounding a higher note, producing a chord above the fundamental tone. Our well-tempered scale, introduced in the latter part of the 1600s, which I often call the "ill-tampered scale," is slightly out of tune—a compromise on natural law. Even in this scale, inspired musicians compose using chords built in 3rds which imply the third octave of the Overtone Series. These are still very grounding and uplifting for us since the overtone series is built into us. I will be explaining the Overtone Series in more depth later in this book. For 25 years, I have occasionally retuned my harp to an Overtone Series and listeners often say, "That takes me home!" Some of these channelings are very healing and are available. So the Overtone Series Tuning is coming back as we return to greater respect for, and harmony with, nature.

MAJOR LIFE CHANGES, CLARIFICATION OF LIFE PURPOSES, OPENING OF NEW LIFE DIRECTIONS

> "It's after midnight, and in five hours it will be time to get up, but I can't close my eyes without thanking you for all the healing you generated this weekend. Saturday evening our "psychic encounter" and the conversation with the masters in spirit was, and will be forever, a turning point in my life. For the first time since day one of this incarnation, I feel at home in this body and on this planet. It prepared me for Sunday's healing music, when I experienced something being pulled out of me! I am free to go, now that the doubts are gone. Bless you with all of my heart, which feels so opened and alive. Om." – R.
>
> "I wanted to listen and absorb the music for a while before writing you. I am uplifted and inspired. Music certainly resonates with me at certain moments in my life, particularly music of a higher order, and it reaches and impresses me with a certain quality of beauty. The notes seem to resonate with the point I have reached

in my life. Many years ago, when I first heard your music, it was as if I already understood where it comes from, as if I was listening to something very familiar, and the same applies now. The beautiful quality of lightness of this music is something I feel very at home with, and certainly more than any other music. Thank you for bringing so much beauty into the world".—A.F.

This mostly speaks for itself. Often, after a concert, just before I invite the audience to share their experiences, I ask them if they can still hear the music. Most of them report that they can and I say, "You're probably tuning in to the same Sources I am." And it sounds as if the above client had heard it before he heard what I brought through for him.

I am so profoundly grateful for these reports and for the opportunity to share them with you. I have lost track of most of these dear souls, so I hope they will be guided to read this book and know that their testimonials were able to inspire others.

INSIGHTS AND OPENINGS

The hour before sunset is one of the most beautiful and inspiring times of day on the Pacific Coast. A few clouds over the ocean can create exquisite plumes of subtly changing colors and the slanting rays striking the foliage around my house create a soft green-gold, one of my favorite colors. Corinne Helene, in her book *Color in the New Age*, associates this color with artistic creativity so it is no wonder I am drawn to it

I had just finished the previous chapter and had invited my friend to come over and give me his reactions. We had just settled down with our drinks to watch the light show, celebrate the day and the great gifts of the departing sun, when he said, "This variety of responses takes your readers much farther than your last book and your comments take them much deeper into the essence of your work. You have been able to share much that should be of value to them. I find their reports fascinating and it's encouraging to find so many people seriously dedicated to their spiritual growth. Their insights should answer many questions and be inspiring and uplifting for your readers."

I agreed with him and said, "I was profoundly moved by these responses in that they prove to me, beyond the shadow of a doubt, that I could not have created music that so perfectly fits each client and situation. That seems to me to require much higher perception than I possess. These testimonials show me for the first time the extent of my work; that I am actually manifesting the vision I was given forty years ago, that the highest destiny of music might be healing and setting people, as well as other forms of life, on the path to higher consciousness and Divinity Realization. This is not to mention all the related benefits of peace, harmony, raising of consciousness, release from stress, remembering their true purposes, and the resulting physical healing. These miracles and more are found in these reports and I have another file of them, covering different areas of service, I would like to share with you. I'll begin the new chapter tomorrow and let you know when I've finished."

My friend thanked me, saying he would be looking forward to that, and we sat for some minutes just drinking in the gradual modulations of the sphere-fire to the West.

6

More Responses: The Spectrum Widens

The following testimonies do not seem to need comment.

AN APPRECIATION BY A HARPIST, THE DAUGHTER OF THE FOREMOST HARPIST OF KANSAS CITY, AFTER ATTENDING MY CONCERT

"We admired your technique, musicality, and your relaxed, expert delivery; I've seen many harpists in concert and I've never seen anyone with a more perfect hand position. You have a background from which you draw rich content and are able to form it into a coherent whole. The harp is truly an instrument of beauty and healing." —R.L.

PHYSICAL HEALING—HEADACHES

"Joel, I love my CD! It may be worn out; I've played it so much. It really does have an effect on me. I've been having headaches and your beautiful music has been the only relief from pain I have had." —D.Y.

MIGRAINE

"I woke up this morning with a 'sick headache' (migraine). I don't have them much anymore but when they come they usually last 2-3 days unless I can get to a chiropractor. This morning I took a shower and lay down to put on my Attunement Music. I was sick for only one hour. What else can I say? Bless you!" —L.N.

SPINAL AND NECK ADJUSTMENTS

"Thank you so much. We are enjoying the uplifting effects (and the musicality) of our Healing Music. Audrey feels she definitely had some sort of spinal healing during the channeling, and then, as I said, my neck adjusted! We were all uplifted." —G.J.

PERSONAL CDS FOR INDIVIDUALS

"Your music had a powerful effect on me. It generated an experience that was absolutely mind-boggling in its intensity and beauty. I can't tell you how much it has meant to me!" – R.H., M.D.

"Your CDs mean so much to me that I play them not only when meditating, going to sleep, and creative pursuits, but in the midst of household chores. They beautify the whole world!" —M.L.

"I have found my own soul's music, placed safely in Mr. Andrews' harp and hands, so valuable for the edification and healing of my mind, bringing into awareness greater harmony, wisdom, and understanding in living my daily life. There has been release of muscular and nerve tensions throughout the body under the sounds of 'my own' music."— M.W. (metaphysical consultant)

"During the session I truly did feel that I became part of the music and it was beautiful beyond description! I am finding it a very good tool to use in meditation." —S.B.

"…(my music) has really meant very much to me. It's the most positive, helpful, and beautiful aid I've ever found to become uplifted and "attuned." I cannot adequately thank you." —N.L.

"It was a high point for me. I experienced such an intense inflow of pure unconditional love. It is a source of inspiration which still guides me so I have always deeply appreciated the experience and your work." —G.A.

"This is one of the most beautiful gifts I have ever gotten. It's like bathing in a clear, clean, crystal fountain of light. I had almost forgotten my origin." —I.

"Thank you so much for such *divine* music. It has helped me through some difficult moments! God bless you." —D.P.

"I was very strangely moved: I felt as if I were being turned inside out! I guess my psychic centers were all twanging away in some marvelous fashion —and it lasted for some time." —H.K.

"You touched my soul and healed some deep, non-verbal wounds. I love you beyond words." —C.E.

"What impressed us most was the "anointing" through the harp playing and the effect it had on us—even through the TV set into our living room!" —E. and D. B.

The Spectrum Widens

"[During a concert] my pragmatic husband had all sorts of nature visions: rivers, falling leaves, and melting icicles. I experienced violet light shows in the third eye, ice caverns of blue light in the solar plexus, and flying—great spiritual energy!" —L.

"Your music is like a beautiful, golden angel's wing brushing gently against one's cheek." —D. & R. P.

"The CD of my music arrived and it is a great comfort to me. It gives me courage to hang on until the change comes." —Anon.

"I intended to contact my doctor about a bronchial condition of asthmatic proportions, also a bout of cystitis. The latter condition was cured with the initial playing of 'my music'. The bronchial condition took a little longer—two days!" —A.M.

Two Comments From Holland

I have toured this wonderful country 16 times.

"You and your music have led me out of the fear of 'outside authorities' and right into the authority of my innermost being where there is only love, joy, acceptance, and overflowing gratitude." — E. van der K.

"My music is wonderful and gives me already peace. It does my tiredness away and makes me enthusiasm and joy!"

Responses To My CDs Available To The General Public

Keep in mind these clients did not hear me in person. Please see the Appendix for descriptions of these CDs.

"I felt more pure joy from your CD with the 'dolphin' sounds than I have *ever* felt from anyone or anything 'outside' myself. Thank you for helping to create this magnificent CD."—A.S.

While bringing through the music, I am often guided to sing in a high falsetto. The clairvoyants tell me this is usually an angel communicating something to us which couldn't best be done on the harp. The listeners say it sets the entire room to vibrating to each note. It's a very pure, focused tone without vibrato.

Ave Maria calls forth the Love, Compassion, and Nurturing of Divine Mother.

"Your *Ave Maria* puts us in touch with that 'special place' after a busy day. I am ordering a Soul-Path Re-Alignment."—R.C.

"Your expression and sensitivity in *Ave Maria* is so moving! And I love the way you repeated it many times. I love its flowing texture and its calming, tranquil effect on my clients."—S.L.

"Your *Ave Maria* has an immense impact on me! It connects me with my subtle, inner being. Also, while sitting in front of you at the concert, my aura was cleansed. – J. van der H.

"The *Ave Maria* CD was played after Joel's concert, just before going to sleep the same night. The following morning I noticed that the pain in my right shoulder was gone and I had free movement of my arm and shoulder! I have been diagnosed with rheumatoid arthritis."—D.D.

"Your new CD channeled from our beloved St. Germaine of The Violet Transmuting Flame is sublime!!—M.R.

"Your *Violet Flame* is quite amazing. I felt the healing power enter the room the second time I played it. I was recently hospitalized, so this is a tool I can really use at this time!" – S.R.

"Your *Violet Flame* is rather effective. Immediately a misunderstanding had to be corrected in a family relationship, over the phone. Peace and uplifting transmutation of negativity into harmonious positivity became evident. Just listening to the selection created the response. Amazing: four lives now in flowing balance and attitudes. Praise the Lord!"—N.O.

"I have enjoyed *The Violet Flame* very much. May the Lord of Hosts bless your work so that everyone can hear the 'songs of Light.'—S.M.

The ascended master, Kuthumi, is also the chohan of the second Ray, Love/Wisdom. This music from him helps the listener manifest Spiritual Renaissance principles, and also helps connect with higher planes of being.

"I love the music from the master Kuthumi that is played at the beginning of our meditation group. I thank the Infinite One for the music brought to Terra through you." – L.B.

The Spectrum Widens

"I have no words to describe my wife's and my appreciation for this music from Kuthumi. It is certainly a part of that music which my soul has sensed and searched for." – K.A.

"This music from Kuthumi has stirred me to the very depths!"— E.P.

"I am profoundly moved by this music of Kuthumi flowing through you. I experienced intense sensations in my Solar Plexus, Heart, Throat, and Third Eye chakras, and tears came to my eyes."— A.

"Immediately I felt a strong super-conscious response and attunement to the high spiritual purpose of this beautiful Kuthumi music."—J.M.

"Never before have I been privileged with such an intimate contact with the master Kuthumi. You have truly opened a channel with this recording. I thank you for all who will benefit by its influence."—J.W.

Journey Toward the Sun is a potpourri of heart-opening pieces. It is my first recording of Harp with Orchestra, a collaboration with Soren Hyldgaard, the Danish composer.

"While listening to *Journey toward the Sun* I burst into creative dancing in my room. I moved in ways I wouldn't have dared before with my Meniere's Disease. and extensive orthopedic surgery."— D.M.

Iridescence I has been found to clear the blocks to creativity. *Iridescence II* brings deep peace.

"I listen to *Iridescence II* every evening before going to sleep, with the deepest heartfelt appreciation for your inspiring music."— A.H.

"I am a life-long insomniac and your *Iridescence II* has been so helpful in giving me a deeper sleep. I feel changed every time I listen to it. I am mesmerized by your playing!"—S.L.

Seven Wheels of Light energizes, heals, and balances the seven chakra system.

"Around 1990 I purchased your *Seven Wheels of Light*. I lost it, but just found the CD cover! On playing that CD, I would feel harmony, balance, and peace almost immediately; and if I didn't feel well, and I listened to it, within a short time, sometimes within one day, I would *get well*! Can I still order it?"—M.P.

Responses Suggesting Spiritual Upliftment

"Your CDs have healed my Thyroid, my Heart, and united me with The Heart of God. Blessed one, we love you. Your CDs have revolutionized our lives." —E von P (a spiritual teacher and founder of an organization disseminating the teachings of the Masters.)

"Your music is giving me effects beyond words! I am imbued and there is great creative action which I know will manifest eventually." — G. von P. (husband, and co-worker of the above)

"Your music is so inspiring, but your presence in your music is truly amazing. You have a wonderful quality of encircling the listener and drawing them into your experience. Then I feel a deep connection with our Source."—S.L.

"I feel that the Kuthumi music is opening me in ways I do not understand but sense and accept as part of my evolution into higher consciousness. You have been given a very special gift and opportunity to serve in aiding this evolution for many. Thank you for answering that call."—A.

"I have a precious memory of your concert at the Theo Gimbel Color Healing Centre in England. You played unimaginable, spontaneous music, translating soul substance into sounds—just wonderful!"—J.M.

"When I listen to your music I have the awareness that I truly am one with All That Is! You have enriched our lives."—L.M.

Emotional Cleansing

"This morning I was feeling dispirited, so I meditated with your music playing in the background. After a strong emotional reaction (it had never made me weep before!) I felt a pervading peace, and then at the end, joy. I emerged fully renewed." – S.M.

The Spectrum Widens

"When the mental and emotional bodies need to be put back into alignment I just lie down and put on the music. Then I can feel the subtle energies as they heal—remarkable!" – D.G.

Name Analysis

"Your work with The Mystical English Alphabet is fascinating. I have been interested for a while in number and letter symbolism, so I signed up for the all-day seminar. The depth and range of application of this material appears vast!"—J.W.

"I must tell you how much we have enjoyed listening to our CD. It is amazing and fascinating that you can do that. The information was terrific, so meaningful, and seemed pretty much 'right on'.—B.

Doctors, Chiropractors, And Hypnotherapists

"What a talent and gift! I am anxious to get this music going throughout my office." – W.L.B., Chiropractor

"I'm getting very positive feedback from my mentally-ill patients with the healing music. I'm thrilled with the results! I can't say enough good things about your work. Bless you." – K.M. (a mental institution)

"For the past two months I have used your beautiful music as background for my hypnotherapy sessions. After many years in practice using other music, I have found *Iridescence* to be the most pleasant, relaxing, and helpful music of its kind. It makes the session more effective. Thank you, Joel; your work is wonderful and deeply appreciated.—Anon.

An Interview

"I'm intrigued, excited, and just wholly impressed by the interview you did for the Earth Nation Sunrise. It was a wonderful experience!"

After A Concert At A Retirement Home

"Words can never express the wonder of your performance! The sounds still linger in the air, and your beautiful golden harp will long be remembered! Continued blessings on you and your dedicated work!" —Sister C.B.

"The notes of the harp were like tiny raindrops,

cleansing every part of my dancing being!"—N.F.

"Words would have intruded in the state of being I reached Friday night at the concert. We touched and my soul rejoices in that touch. I leave you with a radiance of love and laughter."—J.

"The most celestial music I have ever heard!" —S.L.

"Your music truly comes from the fount of all healing."—G.S.

Appreciation Through Me To The Source

"We want to thank you again for your efforts on our behalf. We know that Steven will be helped by your healing music just as Arnold and I were. We deeply appreciate our relationship with you. It has given us the confidence we need for our challenges in life.— B.M.

After Concerts At New Thought Churches

"It was a very special experience for me. The frequencies were high, The Lords of Light were present, and I felt surrounded in total love and protection."—J.W.

"Please accept our gratitude for the beautiful expressions of love that you are and the generosity of Spirit you shared in our presence. The music (that term seems inadequate), the golden tones of peace and harmony, seemed to prompt inner 'remembering' of a long ago and future time and I know will continue to resonate with us here."—Anon.

A Workshop At A Conference Of Harpists

"On behalf of the American Harp Society. I thank you for your presentation of the workshop 'Improvising Effective Patterns for Healing'. We appreciate your sharing your expertise on a topic which is of great interest to harpists."—J.B.

Name Analysis Applied

"I was amazed to find that I had composed a tune at sunrise, and later found, through the meanings you've channeled, that it is a tune apropos for a sunrise: the symbolism of the notes supporting that concept. Since then I've analyzed other tunes with similar results. Does this mean my rapport with my "muse" is improving?"—H.E.

The Spectrum Widens

Name Analysis Helps Unreturned Love

"Your *Name Analysis* just arrived—very interesting, centering, and healing—particularly about 'spiritualizing human love.' I'm learning to be more positive about my latest attraction, who isn't responding, and to see him more as my brother. Actually he was born on the same day as my brother, although in a different year. I'm trying to acknowledge the love that is there, instead of whining about what isn't."—F.

Yoga Class

"I am playing your beautiful CDs at my Hatha Yoga classes. We are having miracles and healings through your divine help."—J.

T'ai Chi

"I am very enthusiastic about the lovely harp music of *Emblissening Movement!* This CD creates the perfect background for my practice of T'ai Chi."—M.H.

Childbirth

Note: Pilar Farnsworth commissioned this music and her five-year-old son sat with us. I left his voice on the recording.

"The co-creation of this very beautiful music was one of the highest experiences of my life. The music that your hands and harp brought to earth truly expresses the sacred energy of birth. God bless you, Joel, and your work!"—P.F. (Champion of Home Birth)

"I cannot explain with mere words the strength, beauty, and calm I have derived from this music. I am intending to use it in my birth experience, which it has shown me in a spiritual and joyous light."—J.D.

Massage And Reflexology

"The beauty and harmony of Joel's music has a very relaxing and balancing effect on my clients. It rejuvenates the spirit and calms the mind. Some clients have reported it helps them remember who they are." —R.A., Massage Therapist

"I shall use this music when giving reflexology treatments to others—a double healing!"—J.

Dentistry

"I have been playing the relaxation CDs of Joel Andrews for my patients. The effects have been profound. The music greatly enhances my ability to provide a safe, trusting, and healing environment in my office. Research indicates that music acts on the vagus nerve, a central component in the pain response."—W.W., DDS

Feedback From A College Class

"Interesting is not a good enough adjective to describe this presentation. To begin with, the music was incredible—very captivating! Although I wasn't convinced about angels existing, it is fascinating to think about."— J.I., Student

"Joel Andrews' mode of presentation was a welcome change. His body language was very smooth, gentle, and sophisticated. Apparently angels at least symbolize everything that is good and beautiful. There was a great serenity during the performance."—R.A.

"Excellent. The music made me feel as if I was in heaven! It was great! Mr. Andrews could have told us more about angels, when they respond to music and what they're doing while they're here."—C.J.

Professor Plays Music Before Class

"As a training consultant and college professor, I use this music to set a light, relaxing tone in my seminars and classes. I'm not sure that the students appreciate it as much as I do, but it consistently calms me and supports me to center myself before class. Thank you for giving the world these wonderful sounds."—L.P.

The "Music Of The Spheres"

"Thank you, thank you, thank you, a million times for introducing so much music of the spheres to me. I've loved all of our adventures together."—M

Attunement Of The Whole Being

"By complete attunement with the harp, Joel Andrews brings through inspirations from subtler realms which can harmonize your whole being. Through vast realms of finer harmonic intensities this music can purify our whole inner being. Then our physical, emotional, mental, and intuitive bodies are harmonized through a language of pure vibration—truly inspiring!"—Anon.

The Spectrum Widens

From A Great Intuitive Of The Spiritual Renaissance, Ray Stanford, One Of The Successors To Edgar Cayce

"Joel, you have come with a most unique gift into the earth this lifetime: Music expressed through the Harp! With it you can, and *are*, leading many back to The Father from whom all of us came. *By the mercy and grace of God through the Christ*, do that!"—R.S.

General Appreciations Of The Healing Ministry

"I received the CDs and *love* them. Your work in this field is *awe-inspiring*"—Anon.

"Joel is an angelic presence in the sound healing community. His gentle, heavenly harp playing speaks to us directly from the spiritual realms. I recently had a Soul-Path Session where he played my life themes. Whenever I forget who I am, or my path, this CD inspires me to my core self again."—J.C. (a healer with the voice)

"His golden harp helps your soul re-harmonize. Since 1971, Andrews has been transcribing music he overhears in higher dimensions, becoming a harbinger of peace, love and ecstasy and, even at times, acting as a prescription for pain." —C.O. (from a newspaper review in Santa Cruz, CA)

"Thank you and all those involved in bringing this celestial music through. Your efforts and responsibility to this important work is surely blessed. It is helping to form the foundations of the new divine medicine."—J.W.

"Your work has made a tremendous difference in my life!" — D.G.

"Thank you for bringing the music of the heavens to those of us here who are not yet able to perceive those glorious, loving sounds. Words cannot describe the peace and love I felt in your presence. I know you are a true man of God and I thank you with all my heart for being that."—C.D.

From Readers Of My Book, *A Harp Full of Stars*

"I just finished it!…excellent, very inspirational, very moving. When my daughter tuned into it she said, 'It's like coming home to the angels and devas!'"—H.D.

"I'm half-way through it and am savoring each page! You have so many insights into the harmonies of all living things that I would like to read your book again and again"—J.F.

What an experience it is for me to read these client responses after some years have passed. I've been fairly faithful putting them in a file over the years, but I have never seen so many all in one place.

I would love to hear your reaction to these responses, and let me share a little of mine. First, I am almost as moved, impressed, uplifted, amazed, and even astonished as my clients, that this unbelievable variety of miracles could take place through music, and through me. On the other hand, it is staggering to be reminded of the physical work involved in moving the harp, my heart, and my body through hundreds of concerts, 16 tours of Europe and the Far East. And yet, I am young for my years, and still playing some of the best concerts of my career. Of course, I have learned, and practice, many techniques for optimum health, but I attribute my youthfulness mainly to the healing vibrations coming through me.

It is certainly humbling to read these responses, because when I see the volume and depth of them it becomes clear that I could never have done them without the help of the beings in spirit—my muses. So, if nothing else, it is proof of their existence. And beyond this, it demonstrates their infinite love and wisdom. And, of course, these healing effects would have been impossible without the desire and willingness of the clients for healing. This pulls the healing vibrations through me.

It has not always been easy, to "stay the course" in a world so full of hyper-confusion and stress, and therefore doubt about spiritual matters—another reason I deeply appreciate the personal gratitude so many of these clients have expressed.

In a way, these miracles are like the rounding of a circle, the fulfillment of what was only a vision and a trust in 1971, when I turned away from a career as a professional concert harpist. See chapter 12 for this story. As I read these heartfelt responses, I see the fulfillment of that radical change in the direction of my life, and it has gone far beyond my wildest dreams.

These testimonies are also a demonstration that everyone has a unique work to do, and can be guided and prepared to do it. This comes with one of The Creator's incredible gifts to us, our individuality. I am not referring to the *ego*, which separates us from our brothers and sisters, life, and The All That Is, but the inexhaustible love our Source obviously has for *diversity*.

Also, they are a reminder again of the universality of the language of music, that it can carry such a wide spectrum of human messages, not to mention serve as a vehicle for love and light, harmony and healing on so many levels—and all this coming from beings in spirit.

Do not these personal stories suggest the fundamental Divinity of these brothers and sisters of ours? And has there not been a wealth of information and wisdom embodied in these responses?

So it has been an honor and a privilege to have been able to facilitate these miracles. Of course, as *A Course in Miracles* reminds us, "You never teach without learning. They are one." I am also grateful to have had the opportunity to learn so much from the Interpretations of my client's music about what's really going on with humans at this crucial time in our evolution. Add to this the many suggestions for successful living we can extract from these responses. I'd like to share with you some of these more thought-provoking revelations in the chapters that follow.

7

Cornerstone of the Spiritual Renaissance:

Co-creation

The principle of co-creation is one of the most important characteristics of the Aquarian Age. Creating and collaborating with "higher" forces not only brings us into a greater ecstasy but also is one of the primary ways we actually experience oneness with life. The Piscean Age helped us develop our individuality, but often this was at the expense of the group. Now we are emerging from the last 2165 years of that Age with many strong lines of demarcation between levels of our own being as well as between aspects of the life around us. Now, in one after another of these areas, we are seeing the dropping of barriers to communication, then to understanding, then co-creation, and finally love. We will not go into why or how these barriers were erected but suffice it to say that they were built through fears of one kind or another of which we seem to be past masters on this planet. The dropping of these barriers can provide enormous amounts of growth for those whose curiosity and desire to expand will sustain them through the process of transmutation and release.

Now we have the opportunity—and the necessity—of opening up our relations with the group around us, of embracing the oneness, support and power of the human family. Even beyond this, we are being offered the opportunity to know that we are all children of The Divine Source, are loved and have the potential to reap the manifold benefits of co-creating with that All-That-Is. Then we can not only draw on the accumulated wisdom of the history of our life wave for the good of everyone, but also co-create with the higher guidance of angels, archangels, and ascended masters and even draw on the experience of a vast universe.

To begin, let us explore together some of the parts of our own nature that we are trying to harmonize and unify. Then we could move on to the various orders of life with which we might enjoy playing and creating. By way of introduction, here's a story.

Probably the two most terrifying creatures of the sea have been the whale and the giant octopus. For well over 200 years, sea sagas have relied on the unimaginable power of the whale and the awesome arms of the octopus for their climaxes. Just in the last decade, we have adventuresome souls rowing right up to the whales in dinghies armed with only their love to protect them. The whales, even though we slaughter them constantly, respond to the innocence of this love with unbelievable care and concern for the life in these boats. In addition, a man has danced with an octopus. At a lecture in Los Angeles my friend, Alan Watts, was commenting on this dropping of barriers and fears and he told the story of the man who danced with an octopus. After the lecture, a man who had been standing in the back of the hall came forward and introduced himself. He said, "Alan, I'm the man who danced with the octopus. My name is Jacques Cousteau." Alan replied, "What a pleasure. I've always wanted to meet you. But tell me, how did you dance with the octopus?" And Jacques replied, with a toss of the head typical of the French, "I tickled her private places." Now this story does show the expanded awareness of sex in this age, as a special case of co-creation, but on a much deeper level, it illustrates the rewarding experiences that await the pioneer who has the courage to act on his belief in the oneness and playfulness of the Divine Mother, The Infinite Spirit aspect of Deity.

So let us begin with our own natures. Thousands of years of evolution have produced a degree of cooperation and harmony between our basic aspects and yet we have such a long way to go in this regard. Since this is an experimental planet the humanoid type is not yet completely standardized here. There are variations, but let us consider the majority. The average human enters life embodying two fundamental levels of consciousness: 1) the mind, the initiator, with its reasoning and memory capabilities and 2) the body-consciousness, what has been called the subconscious and what we will prefer to call our Basic Selves. They carry with them many fine sensibilities and instincts gleaned from the animal kingdom, plus a wealth of much human experience. Then, under the watch-care of the guardian seraphim and parents, sometime just before the sixth year, co-incident with the first moral decision, the awareness of right and wrong for the individual, a third aspect is added. What has variously been called the High Self, the beloved I AM Presence, the super-consciousness, an undiluted fragment of the Universal Father, the First Aspect of the Deity Trinity, is assigned to the human. Its primary function is to indwell the mind, adjust thoughts, and draw the individual ever inward to the First Source and Center. In the process, we achieve personhood—identity.

Therefore, your basic nature is triune: your Father fragment could be called "Oneness," your subconscious or Basic Selves could be called "Separated Aspect," and your conscious mind is that which "mediates" between the two. Through this mediation, hopefully, you will develop soul qualities and survive this planet. This is the desire of Deity but, of course, for the plan to work you must choose it with your Creator-given free will. Edgar Cayce said, "The mind is the builder," and it is in this part of us that directives originate. Mind really is "over" matter. Basic Selves evolve through providing the vehicle for the growth of consciousness and can only bypass the mind when it has threatened survival.

Here is the perfect example: A friend of mine was driving in heavy traffic on a six-lane highway with a divider strip. There was a pile-up directly in front of him and he knew he was going to be involved in the accident. At that instant he blacked out, his body got out of the car, picked its way through the heavy traffic, and when he awoke he was sitting on the grass on the divider strip—without a scratch. It is miraculous the physical feats the body consciousness can accomplish when it is not held back by the beliefs and slowness of the mind.

Employing kinesiology—muscle-testing—I have done extensive research into the nature of this aspect of us. I will report on this in detail in Chapter X but here is a brief introduction: The five areas of which the Body Consciousness, or Basic Selves, are in charge are: 1) care of the body, 2) the emotional nature, 3) the chakras, 4) the karmic memory patterns, and 5) most of the intuitions, even though they may come to our awareness through the mind. Your Basic Selves take care of the 500 functions of the liver and this is one organ among many. How much better off we would be and how much faster we would evolve if we provided the Basic Selves with positive, idealistic thought forms, love and friendship, and appreciation for the thousands of things they are doing right and more creative understanding in the areas in which they are having difficulty.

So we are trying to harmonize and integrate these three aspects and this integration is fundamental to our spiritual growth. In a "realized" master, surely these three aspects are working together, but *wherever we are* in our development we can begin to study the nature of these three aspects and begin to observe who is doing what. Even before we fully understand these three we can begin to work toward their integration. Since the conscious mind is the initiator and the builder, our best beginning will be to decree, accept, and visualize this integration. A very effective practice would be, first thing in the morning, to say a mantram something like this: "I decree and accept understanding, cooperation, harmony, and love between my High Self, my Conscious Mind and my Basic Selves." Actually, this harmony has already been decreed for you and you can begin clearing away the blocks that stand in the way of its expression. Then, see if you can feel this harmony and oneness. Of course, it will speed up your progress if you call on higher forces for guidance: your guardian seraphim, your High Self, the Holy Spirit, the Christ, and whatever you call The Supreme.

In this way, you will be developing the art of co-creation between aspects of your own being. As you develop this art, more and more you will free the energy that has been tied up in conflicts of various kinds and you will experience quite an increase in your potential. At this point, most people find an unexpected bonus: as creative harmony is achieved within: you will find it easier to co-create with aspects of life outside of you.

What are the basic orders of life with which you co-create in your environment? These are the mineral kingdom, the plant kingdom, the animal kingdom, the human, and the angelic. These are also called dimensions of consciousness here on this planet and can also be found within you. They are perhaps a little easier to see outside of you and so, once you are learning to co-create with them in your exterior world, then you can internalize this process.

First, we must realize that everything on this planet is alive—has consciousness. The planet itself is a being and has outer bodies just as we have outer bodies. It is as if we are cells in the body of the planet's very being while we are here—although our destiny lies beyond the stars. The fact that the mineral level of consciousness is alive is demonstrated by the fact that the walls, floor and ceiling of a room and the objects within it respond to the vibrations of the people who have been in the room and reflect these back to those who enter it. A person who has developed psychometric ability can read these impressions. How could these material objects carry human patterns of vibration if they were "only matter"? Do you remember how different your car feels after you have loaned it to someone? Have you noticed how cars take on the patterns of their owners, often developing similar ailments? In any case, if the objects around us are going to be reflecting our vibrational patterns back to us it might be a good idea to begin projecting love to this level of consciousness.

You might begin by sending love and then talking to your car, your computer, your cell phone and your washing machine—after first noticing who might be present. Over a period of time, you will begin to notice results. When you begin to develop this rapport, you might even start to notice miracles. You know, there are a few individuals on the earth plane who have developed this co-creation to the point of being able to bend metal and move objects from one place to another.

Even apart from miracles, we have a lot for which to thank the mineral kingdom. It is what gives our world a great deal of its stability. Can you imagine what your flesh would look like without the shape and design given it by your skeleton? Then we have the wonders of precious gems, created over thousands of years, and the reliable qualities of the stones that make up our buildings—not to mention the soil in which we grow our food. There is no question about it: the mineral kingdom responds to your love.

Next, we come to the plants. The research of Cleve Backster with the polygraph and the extensive work reported in *The Secret Life of Plants*, by P. Tompkins and C. Bird, demonstrates the almost unbelievable sensitivity of the plant kingdom. What a revelation it is to know that plants in the next room, or even farther, are registering our thoughts and emotions. In the next chapter I give an account of a friend who developed a close relationship with a small plant in his apartment. He went on vacation for two weeks and when he returned, his plant wrapped a tendril around his finger. Anyone who has seen time-lapse photography of plant growth knows that movement is one of the plant's specialties, but usually takes place just under the ability of our eyes to register it. Of course, the wind shows the great flexibility of plants. In the case of my friend's plant, the movement was slightly accelerated—probably by the resident deva—and its emotion of joy. The emotions of plants cover a broad spectrum from fear to gladness and the needles of the polygraph sometimes register wild movement as they register to these emotions.

So the vegetative dimension of consciousness adds expansion and contraction to the mineral dimension and it is perhaps in these two qualities that we recognize it most easily in our own bodies. So, through this quality of movement we can empathize and co-create with the plant kingdom. Recent research seems to indicate that plants in some way actually take in our negativity and transmute it and this is beyond just the ingestion of our carbon dioxide from which they give back oxygen. We are certainly dependent for life on the plants not only physically but also aesthetically. The exquisite beauty and fragrance of the flowers heals us and raises our spirits and our consciousness. There are those who have devoted years to the study and successful practice of aromatherapy. Herbal healing has also proven itself.

At this point let us say that we can effectively send our love to minerals and plants as they appear to be, but when we consider the full range of their expression—and this includes the animals and the humans—we must take into account the action of the devas and angels in charge of these forms of life. To psychic sight, small points of light are seen hovering around plants charging themselves up with prana—vitality—then flying into the interior of the plant and discharging it. A group or clump of small plants will have a deva hovering over it and any plant of any size usually has a resident deva. The word *deva* comes from the East Indian, and means *angel*, but in the West is usually used to describe an angel of four feet or under working with the mineral, plant or animal kingdoms. However, there are also some large devas over mountains and lakes. The angels are the builders of form on the planet and these tireless artisans help the species to reach their full potential, working directly with Light—they know no negativity. When communicating with these forms of life it is well to address your thoughts to the deva in charge. I have been tuning in to plants and trees for some years now, have received words from them, healing from them, and even channeled music from them. We can certainly gain timeless wisdom from some of the old trees. Plants wish to serve us but they do like to be asked. There are joys unending in co-creating with the plant kingdom.

How could we ever have come this far without the help and companionship of the animals? And this joint evolution has been in spite of a good deal of fear that still exists between the two forms of life. Relating to an animal is quite similar to the challenge of relating to your own subconscious—Basic Selves. An animal is fundamentally a Basic Self and while it has rudimentary brain and mind capability, it does not have a conscious mind as we know it, with the functions of reasoning. Therefore, wisdom and experience are gained primarily through trial and error but a Basic Self may draw on experience from the past through embodiment in previous animals, humans or from the accumulated fund of experience through the devas. The animals begin under group spirit and then through their association with us as pets begin to develop more and more individualized consciousness in preparation for one day being in a human. A cat recently came to me to be trained by my Basic Self, whose last animal embodiment was a cat, in preparation to be in a human for the first time. She has now gone on to that exciting experience.

It is through this knowledge that I have finally found one explanation for the strange concept of transmigration of souls. Let us imagine a Basic Self of animal origin who has just completed its first life in a human and really couldn't quite do it well enough. It is decided by the angels of destiny that another life in an animal might provide the optimal growth. This does not mean that the human *as a whole* is reincarnated in the animal. While anomalies do happen on this experimental planet, it would be extremely rare, if it is possible at all, to find a human conscious mind in an animal. The presence of a High Self would also be somewhat superfluous. The over-lighting deva performs this higher attunement. While animals are most beautiful creations of The Supreme, they do not have the kind of minds that conceive of spiritual values; and so would not be responsive to the leadings and indwelling of a High Self. On the rare occasions when animals have performed human-type mental functions I think it is the guiding deva teaching us something or it is an experiment of some kind.

We can certainly learn much and profit much by co-creating, in love, with the animals. In the process, we will learn much that we can apply to our own natures.

What about communication between humans? Man's myriad fears have stood in the way of the ecstasy and power wrapped up in the potentialities of men and women linking, working together in minds, hearts and bodies, and taking harmonious action in the world. In addition, these fears have often blocked humans from supporting each other's spiritual growth. The Aquarian Age is certainly the age of the group and with meditation groups, healing groups, mass meditations and international organizations of people with a purpose of oneness, we are beginning to see some of the wonderful things that can be accomplished when people can resonate together in love and concerted action. More and more of our visionaries are realizing that this may be essential if we are to counteract the growing threats to our survival.

In past ages the human order and the angelic order have been in much closer rapport. In more recent times, and during the so-called scientific age, we humans seem to have lost the sensitivities to be aware of the vast work of the angels. The seraphim, as a general class of beings, are the creations of the Infinite Spirit, the Third Aspect of Deity, through the Creative Mother Spirit of the local universe. Their primary function is to minister to all forms of life on the inhabited planets and so they might be thought of as the custodians of the planet. They do not die and are more or less permanently assigned to a planet. In 1953, the publication date of *The Urantia Book*, it listed 597,196,800 pairs of seraphim assigned to service on this planet. There are a similar number of their helpers, the cherubim. While they can work alone, their most important work is done as a polarized pair, yang and yin, aggressive and receptive. This order includes a vast hierarchy of beings who do not work with duality as do we humans, thus they know not negativity and channel the Light of the Holy Spirit into a thousand jobs supportive of life. They range from the tiny points of light that carry prana into the plants, called elementals, to the plant devas, to devas working with minerals and animals, to the seraphim assigned to human progression toward the Light, to the larger angels of the weather and those in charge of nations and races.

There is no doubt anymore that each human has a guardian angel—actually two. Whether you are in a group of a thousand with a pair or one hundred or ten or even one, should you have enough Light work to keep one pair busy, you can consider that you have a pair. Whatever grouping you are in, the guardian angels are able to take care of you. They see very well your life plan and they work in two primary areas: to guide you toward things, places, people and beings for your highest growth and to warn you of situations which might threaten your survival. The guardian seraphim role is a highly sought-after assignment and there can sometimes be a hundred applicants for an opening.

Did you know that many mentions of angels and reports of communications with them were taken out of the Bible around 500 A.D. in order to strengthen the story of Jesus? Nowadays we are seeing a shift from the left brain, rational and scientific approach to life to the right brain, intuitive-artistic approach and we are seeing more and more people developing the sensitivities to attune to, and communicate with, the angels.

My miracle at Findhorn is a good example. Ever since 1973, when I channeled for a presence over my harp there, one of the most beautiful experience of my life, I have enjoyed a growing rapport with many types of angelic beings. I work closely with my guarding seraphim in bringing through music from higher planets in my human and planetary healing ministry with music. My experiences with trees alone have been richly rewarding and fulfilling, as I will be reporting. Then for a number of years at every healing concert-celebration these shining presences are seen on the stage around me and in the audience working with those people who are open to their healing care. I owe much of the success of my ministry to their love and wisdom.

I invite you to reach out with love and sensitivity to these beautiful beings. There are no longer any diabolic or negative angels on this planet. You might begin by giving thanks to them when you eat your food, for you are about to partake of their handiwork. Whenever you wish to use a mineral, a plant, an animal or even work with another human being, ask if this form of life, and especially the devic forces connected with it, would like to co-create with you. Again, they do wish to serve but they like to be asked. Out of the many evidences of the success of this in my life have been the countless times I have received a break in the rain to load or unload my harp. They always try to do their best but it's probably easier if the request involves service to others.

We are created to be creators. It is our destiny. The entire ascension career, through our system, the constellation, the universe, the minor and major sectors, the super universe and on to the central sun universe, is a vast schooling in creativity, that we might come into the presence of the Universal Father of all, able to create with Him. Actually I prefer to use the word "Hirm," Him-Her. During this panoramic adventure, we are told that we will exchange energy with a host of marvelous places and beings. We are also told that once we leave this isolated planet, any contactable being will be friendly and that we will never be without access to a guide or companion.

People ask. "How do you relate to a space being?" I tell them that there are many kinds of space beings walking around in bodies on the earth today, so we can start practicing tomorrow. Also, we are provided with various forms of life here with which to work out co-creative relationships: minerals, plants, animals and angels—fascinating opportunities to prepare us for socializing in space.

What holds us back? Most often, contraction caused by a host of fears. To visitors from space, this planet is often known as the planet of fears—we are masters of them, and we have hundreds. Since most of them are connected with the physical vehicle, the first step in deflating fear is to learn and know that you are much more than your body. As grateful as you are for a smooth-running, healthy vehicle for your spiritual quest, your outer, finer bodies are the ones that have more survival potential. These would be those extending out past your Etheric Body, which is your true physical body and is found roughly five inches past your skin. These are your Emotional-Astral Body, your Mental Body, and your more subtle bodies: the Intuitional, Spiritual, Monadic, and Divine. These names are from the ascended masters through Theosophy.

As you learn about them and put more energy into them, you will find that they protect the physical and you will begin to lose the fear of death. You can drop other fears as well, as you develop more and more faith in the higher forces that are at all times working for you and offering their guidance and protection. The basic ones are: 1) your High Self—the fragment of the Universal Father assigned to you; 2) your guardian seraphim—they can see your optimum life plan and guide you toward it and protect you; 3) the Spirit of Truth and Beauty—the personal spiritual circuit of Christ Michael, the Creator of this local universe, ever-present on the earth; and 4) the Holy Spirit—

the personal spiritual circuit of the Creative Mother Spirit of the local universe, ever-present on the earth.

THIS IS AN INVITATION, THEN, TO CO-CREATE WITH ASPECTS OF YOUR WONDERFUL SELF, ALL FORMS OF EXQUISITE LIFE ON THIS PLANET AND THESE HIGHER FORCES SO SHINING WITH LOVE; TO USE YOUR SENSE OF SELF, NOT TO LIMIT YOURSELF, BUT TO EXPAND YOURSELF TO INCLUDE AS MUCH OF LIFE AS POSSIBLE. MEDITATE ON THIS EXPANSION, VISUALIZE IT, DECREE IT AND ACCEPT IT. THEN EXPECT TO NEVER FEEL LONELINESS AGAIN BUT TO EMBRACE THE PLAYFULNESS AND ECSTASY THAT IS THE BIRTHRIGHT OF THE PLANETARY AND UNIVERSE CITIZEN.

8

Interspecies Communication: Talking to Plants

The ancient wisdom tells us, and our adepts, masters, and spiritual teachers echo this, that all life is one. Is it not possible, then, that the life forms on this planet have the capability of communicating with each other? And, in addition, that this rapport might be going on somewhat constantly? Science is reporting that there is not as much difference between the basic building blocks of the various species of life as we thought, that very slight re-arrangements of DNA and chromosomes produce the kaleidoscope of life forms we observe around us, including us humans.

In this chapter, I would like to support these hypotheses with examples (evidential) and insights from my many years of practicing my belief in the oneness of all life by developing the art of talking to the plant kingdom. In the next chapter, when I talk to animals, I will include some experiences by an expert in this field.

Now, of course, I am not the only one who has experienced this kind of communication, so first I will share a very special story of what a close friend of mine experienced.

A POTTED PLANT REACHES OUT

I met David at the Oasis Human Potential Center in Chicago when he was the director. After my workshop, we spent some time together. We hit it off, and he told me this amazing story. He was living alone, he loved plants, and he had just acquired a potted flower—I wish I could remember what variety. After three weeks of taking care of it, he was called unexpectedly away on business. He asked a friend to come in every few days and water the plant. He missed his new flower friend over the three weeks he was away, so the first thing he did on his return was draw up a chair right next to the plant. He put out his hand in a gesture of love and the plant sent out a tendril which *wrapped around his finger.* Can you imagine that? He said that, at first, it was a bit of a shock, as he had never seen a plant move like that—who has?—unless it was one of those rare African flowers that snaps shut to trap an insect.

My friend realized how much his plant had missed him and felt privileged to experience this interspecies love.

The Deep Peace Of Trees

I have always had a special love for trees and have been practicing talking to them for many years. It was slow going for the first three years until I realized that I just was not achieving a deep enough state of peace. Trees, in spite of their height and size, are *very peaceful*. So for many months I talked to the trees, telling them how beautiful they were and how much I loved them and asking my guardian seraphim to carry my message to the deva of the tree. All plants have guiding spirits, which are members of the vast angelic order, and they attract the elementals, the tiny points of light which help to sustain them. These tireless little workers take in prana, or life force, outside the plant, then fly inside the plant and release their charge. They love their work and they work happily, under the direction of the larger devas and angels.

After a long time, speaking lovingly to the trees, in a deepening state of peace, I began to receive messages from them. How exciting and rewarding this was.

Music From A Magnificent Sacred Cedar

The Sierra mountain range rises in the easternmost part of California, and opposite Sacramento, about half way up the foothills, at about 3,000 feet, lies the tree-filled town of Nevada City. One of the foremost disciples of Yogananda, Kryananda, founded a center there and I was asked to give a concert in their 50-foot dome. This was around 1979. The recording engineer could not make the concert so he asked me to record in the dome the next morning. When I stopped in at the coffee shop for tea there was only one member of the community there, a young woman, and she asked me to come with her down a path to a spot where some of the members had been playing volleyball. She wanted to see what kind of vibrations I might pick up. She and some others had felt that it was a sacred space and should not be used for sports. I asked her if I could come after my recording session but she was insistent, feeling that I really should come before the session, so down the path we went.

We came out of some small trees to the edge of a flat, triangular area about 150 feet across. She was behind me and I immediately went into the meditative state I use when I ask my body to act as a dowsing instrument for earth energies. Right away, I found myself rushed forward 30 feet, then turned around 90 degrees and rushed 30 feet to the right. Then turned again and rushed back to my starting position, inscribing a triangle. The force was strong and as I stood there, I experienced a powerful stream of energy coming from directly behind me and extending across the little meadow. Turning around I beheld a magnificent, old cedar, six or seven feet in diameter, with just a few gnarled branches at the top. I walked slowly toward it, asking respectfully if I might enter its aura. I distinctly heard it say, "Come to me." As I approached, I remembered how much I needed some healing and threw my arms as far around the base of the tree as I could reach. This embrace could not have lasted more than two minutes, but its deep peace, grounded life force, and lofty ascension did much to prepare me for the coming session.

As I backed away I gave it the Namasté salutation—palms together, level with the heart, symbolizing "The Divine in me salutes the Divine in you." As I have probably mentioned, I have had some training and experience in receiving names from planets, beings in spirit, and entities in nature, so I asked the cedar its name and heard it clearly: "Ematana."

I quickly analyzed its symbolism according to the master's system. The E is its Purpose of Growth—to seek more direct contact with the Light. Then the rest of the letters are the experience it's drawing on: the M—Intuitive Approach to Survival, the A —Divine Mother Principle itself, the T—the Form Aspect of the Physical, the A—Divine Mother Principle, the N—Physical Energy, and the A—Divine Mother Principle. I noticed also that it had T, N, and A, all in a row, which represents the successful coordination of the three aspects of the Physical Plane—the three ways Divine Mother brings into form the Divine Father blueprints. I did this analysis in about three minutes, gave great thanks to Ematana, and as we walked on up the hill to the dome, I explained it to the girl.

At this point, I still did not know what the subject of my channeling would be, but I was guided to tune my harp to the Overtone Series of F—the angels and devas of nature. While I tuned, the engineer, in order to capture the unique sonority of the space, aimed the microphones directly at the top of the dome instead of toward the harp. The effect is as if the listener is on top of the dome listening through an opening and it lends an unusually eerie and devic quality to the music.

The music was most distinctive and filled with the qualities of power, beauty, and dedication. It covered the whole range of the harp and seemed to emphasize the deepest register and the very highest octaves. When it was over, I announced to the seven people who were present that we had just brought through the music of the old cedar tree at the foot of the hill. I explained that the parts of the music in the bass symbolized the roots going deep into the earth and the high parts symbolized the highest branches reaching to the sun and to the Light. I asked them if they would like to meet Ematana. As we walked down the path, I had an incredible surprise. The first time down the path, I had not noticed the top of this tree and, of course, had not seen it walking back up the path. What I saw now stopped me in my tracks. Above the branches at the top of the tree was a fifteen-foot spire, silver from having been struck by lightning, and shining in the sun. Here was one tree, which certainly had achieved its Purpose of Growth: To make Direct Contact with the Light. I told my new friends my experience before the session and we gave our love and wonder to this "Warrior of the Difficult Path" and now "Carrier of the Light."

Two-Way Conversation With A Ponderosa Pine

Here is an account of the first time, after years of practice, I had a two-way conversation with a tree. It was in the mountains above Taos, New Mexico. After I had been admiring it for a while, the tree replied with a "Thank you." Then I explained that I play music on an instrument that is made from a tree and projected to it a picture of my harp. I wished I could play for my new friend so I asked my guardian seraphim to send the tree a sample of my music. The pine said. "Oh, that's very nice." By then its voice, through me, was taking on an individual quality, giving me some evidence that I was not imagining the conversation—I do have a skeptical side. Probably, at first, my guardian angel was "translating"—however that works.

Then I asked the pine, "Have you ever heard any other human music?" The tree answered in its soft, innocent voice, "Yes, a young man came near me and played what I think you call a violin. I enjoyed it very much, but being a single melody, his music was quite different from yours. You're the first human to talk to me but I often receive the thoughts and feelings of the humans who walk near me." We talked for a while longer but then I had to leave, so I sent my love to the tree, thanking it for talking to me.

I came down the mountain filled with awe, the satisfaction of long-awaited success, and the heart-felt appreciation of the humility of this fellow creature who was so much larger than I. Later I was to find this childlike naïveté common in subsequent talks with trees and other members of the plant kingdom—a refreshing contrast with most of the human clan, although I suspect it still lurks just under our facades.

I Am Gifted A Christmas Tree

Just a few months later, I was living in a house I built on the family property in the foothills above Santa Barbara, California. Christmas was approaching and I wondered if I might be allowed to cut the top off a tree to help us celebrate the Rebirth of the Light in my living room. I did not want to cut down a tree but there grew a number of pines nearby and one of them was about to grow into the power lines and would have to be trimmed sometime soon. So I asked it if I could just take the top five or six feet, but I got a lukewarm response. I thanked it, sent it my love, and turned away. Then I saw two taller pines that were growing quite close to each other. They were even more crowded since one had divided into two trunks. The thought struck me that if I took the middle trunk it would leave more room for the other two.

When I asked, the tree replied, "That would be all right, if you will doctor the wound." Now I am not an experienced horticulturist so this would not have occurred to me, and so was "evidential." When I asked, "Are you sure this would be O.K.?" the tree answered, "I wish to serve." So I learned here, and from other trees, that in most cases they do wish to serve life, but not always, so we should always ask, out of respect. I went downtown and bought the proper salve, and then once more asked the tree if it was all right. It said again, "I wish to serve." I cut the tree and took it into my living room. It reached exactly to the ceiling—twelve feet above the floor. This was rather magnificent—much better than the six-foot treetop would have been.

I Record The Music Of A Giant Cypress

Around the same time, a friend told me of an enormous cypress tree on an estate just south of where I lived. It was a beautiful retreat center with many gardens. I love cypresses for their strength and curvaceous limbs which, when they grow near the sea, are sculptured by the offshore winds. When I met this magnificent tree, I was taken aback by its size. It looked as if five trees had gown together. After I bowed to it in reverence, I walked around it and estimated that it could not have been less than eight feet in diameter and probably at least 200, or more, years old.

When I stepped back and looked at the top of it there were only a few branches of leaves and I remembered that my friend was afraid it was dying. When I spoke to the tree, it said it had lost a friend and I wondered if it had not been watered lately. I was about to leave on a four-week concert tour of the Northwest and told the tree I wanted to see it better when I returned. Then I remembered that I was beginning to request, and receive, names for trees, so I asked and heard, with great strength and emphasis, "Mo, Momana, Momanadek." What a perfect name for this powerful representative of his species.

Deeply concerned, I went to the office. They did not realize the tree might be dying, but they said their Japanese gardener had recently left and they had not found a replacement. It also came out that the water table had been receding over the last few months. I reminded them that this rare treasure must be a valued feature of the estate, they could not let it die, and could they please give it some extra water? I also pointed out that if it did die it would be a huge and costly job to cut it up and remove it. Then I knew that the Japanese gardener was Momanadek's lost friend.

Filled with concern that my new friend might not last long, I had an inspiration and I returned to Momanadek. I asked him if he would give me his personal vibrations—his music—and I asked my master guides and angels that I might be able to record it and retain it. With the hope that this was successful, I bid Momanadek a loving farewell. I left on tour with the hope that I would be guided when to play this unusual music and that I would be able to re-create it on the harp.

In Vancouver, Washington, I was to play a concert and was meeting with the minister of the New Thought Church. Without any nudging from me, she said that many members of her congregation were interested in the environment, especially trees. That was my cue. So at the concert, after Intermission, I briefly told my story of meeting Momanadek and then, with a little trepidation, I brought through his music. It was unique, obviously "tree music," and I truly felt I was sharing this great tree's spirit with these tree lovers. As soon as I returned home I visited Momanadek and he seemed to be somewhat improved.

A Cork Oak Donates The Perfect Cork

In 1997, we moved to a 100-year-old apple farm on the Mendocino Coast north of San Francisco. We were not ready to hook up our hot tub, but we thought we would fill it with water for emergencies. To plug one of the hoses I needed a cork about an inch-and-a-half in diameter and about four inches long. Now it just so happened that there grew on the farm six cork oak trees—the ones that supply the cork for the wine bottles. Not indigenous, they had been imported from Portugal seventy years ago for a High School project. The tallest, just outside our kitchen window, had attained some 45 feet in height. Their bark is soft and a little rubbery—a special pleasure to touch—and I often talk to them.

An arborist came once to cut down acacias that were threatening the house. We saved the wood for firewood and gave great thanks to the acacias. He told me the story of the High School project and then added that I could harvest the cork and sell it to the burgeoning wine industry in northern California. I asked him how long it would take the tree to regrow its bark and he said, "Only about seven years." I said, "Forget it. This tree is my special friend and I'm not going to denude it of its protective clothes." He was a little taken aback, but how could he know my history of communication with our sylvan siblings?

To get back to my need for a cork for the hot tub: I went around asking each cork oak if I could have enough cork to make the plug. The first four resulted in subdued and hesitant arm tests. By this time, I would hold a branch or leaf as I asked the question and then muscle-test for the answer. This works well for a quick answer to a yes-or-no question, and sometimes words are added. When I got a negative response, I showed respect and move right on to the next tree. When I asked the fifth tree, it said, "You may take it if you take it down there where I come out of the earth. I looked down and, sure enough, just above the leaves, was a thickening of the cork. But, just to check, I asked, "Are you sure?" and it replied, "I wish to serve." I was so moved by this!

I carved out a chunk, covered up the place with soil and leaves, thanked the oak, and fashioned a perfect cork for the hot tub hose.

An Oak Tree Curious About Traffic

In the summer of 1992, in Ben Lomand, near Santa Cruz, I was giving a workshop in my house for harpists in the fine art of improvisation and performance. We had been concentrating on creating music for three hours and I felt we all needed a break. So I invited my students out behind my house to sit around my live oak tree, settle into a deep peace, and then become receptive to what they might pick up from the tree. I had not actually had a conversation with this tree, though for some years I had often sent my love to it. About ten feet from our back door the tree had a spray of tiny branches and my wife and I had wondered if it might look better if I trimmed them. I had imagined that perhaps some kind of wound or eggs of an insect had produced this spray, which was about two-and-one-half feet in diameter. After I had closed out the outside world and gone within, I reached a deep enough level to ask the tree if it would like me to prune the spray. Immediately I heard "Please don't do it. That's my antennae." I already had learned that trees, although stationary, are in touch with other trees, especially of their own species, over large distances. I learned that this spray of fine branches was acting as an aerial, picking up messages from its brothers and sisters all over the valley.

We lived on a busy street and, as I sat there thinking about its antennae, this tree asked me "Where are all these cars going?" When this unusual question—possible evidential—sank in, I could understand how puzzling it could be for a life form without mobility to have cars whizzing by 20 feet from its branches. For a moment, I felt a little embarrassed to be part of the human race but, trying to answer the tree's question, I said, "Please forgive the humans. They are going through a phase in their development right now where they think life will be better 'over there.' The wiser ones are realizing that the one who arrives is much the same as the one who left. Of course, they are also about the business of survival and experiencing being closer to their friends and family as well as exploring their mobility. Please excuse the smell and the noise. We are working on healthier means of transportation."

An entire year passed and again I gathered with my class around the oak. When I attuned myself to the tree it said, "We have been tracking these cars, and we have figured out where they are going." I was astonished. Surely, you will agree that I could never have imagined such a thing. First, they would have to identify each car. Then somehow pass along a picture of it from tree to tree, or did they broadcast the sound it made? Then I remembered that I had been studying the shapes in boards and paneling sawn from trees and had formed the hypothesis that trees take pictures of people and animals they see around them. If you study these shapes, you will see them.

I hope these few accounts will give a rich picture of some of the possibilities that await the diligent and patient student who wishes to converse with plants and trees. They are chosen out of many such experiences—some major, some minor. You will find more in my first book *A Harp Full of Stars*. Some of the shorter ones have been no less important and educational. In my garden and greenhouse I often need to know whether a plant has enough water, fertilizer, sun, or shade and these questions can be settled in five or six minutes by holding on to a leaf, asking the question, and muscle-testing. Then, all plants have an aura, or more exactly, an extended "etheric" body. Often I can feel how far out the plant's true body extends, as I can with the outer bodies of humans, including my own—a skill most people can learn with a little guidance and practice. But to find out if a certain plant is too close to its neighbor, and feels crowded, I have to ask. Only on rare occasions do I see, with inner sight, these outer bodies. Later on in this book, I will discuss the basic human bodies. And now: animals.

9

Interspecies Communication: Talking to Animals

From my research into the nature of our subconscious, which I call our "Basic Selves," and which I explore in depth in the next chapter, I know that a large percentage of them have had origin in the animals. This is where we developed our keen and remarkable five senses. So it is not surprising that I have become increasingly aware that our pets, especially dogs and cats, are in close rapport with our Basic Selves. It could even be said that your pet animal is primarily the companion of your body consciousness. As you have probably noticed, they often show uncanny awareness of what you are feeling, sometimes even before your conscious mind knows it. So it should not be surprising that one can develop the art of communicating with animals. Of course, a little higher guidance and some clues from the experts can help. Here are some examples, out of many:

CAT DEALS WITH NIGHTMARE

A friend of mine told me that often, when she was having a nightmare, her cat would awaken her. Then she would just sit there, staring at her, until my friend worked it through enough to go back to sleep. In other words, her cat was woken up by the scary dreams her Basic Self companion was having. I have observed that cats require, and are champions for, peace and harmony. One reason they purr is to release extra tension.

HOW TO LOVE A FERAL CAT

Here is another story from my own experience: When my wife and I moved onto our five-acre, 100-year-old apple farm, there was a wild cat already in residence. I love cats and I was frustrated that I couldn't pet her. We named her "Gloria," thought of her as our cat, and let her forage in our compost pile. It was a challenge to love her from afar. When I put focused energy into this, Gloria would bat her eyes. I gradually came to know that this meant that she had received my love.

Then we met a woman who lives in our neighborhood and is an expert in communicating with animals. Serafina shared our frustration with Gloria and the woman said, "Cats communicate through pictures. Try forming a strong image in your mind and sending it to her." It worked like a charm. The next day Gloria, who never came near us unless we fed her, was brushing against Serafina's legs.

A Garden Spider Repositions Its Web

The path to my greenhouse passes through a narrow place next to a falling-down goat house. One morning, on my way out to water the green house, I ran right into a spider web. I just narrowly escaped getting the huge yellow spider on my face. I felt stupid, running into, and damaging, his carefully fashioned web, but in eight years, I had never seen one there. It was somewhat comforting when I realized that to be a success a web is intentionally created to be invisible. Then I asked to be able to communicate with the spider and apologetically said, "I don't want to hurt you, or your web, but I need to pass through here almost every day. Could you just make your web higher?"

Two days later, when I walked out to the greenhouse, the spider's web was just over my head and *horizontal*. I had never seen such a thing, have you? I thought this was a miracle since webs are usually vertical to catch the most flying insects. I should note that after three years a vertical web has again appeared.

Gophers In My Vegetable Garden!

I have had some success with gophers, but have found that it only lasts one full cycle of the year. I have assumed that by then I was dealing with a new generation and that my contract was not inherited. It could have been the same with the spider. Now, so you will not think I am the only one who has developed communication with animals, I will share two accounts by an expert in this field.

Conference On Interspecies Communication

Sometime in the late '80s my wife and I were invited to take part in this unusual gathering, which took place in Tucson, Arizona. I had been talking to trees and the ascended masters for a few years, and of course, co-creating music with the masters and angels and Serafina had begun to channel from her seraphim, so we were excited to hear what other intuitives were experiencing. Serafina read some of her channeled poetry, punctuated here and there with my Celtic Harp, in the style of the Irish bards. I brought through a 15-minute piece to bring peace and love to the audience, to help dissolve the barriers between the planes of being, and help them attune to each other and their highest guidance. About 200 attendees took part in this unique conference, and a number of people with origin on other planets, and two or three "walk-ins" were emboldened to confess, and comment on their outer space connections. Of course, I cannot vouch for the veracity of these confessions, but can certainly report that some of them seemed genuine.

There was one very impressive woman who presented there and told a number of stories. I believe her name was Samantha. She is fairly well-known for her service work with animals. I will tell two of her stories that are indelibly written on my memory. By their very nature, and detail, you will be able to tell that they are authentic. At the time of the conference she was writing a book—perhaps it has been published.

A Robin And A Cat Patch It Up

When Samantha was living in the Midwest, she was called to New York to work with a friend's cat who was acting up in strange ways. Samantha had a pet robin with whom she was very close and so she arranged proper care for the robin while she would be away. She told the robin that she had to go on a trip to help heal a cat and would be back in ten days. Now you and I know, and the robin knew, that cats instinctively feel that birds are their dinner. Nevertheless the Robin said, "I don't want to stay here; please let me come with you." After some back and forth, Samantha agreed, but when she was packing, she included a cage and they set off by car for New York. Slides accompanied this story and the first one showed Samantha driving along the highway with the robin on her *left* shoulder *with the window open*. She said truckers who passed her would hang back just to get an eyeful of this incredible sight.

The owner of the cat was away on business so there were just the three of them in the apartment. Samantha greeted the cat on entering and explained to him that the robin was her dear friend and that she expected him to behave himself. At the same time, she deemed it wise to keep the robin in the cage, high off the floor, in a safe place. Then she showed a slide of the first time, after two days, she put the cage on the floor. The cat is crouching about 20 feet away, alert, with its tail twitching. Two days later, a slide shows the cat halfway across the floor toward the cage and much more peaceful. Three days after that the cat is snuggled up against the cage, asleep. Of course, every day Samantha is talking to, and working with, the cat.

What an amazing and inspiring picture: these traditional enemies, not only at peace, but enjoying the close company of each other.

Moreover, a human, one of the more warlike species on Earth, negotiated it. In the last few years, on the internet, I have seen more and more animals snuggling up who are normally enemies.

Crisis At The San Diego Zoo

The keepers were having some serious problems with the elephants. In the morning, when they rolled up the big metal doors, the elephants would rush out, led by their larger leader. The keeper's methods had not proved effective, the situation had grown worse, and they finally called in Samantha. First off, she asked the lead elephant how she was. The answer, with emotion, was "My foot hurts." With guidance from Samantha, the keepers were able to lift the elephant's foot and found a sizable thorn in it.

After the thorn was removed, Samantha was talking to the elephant, explaining the anxiety of the keepers when the elephants rushed out in the morning. Just then, the head keeper called to her from a distance away. She turned to walk toward him and the elephant followed her, dangerously close to her foot, obviously upset. Samantha stopped and asked what the problem was. The elephant replied, "We were having a conversation and you just turned away." Samantha said, "I am so sorry. Please forgive me." Then we see a slide showing the elephant *kneeling down in front of Samantha and she's embracing the elephant's head.* I wager you have never contemplated just how you would embrace an elephant, but now we know how it is done, thanks to the amazing Samantha—an example of "Love will find a way." Then Samantha asks her enormous friend if there was anything else bothering the elephants. She received this reply: "Some weeks ago one of our older members died and the body was taken out of our compound before we could do our ritual of releasing and passing over. Samantha could tell that this could be contributing to the problems the elephants were causing. When she questioned the keepers about this they said, "Most of that animal has been removed, but we might still have the head. Do you think that would help?" Samantha replied, "It's certainly worth a try."

As soon as they put the head in the compound, all the elephants started circling it, making strange sounds, and pushing the head around with their trunks. After some 45 minutes of this seemingly well-organized ceremony, they all stopped at once. Samantha said that later the lead elephant expressed thanks.

The very next morning, when the attendants rolled up the big doors, the elephants came out peacefully, connected trunk to tail, trunk to tail, trunk to tail. As we can see here, communication with animals can reveal the "inside story" as little else can.

My Work With Dolphins

This was one of my most fascinating adventures in communication between species.

Around 1980 in Santa Barbara, I met Eric Lichtman who, for some years, had been "lending" his vocal equipment, as well as his mind, to a dolphin named Yuke ("you-kuh"). When she was speaking through him, his voice would go up an octave above his normal range with an energy noticeably higher than human.

Eric and I hit it off and I was intrigued and excited when he asked me to record with Yuke. He felt that the harp could provide a background like her natural environment, the glissandos of the harp sounding closer to the sea than probably any instrument short of the orchestra. Then he felt that my Sources would enhance the transmission. We ended up recording six sessions of this unique collaboration. As I write I am remembering that they took place in my studio in the basement of the Unity Church, one of the lowest places in the city—down near sea level. Our work culminated in a breakthrough in human/dolphin communication, something the experts, John Lilly and others, had been unsuccessful in doing, even though they had recorded and analyzed countless hours of dolphins conversing.

I began the first session with glissandos in the deepest range of the harp, which I felt would invoke Earth Mother's aspect as Mother Sea. I chose the key of F, which in the system of pitch symbolism revealed by my masters over the years, symbolizes the natural world of the angels, devas, and elementals. When Yuke entered, it was with her high voice, which was familiar to us, but soon began going through the many voices of the creatures of the Pacific. Eric later corroborated that these were the painful cries of the sea and land creatures the humans have mistreated. Both Eric and I were deeply moved. We also agreed that the music of this unusual duet was most special.

For the second session, Eric and I decided that the opening should express compassion from the humans. When Yuke's voice entered, her anguish had somewhat diminished. It softened more in the third session and then she began to imitate what I had just played, proving that she had heard me. These back-and-forth patterns became more and more playful, ending up in a humorous section, all of which was suggestive of healing and forgiveness.

There were one or two more sessions, each becoming higher and more positive, and then I had an inspiration. If I could teach Yuke the master's system of Letter-Pitch Equivalents she might answer simple, "yes" or "no" questions by singing pitches which could be translated into words. It took something like an hour to go through the entire alphabet, but before Eric came out of trance, I asked Yuke two questions and received definite answers, since "yes" is three letters and "no" is two.

The first question was whether Yuke was the spirit of a dolphin that had passed on, or a spirit in the invisible realms taking on that name. The answer was "no" to both of these. The answer was "yes" to whether she was a living dolphin. In addition, it became clear that she was right off the Santa Barbara coast.

Eric said later that she was pleased with our sessions, that she loved us and that she would be willing to explore the collaboration further. He also said that going through the 26 letters of the alphabet and their equivalents—which, by the way I had played on the harp—was the most difficult and exhausting clairvoyant and clairaudient work he had ever done, but that for Yuke it was easy. This reminds me that once John Lilly set up a tank with a glass partition and put a dolphin couple—friends? mates?—one on each side, separated by the glass. Then he recorded their conversation for some hours. When it was brought down a few octaves, analysis revealed that they had conversed for eight hours *without repeating themselves.* My comment: "Amazing, now *that's* a relationship that could last."

This was the last session with Eric as the next step on his spiritual path took him 3,000 miles away to the East Coast. I felt most privileged to take part in this exploration with Eric and Yuke. Moreover, to have had the opportunity to show Yuke that there are at least some humans with compassion for our brothers and sisters, the sea and island creatures of the Pacific Basin.

Another friend of mine, who has developed psychic rapport with dolphins, reported that she has had success using the system given me by my Sources. It is called "The Mystical English Alphabet for the Spiritual Renaissance" and can be found in the Appendix of this book and in *A Harp Full of Stars*. Through the years, it has enabled me to complete over 1600 analyses of client's names. They have found them most helpful in understanding who they are, what they are drawing on from their past lives, and what their chosen purposes of growth are in the three basic areas: Personality, Subconscious, and Activity in the World. Chapter XIV is devoted to a number of my favorite applications of this code. I have carefully saved the cassettes of the Yuke sessions.

IF WE CAN TALK TO AN ELEPHANT, COULD WE TALK TO A WHALE?

For two years, I was a member of The Paul Winter Consort, a multi-styled jazz group. We toured the East Coast, especially the colleges. Those young people responded to Paul's great concern for the endangered species, especially wolves and whales, and we played music accompanying their recorded voices. Around 1986, The Consort journeyed to Magdalena Bay on the west coast of Baja California, Mexico, where the whales gather on their southward migration.

The plan was to play for the whales on a raft, right in the middle of the Bay, broadcast our music into the water with hydrophones, and try to ascertain their response. There was a group filming a documentary on the whales and when Paul heard that their helicopter would be over us at the time, he asked them to notice any signs that might suggest a response.

Before I ever got to the Bay, I had three experiences. As soon as I arrived at the base camp I met a girl who had gone out to the water's edge at dusk with her guitar. As she played, she reached out with love to the whales. After a while, a dolphin came up out of the water and just stared at her for some time. She was deeply moved by this appearance.

My second experience happened in this way: Paul had invited a well-known psychic to join us the next day. She said she would try to contact a whale and could I improvise some ocean background for her intuitive journey. It went well and later she said she entered the whale through its eye—and I remembered seeing an image of a great, iridescent iris. She reported that the whale was not angry with the humans. This in spite of the fact that we have seriously mistreated them, killing them and polluting their environment with chemicals, plastics, and sound until they can hardly navigate. They used to be in touch with each other over thousands of miles, through their sonar, and this has been reduced to something like 1500 miles. In spite of this, the whale was concerned for the human race.

The night before we were to leave for the raft in the middle of the Bay, Paul told us we would need to wake up at four in the morning. I have an inner clock so this was no problem, but when I got up everyone was still asleep. Remembering my guitarist friend's experience with the dolphin, I took my harp out to the water's edge of the bay and began to play. There did not seem to be any response. On inspiration, I retuned my harp to an Overtone Scale, the chord of Nature. After just six or seven minutes, a flock of birds began chirping, squawking, and flapping their wings. They had been asleep, standing on an island just off the bay shore that was about six inches under the surface of the water. The Overtone Series is a Law of Resonance, so I guess animals are not used to hearing it from us and it wakes them up. Also, birds sleep only lightly and usually on one leg, for safety.

On my return to camp, I asked after Paul and was told that he was seen on the beach snuggling up with a seal. When he came in from the beach, he seemed to be in some kind of trance. He explained that for much of his life he had had a dream of sleeping with an animal and now he had done it, and it had exceeded his imaginings. On top of that, this seal had beached itself and *needed him* so he had the added satisfaction of providing some loving healing.

When we had all assembled, including the recording engineer with his hydrophones and his walkie-talkie for communicating with our friends in the helicopter, we embarked in a small rowboat for the raft. Twice, on the way out, a whale came right under the boat, which was a little scary, but the whale never disturbed our passage. We hoped it was just checking us out and that we had passed inspection.

Paul had brought a bass sarousaphone, a first cousin of the saxophone, his primary instrument. This unusual "piece of plumbing" rises above just about everything in the orchestra except the basses and the conductor. Paul felt its lowest tones might carry best under the water and speak to these leviathan whales.

David Darling with his cello and I with my Celtic Harp filled out this valiant trio. We meditated a few minutes, reaching out from our hearts to the whales. After a few minutes of improvising, all three of us began to feel a strong emotion. Later the engineer said that at that moment our friends came through from the helicopter saying, "We don't know if you can see this, but the whales are making *a perfect circle around your raft.* What a miraculous demonstration, manifesting as a mandala probably three-quarters-of-a-mile across, involving much planning on Paul's part, the cooperation of the musicians, the recording man and his equipment, the helicopter crew, and, of course, the pod of whales.

A Duet Between My Harp And A Nightingale

On a European tour we stopped at a charming Bed-and-Breakfast on our way to the Provence Coast. On arrival they served us a summer dinner out under the trees. After dessert the owner's wife drew me aside, saying that she had a harp and would I play for the guests. I replied that it would be my pleasure. (I've had experience playing on many strange harps all over the world.) I said my affirmations and put heart and soul into two improvisations. They went very well and Serafina said that a two-year-old child, who had never seen or heard a harp before, was mesmerized by the music. She was clutching her knees in an ecstatic embrace.

Afterwards a man asked me, "Did you hear the nightingale singing with you?" I was so involved with my improvisation that I wasn't aware of it. He must have been a musician because he said, "Not only was the bird singing WHILE you were playing but it made music WITH YOU. This was most satisfying for me as I offer my music for all of life around me, including plants, animals, and angels. But here was such a beautiful example of co-creation coming from the bird kingdom.

10

The Treasure Chest:

A New Method for Directly Accessing

The Subconscious with Kinesiology

In this chapter I will report on research I have done over a period of 25 years, with over 200 clients with a new form of muscle-testing I developed which reveals many new aspects of a person's subconscious.

THE QUEST FOR BETTER COMMUNICATION WITH YOUR SUBCONSCIOUS SELF

Have you ever wished you could better communicate with your subconscious? As a young musician and harp student, I was deeply impressed with the wonders the body could accomplish in a musical performance and so was always working on better rapport between my mind and my body. Then, as I began trying to understand the strange behavior of others, *and* myself, I would often, out of frustration, wish there was some magical way of talking to my deeper self. I took some psychology courses in college, spending many a late night discussing how this hidden side of us operates, and learned a few valuable principles. Of course, Freud, the accepted father of psychology, called it the "*Un*conscious," as if it were not alive with awareness. How could a part of you that performs wonders for you every day, without which you could not live one day here on earth, be called by a name which describes what it is not? But let us honor Freud's great contribution and remember that in his time the scientific age was dawning and with it an emphasis on the mind, so it might have seemed natural to call the body consciousness the "*UN*conscious"—*other* than the mind.

Now we know that there were experts in this knowledge back through history, especially the Kahunas of the Hawaiian culture. They reported great sensitivities, intuitions, and abilities lying "below" the conscious mind. American films of the last 40 years have certainly explored and exploited the negative potential of the subconscious. Hollywood writers must have psychology degrees or psychologists on staff. Unfortunately their overall message rarely focuses on love triumphing over fear and the unresolved patterns from the past. Books reporting research by psychologists have revealed much about how this elusive aspect of us operates and hypnosis has often been quite effective. But we still don't have a practical language with which a person can bridge the gap between the mind and the subconscious, tap its awareness, gifts and powers, and set up a working, and eventually effective and loving relationship with it. Such a language is what I offer in this chapter.

We have received valuable revelations from *highly* reliable beings in spirit through some of our most respected intuitives, and I am most grateful for my own higher guidance, but I had to wait for the art of muscle-testing to provide a more direct, and much quicker, mode of communication.

How Does Muscle-Testing Work?

Muscle-testing, or "kinesiology," as it is called among its practitioners, consists basically of the practitioner, the "tester," and the client or patient, the "testee." They're standing or sitting. The client is asked to make the mind a blank and let the body answer. He, or she, extends the arm out horizontally, to the front or to the side, palm down. The practitioner reaches out to the subconscious, asks the question, and then says "Resist" and presses down. You will need to learn not to press down too hard, because you could overcome a strong answer; and you press, not on the hand, but just inward from it on the wrist. The client tries to keep the arm up but allows the body to express its own strength. The arm either 1) stays in the high position 2) is weak and goes all the way down, or 3) goes part of the way down. The high position indicates a "yes," the bottom position indicates a "no" and part way indicates a degree of answer between "no" and "yes." If the client has never been muscle-tested, you need to tell their body about these responses. We see, then, that there are basically two kinds of questions we can ask: a "yes or no" question or a "matter of degree" question. There is a third type of information the more experienced practitioner can receive and that is the quality of the response: immediate or delayed, forthright or shy.

You can readily see that these types of answers alone can open up a vast storehouse of information, especially if there is time to ask many follow-up questions. This aspect of my patients—later I will suggest a shorter and better name for them—are perfectly willing to answer almost any question put to them. It's as if they are honored to be asked. But it does help to reach out to them with love and respect, and also to affirm that you are asking *only for truth* each time you test. Extremely rarely it becomes clear that something is blocking the truthful answering. I developed a solution for this and will present it later, but your subconscious selves and those of your partner and close friends are just waiting to provide reliable information in the many areas of their knowledge. I believe we should try to figure out solutions to our everyday challenges, but when I'm stumped I ask my partner to muscle-test me, and am often surprised when it comes out the opposite of what my mind imagined. I have developed such faith in this information, and so has my partner, that I have been consulting it almost every other day for 30 years.

To support this I should mention at the outset, that your body consciousness has more direct rapport with your High Self than your conscious mind. This takes place especially at night, after it has dealt with the accumulation of tensions and imbalances from the stresses of the day's activities. Our great seer, Edgar Cayce, one of the most trustworthy intuitives of this country, and from whom I have learned much, corroborates this. Of course there are those who have developed the ability to go into meditation and receive clairvoyant guidance which seems to drop into the open, questioning mind. But we should still explore the role the subconscious may have played in that transmission. Most of the great sensitives put the conscious mind aside before they open to higher truth. All of Cayce's 14,000 readings were conducted in full trance.

WHAT KIND OF GIFTS ARE IN YOUR TREASURE CHEST?

Obviously, what follows is going to require two of you so I highly recommend that you have a muscle-testing friend, if for some reason you don't develop this invaluable practice with your close partner. This should be someone with whom you can get together at least every other day.

1) You can receive accurate information on what is best to put into your body. The best procedure is for the client to place their "receptive" hand on the food or beverage before the question is asked. Normally, this would be the left hand for right-handed people, the right hand for left-handed people. You can even check out medications. You can ask in general, "Would it be good for this client to have some of this now?" Then you can be more specific as to amounts, and times to take it.

I once took most of a day to go over everything a friend ate, drank, and took in. I remember he wanted to know how much Vitamin C to take. So I started with a small amount, and how often to take it, and the arm went all the way down. So I increased the amount gradually until the arm stayed all the way up. I always go past that and then come back to where it's just a strong response. Then I ask a yes or no question, "Is this correct?" If the answer is yes, we've got it. This was a revelation to him; he made major changes in his diet, realized benefits in many areas of his life, not the least of which was some much-needed weight loss.

What if you're in a restaurant trying to choose what to order from an unfamiliar menu? If you can't place your hand over the food, you can place a finger over the item on the menu, and then use the "restaurant muscle test." This was developed for those who are a little shy about muscle-testing in public, which is most of us. Touch first, then with both hands in your lap, make a circle between you left thumb and forefinger, if you are right-handed, ask the question, and try to break the circle apart with the right hand. If it strongly holds together, that's a "yes." coming easily apart is a "no," how hard it is to break apart shows a "matter of degree." The body consciousness picks up vibrations, so touching the menu works.

2.) In a similar way you can find out how colors and textures influence you. The colors of your walls and the fabrics you wear are affecting you and the people who are looking at you much more than you realize. I remember a dramatic story about a nursing home where they were having all kinds of arguments and friction between the patients. The color expert they called in noticed immediately the sick shade of yellow on the walls. The walls were painted green and the whole place calmed down. There is general esoteric symbolism for the colors (See Appendix), but remember that individuals have associations for colors from past experience also, which can change how the colors affect them.

3.) One of the most remarkable sensitivities of the body is how quickly it tunes in to the subconscious of other people. You can walk into a room and within minutes you have checked out everyone there and something in you knows if there's someone present who really doesn't like you, or is upset, or dangerous. This ability was developed thousands of years ago for survival. I'm sure you've had many experiences like this. So with muscle-testing you can ask questions about your relationships.

4.) Then you can ask about your job, a new job, where to move, or a possible new house. You can ask how certain people affect you, what it might be like to work with them, live with them, or even marry them. Naturally, the more important the question is, the more you want to check.

5.) You can explore many areas of your life, as long as it's not a question about a strictly mental process. Be adventuresome; your subconscious is much more alive and capable than you might imagine, is trying always to get through to you, and will welcome being honored by a closer communication with your conscious mind. Remember, we have three basic aspects: High Self, conscious mind, and body consciousness. One of our major challenges in self-realization is bringing about cooperation and harmony between these three. The rewards are unbelievable. The realized masters embody this rapport and, in response to many requests in my workshops, I have been inspired with a decree for it. (See Appendix.)

As I report on my research you will discover many more talents and abilities of which your subconscious is capable.

An Exciting New Direction Opens Up

Around 1971 I had a "Three Selves Attunement" from Bella Karish, one of the outstanding clairvoyants in this country at that time. The 3-hour session contained revelatory, and highly relevant, information from my past-lives as well as this life concerning my High Self, my conscious mind, and my subconscious, which she called my "Basic Selves."

What commanded my attention the most was the Basic Selves because she had developed the ability to allow my Basic Selves to speak through her. I had two at that time and when they spoke to me I had tears of recognition. They showed love for me and talked about the jobs they do in my body, and made humble requests that would make their jobs easier and my life better.

I was pleasantly shocked and it changed my life. At first I assumed she was creating these entities to speak about what she was reading in my body consciousness—a form of mind reading. But further research confirmed that my Basic Selves were living entities, my body-consciousness. Then the possibility occurred to me that, since I now knew what their activities were, if I had a problem in that area, I could talk to the appropriate one about it. After many years of research I can assure you that they are entities, good, and dedicated ones, most of whom have been with you since birth and stay with you for years—with a few notable exceptions.

At the time, Bella lived in Los Angeles and I was living in Virginia Beach, Virginia and, as far as I knew, she didn't do *in absentia* readings. So I was wishing there was some other way we could access the Basic Selves. I had been introduced to basic muscle-testing a few years earlier, so my partner and I began experimenting to see if we could check out some of the things about the Basic Selves I had learned from Bella. It was very successful—beyond my imaginings—and I gradually developed, I'm sure with guidance from my friends and masters in spirit, the new system I am presenting here.

Let's Up-Level The Name Of Your Subconscious

There are four reasons why I'd like to use the term Basic Selves from now on in this book. Of all the ancient cultures I've studied, it is apparently the Kahuna healers of Hawaii who studied the most extensively the nature and activities of what they called the "Low Selves" or "Basic Selves." We are grateful to Max Freedom Long for collecting this wisdom before much of it would have been lost due to westernization—American and British priests. First, when I read Max Freedom Long's book *The Secret Science behind Miracles* it became evident that the Kahunas knew much more about the subconscious than our American psychologists and psychiatrists. Second, Bella Karish had studied the Kahuna wisdom, called "Huna" in preparation for her work. Third, it respects the Basic Selves as being not "lower than the mind" but just a different level of consciousness. My research supports this as you will see. Fourth, it's much easier to spell and write.

Fundamental Nature Of Our Basic Selves

My Sources have advised me to state the following at the outset: Nothing I say in this chapter is intended to encourage you to get in the habit of thinking of yourself in terms of *parts*. One of your mandates is to unify and make whole and harmonious all aspects of your being. The prime example I often give here is that we cannot do better than emulate "The All That Is" which delights in creating an unbelievably rich diversity and yet is always a harmonious One. "Sohiez" could also be called "One/one." On the other hand, shouldn't it help to know something about the aspects you are bringing into harmony—especially if these aspects have differing experience and skills upon which you might wish to draw?

New Method For Accessing And Getting To Know Your Subconscious

So you're standing or sitting beside your client, partner, or friend. You've arranged to record the session for later study and you have pen and at least two sheets of paper handy. You've asked them to make their mind a blank so it won't affect their responses, and to just let the body give the answers. Their arm is stretched out horizontally, palm down, preferably in front so you're not behind them. At this point, either arm will do, and you can change over if one gets tired. Your hand rests lightly just above the wrist, not on the hand. You might like to say an affirmation, decreeing and accepting the success and upliftment of the session. Call on whatever you hold as the highest. I say "In the Name and Power of the Living Christ, I place this session in Divine Order, and I ask that there be no limit to the information, understanding, and love that could come forth here." Then add something like "I reach out with love to your Basic Selves and invite them to reveal their nature and I ask only for truth," while projecting your love to the solar plexus area of your client. The Basic Selves can be focused anywhere in the body, even outside of it, as we will discover, but their main headquarters is the abdominal cavity. Just know that they hear you, especially when your words are charged with feeling.

Then ask for a strong response in order to feel the person's strength and then a weak response. The Basic Selves are dedicated to carrying out the mind's wishes, unless it threatens survival—more about this later. It has happened where the Basic Selves had such a strong desire to cooperate that when the client says to his body "I want you to try to keep this arm up." there *is* no weak response. Then you ask for a weak response and ask that there be more difference between a strong and a weak.

It is quite rare, but once, a few minutes into the session, I realized that the Basic Selves weren't cooperating with true answers, as they almost always had done. This was due to the presence of a discarnate entity. I sent the entity on its way and then we got honest answers. (See the Appendix for a decree to clear these not-so-nice entities.) This is getting more and more common, but is not to be construed as possession, which is more serious. They are known as eating companions because they enter a person, when they are over tired or filled with a negative emotion, to feed off their energy. Unfortunately they will think nothing of stimulating your energy by stirring your emotions through frustration or arguments. I have found the affirmation quite effective.

Note: One of the wonderful features of the material of this chapter is that, once you have some experience muscle-testing, you can check on everything I say about the Basic Selves for yourself. Just be sure you're getting true answers—you probably are—and remember that there is a vast variety of Basic Selves. I have only scratched the surface and already have discovered an incredibly rich diversification, along with the generic qualities and purposes they all share. You might even be guided to carry this research forward.

First Question: How Many Basic Selves Does This Client Have?

Ask how many are present by saying: Is there one? (test) Are there two? (test) Three? (test) And so on until you get a weak, then ask for a yes if the last number was correct. When you have established how many there are, write them down as half-inch circles across the top of the page. Then ask them if they would please line up, any pairs coming first, starting close to you and stretching away from you across your client's abdomen.

In one fascinating case the number went on and on, and it turned out there was one large Basic Self with many facets. Eventually it came to light that my client had been an actor who played many roles. I have found it amazing, uncovering the rich variety of Basic Selves and I have learned much about people.

Where Do Basic Selves Come From?

I learned from Bella Karish, and I have found this true, that there are three main origins of Basic Selves: the animal kingdom, the devic—a division of the angelic kingdom overlighting the plants and animals—, and space—other inhabited planets. I've found there can also be space-animal and space-devic and these will gladly identify themselves. I ask No.1 its origin, then ask how much it has developed rapport with the other two, and write it down. I use A(animal), D(devic), and S(space) in different sizes, depending how strong the attunement. The ones that are strong in all three are the more experienced and evolved ones who have been around the longest.

Do They Have Masculine And Feminine Polarity?

Next I ask each one, by number, the closest being number one, whether it is masculine or feminine, and they tell me. I write down an "f" or an "m" in the circle. Yes, the arm response is "softer" or "harder" and it's about now that you begin to feel you are communicating with living entities, and it feels more intimate.

Actually, the vast majority of people on this planet have had experience as the body consciousness of animals, sometimes gathering the skills and experience of many different animal forms. So almost all humans have at least one animal Basic Self, and yes, this is where we get our sense of hearing, seeing, smelling, tasting, and touching. I don't know if it's possible to be given these as a gift, but 99% of the time these awarenesses have been developed over thousands of years. This is why different people have different sensitivity skills, some of them quite amazing. (How about fire-walking?) With some practice you can begin to see the last animal in which a Basic Self incarnated. I usually have no problem connecting with cats, because they sense that one of my Basic Selves, many lifetimes ago, was in a cat. This must be why I love and understand them so much.

THEN DO THEY PAIR UP?

Yes, and next you ask numbers one and two if they are a pair. Usually they'll indicate "yes," but you might have to search around to find the other partner. Now, the pairs are growing toward fusion, and I break this down into three stages: Exploring a closer relationship—I write a colon between them; Midway toward fusion—two heads on a stem, the letter "Y" with the two circles on the upper points; and Fusion—one larger head at the top of the stem, but divided, like our brains, the "m" and "f" in each half. So you ask each pair at what stage they are and write it down. Describing the diagram of each stage to them can be helpful and they will pick it up when you visualize it. You will find that the more progressed toward fusion they are the more evolved they are in all three attunements.

Don't expect them to always be m/f. Since they do not reproduce, there are other reasons for pairing up. We find this same-sex pairing, sometimes for a lifetime, also among the animals. It helps to understand same-sex pairing if you know that each one of us is both masculine and feminine, in some balance. You are beginning to get a picture of how they relate to each other. Can you see how this could affect how the person relates to other people—especially a love-partner, where you have four relationships?

At this point in the session you might want to ask your client if their arm is getting a little tired and if they would like to shift to the other arm.

WHAT DO THEY DO FOR US IN THE BODY?
THE FIVE AREAS OF BODY CONSCIOUSNESS

Bella said, and this is borne out in my testing, that the Basic Selves can have five jobs in the body. I have found that they divide these up, perhaps according to past experience in other human embodiments and yes, they have had the "past lives" and they remember them. Only rarely do they duplicate these jobs. These areas of service are: Your (1) Physical Vehicle, (2) Chakras, (3) Karmic Memory Banks, (4) Emotions, and (5) Your Intuitions.

On a fresh sheet of paper, write a vertical column of numbers 1 through 5 for each Basic Self. Label each column. Each vertical number is one of the five areas of service, and you can write opposite it a number from 1 to 5 to represent how much the Basic Self works in that area. This can take a while, but when you're through you have a clear picture of how they divide up these jobs. Later you can add their names under each column.

I was so excited to find out who was doing what that I soon realized that your mind is like the "CEO" of your corporation/business. So now, after this study, if something isn't working in a certain department, you know who to talk to about it. Not only that but later on, after they give us their names, you can speak to them by name. Remember in our spiritual studies the many times we've heard, "You are the captain of your soul." Cayce said "The mind is the builder." The New Thought churches, Christian Science, Unity, Religious Science, and the *Course in Miracles* are based on the enormous power our minds have to create and affect our reality. So we now see what a large role the Basic Selves play in translating "the orders coming down from management" into our life-expression here on Earth.

DO BASIC SELVES REALLY POSITION THEMSELVES IN DIFFERENT PLACES?

This is fairly easy to determine. Just ask your subject to make their right hand, or left if they're left-handed, into a pointer, and ask each Basic Self to indicate where they live most of the time. Often these movements are slow and to me this shows they are being motivated by the Basic Self. Generally the mind is faster, but not always. Often, this positioning can be surprising. I remember how excited I was the first time a Basic Self gave the position as a long line, a swathe, *outside* the body. Then I had to remember that we all have outer bodies: The Etheric, the true physical body that the physical vehicle has to correspond to, extending 3-6 inches out all over the body; the Emotional/Astral, extending 7-10 inches out; and the Mental, as far as you can reach with your hand bent parallel to your body. The distances vary every day and during the day, depending on what you're experiencing and working on. With a little practice you can learn to feel these bodies for yourself. Right after feeling a strong emotion, like love, notice how expanded your Emotional Body has become.

After you have finished this testing you might notice that the positioning of the Basic Selves tallies with their jobs. If it's the emotions, it could be in the solar plexus, where we most often feel emotions. If it's the body, it could be centered in the first two Chakras. If it's the intuitions, perhaps the Sixth Chakra, Third Eye, or clairvoyance. Caution: you don't want to have any such ideas in your mind when you are testing.

Be sure to write down where each Basic Self is centered. I make a rough diagram of a body for each Basic Self and put an "X," or some other sign, at their home base. Or, draw a large body and indicate the location of each one with their number. Keep in mind that they are mobile, can change position, and can even, under certain rare circumstances, leave the body for short periods.

Do Basic Selves Stay With Us Our Whole Lives?

Oftentimes they do, and you probably have at least one or two that will, but it is not uncommon for them to leave and be replaced. There are two main reasons for this. First of all, they have a right to evolve, as do all life forms. So if the free-will decisions of the conscious mind have slowed down their evolution enough they can put in for a transfer. The karmic angels in charge review the case and sometimes grant the request, although it might be somewhat delayed for some reason. The two most common destinations for the Basic Self are: installation in another human, where growth will be forthcoming, or back to the "pool" of Basic Selves for re-assignment when a suitable host is available. Almost always they know which and will tell you. Then an appropriate replacement is selected, which is added to your family of Basic Selves for a training period, so that they can take over when the transferee leaves. You can readily see how important this is for the client's continuing life. A third possibility, which is rare, but which I experienced, is that the Basic Self has earned ascension. I will describe this later.

Here's the procedure: Ask each Basic Self if it is planning to leave anytime soon. If so, ask if it is within five years? One year? The next six months? Then five, four, three, two, one months—until you get a yes—then days. You want to be as accurate as you can because, during the replacement, the person can feel a loss of identity. There have even been accidents if, say, the person was driving at the time the Basic Self left. It helps this transition if the conscious mind of the subject can be supportive of the change, by expressing gratitude and farewell to the Basic Self which has served all this time, and welcome the new one. Who your subject really is hasn't changed but what he or she is working with has, so they may feel a little, or a lot, different. We assume, sooner or later, after the new Basic Self has learned the ropes, the person's life will be going even better than before the changeover.

A rough estimate is that if there are more than five or six Basic Selves one or two are leaving soon and the replacements are present and in training. Usually a pair that has evolved some toward synthesis will go together. Remember you can check again in a few weeks or months and see how their replacements are doing. At that time, if you wish, you can also check to see if the basic attributes of the new arrival are different than the one that moved on. These could be origin, stage of male/female polarity synthesis, jobs, or name. Then again, there may be very few changes.

Early in my research I had speculated on what it would be like to meet someone for the first time in this life who had a Basic Self that had been with one of mine recently, in a past life. I have learned that people are attracted to each other for many reasons and this can be one of them, especially as the body consciousness, the Basic Selves, are most involved in attraction and love-making. I experienced this when I met someone who had a Basic Self who was with one of my Basic Selves in a person around 1500. We did become partners.

Do Basic Selves Have Names?

Just hold the hand, ask your client to make the mind a blank, and ask each Basic Self to give the name they would like to be called. When you've gotten a "yes," make sure it's correct by asking for a spelling and confirming this with a "yes." You will be surprised at the various spellings, but the spelling of a name is most important, as I demonstrated in my last book, *A Harp Full of Stars*, in the chapter on the new method for analyzing names. Remember, as you write a name, say it, answer yes when your name is called, and think of yourself internally as that name, you attract the vibrations of each letter, which are generated by its shape and sound.

Once in a while you get the most surprising names. More than once the name has been a *sound*, and it can be constant, ascending, or descending. These Basic Selves are most often of space origin. Now that your subject knows the names of their Basic Selves they can call them by name, which closes the gap of communication considerably.

This completes the basic process to create what I call a Basic Self Schemata or Model. This is one of the services that I offer, but of course, it has to be done in person.

Now I will give you some of the fine points.

The Treasure Chest

- **PICKING UP THE QUESTIONS TO ASK FROM THE BASIC SELVES** Since you have been reaching out to the Basic Selves of your client with love, your Basic Selves and your client's have established a nice rapport. And you will discover that you are intuitively receiving the questions to ask, which speeds up the process. You will want to be open to this possibility.

- **TESTING YOURSELF** Some people, with practice, can test themselves and I have been able to develop this. You will need to divide yourself into "the tester" and "the testee." I'm a Gemini so it's possible that this is easier for dual astrological signs—also Pisces and Libra. Over the years I have found this technique reliable and a great boon, especially in case my muscle-testing friend is not present. At first, you will want to check everything with a "yes" or "no" response.

- **MAKING AGREEMENTS WITH THE BASIC SELVES** Remember that the Basic Selves have agreed to use a strong response for a "yes" and a weak one for a "no," which is an agreement that could be reversed. With this in mind, I have asked mine if I could test my left arm for my personal life, Emotional/Astral Body, Etheric Body, and Physical Vehicle, and test my right arm for my healing work. This has worked very well, although I could probably test either arm. At first you'll want to get a "yes" of agreement. Included in this request is that your Basic Selves will consult your High Self and your Sources in spirit whenever possible, especially when it comes to questions about your work.

- **STRANGE ANSWERS** Occasionally you'll get an answer that doesn't seem to make sense. First I check to see exactly how I asked the question, because most often I have asked it in an unclear way. Then reframing the question in a more precise and unequivocal way usually produces a sensible answer. Also, the Basic Selves have a harder time with a question which is phrased negatively; that is, asking what a thing is not.

- **THE THIRD DESTINY FOR BASIC SELVES THAT ARE LEAVING** Around 1975, I discovered that the Basic Self that had helped me develop my healing work was about to leave. I was seized with the emotion of separation from something that had been a part of me. On getting a hold of myself I realized that my feeling was natural and to be expected. Then, fortunately, I remembered that I been taught that "we *have* a body, but we *are much more than* the body." Since my muscle-testing mentor was present, we asked John—this was his name. He said "no" to being transferred to another human, and "no" to going back to the pool for reassignment. This was the first time this had come up, and we were really puzzled. Our intuitions provided the questions and we soon learned that he was making his ascension. So we asked if he would be part of me in a life on the higher worlds and John said "no." Then we asked if I might meet him on up the line and he said "yes." Further testing confirmed that the Basic Selves are a different line of evolution than the human. *The Urantia Book* describes some very beautiful and dedicated beings on the higher worlds who had origin as animals and re-incarnate: the *spornagia*. I was finally able to release him to his highest good, not without some deep-felt thanks, and wish him bon voyage on his journey. Then I welcomed his replacement, Jonathan, who already had been in training. All the procedures John had developed were still stored in my memory banks, so there would be no loss in my healing work. Only the essential self of John had gone on.

I found it interesting that since John transcended, my other Basic Selves are even less afraid of death. My hope is that all the Basic Selves who read this will be encouraged to see death as a transition, a graduation.

Do Basic Selves Explain What Is Called "Split Personality"?

Some Basic Selves are quite shy and retiring, due to past-life experience, and then there is usually a strong one that acts as a protector. But every Basic Self has the right to express, so occasionally the strong one retreats and lets the shy one come forward. You can see that where there is a great difference between Basic Selves, this could result in radically different, inconsistent behavior or difficulty in making decisions. Sometimes it has seemed that there was insulation between them—isolation. This could explain what the early psychiatrists called "split personality." Is it possible that they were put together by the karmic angels in the hope that they could works things out? To me there is always an explanation and perhaps through hypnotherapy, or a past-life reader, they could be encouraged to reveal their past lives, since they remember them, and this would help the therapist to help them. This could also be through the intuition of the tester. If this isn't successful, with the permission of the client, I go for the lives myself. I have sometimes been able to help them toward a more harmonious relationship, and this should improve how the whole person interacts with the world.

It has been my great pleasure to open up a vast vista of information for you, and it's possible that I've only scratched the surface. I have found that one of our unalienable rights, one of the gifts from our Creator, is the right to have our questions answered. Certainly one of the exciting, new paths leading to untapped treasures of information is muscle-testing the Basic Selves. Personally I have proven this in how it has enhanced my own life over the past 30 years and the lives of the 200 clients who have had their Basic Self Schematas charted with me. So now you can access higher octaves of physical consciousness through the vibratory resonance of kinesiology.

A Brighter Future For Basic Selves

At the very least, we can thank, honor, and love our wondrous, dedicated, and valiant Basic Selves. It is my hope that this will create a more harmonious, effective, and enjoyable relationship with them. Your body consciousness, with guidance from "The All That Is," makes it possible for you to take advantage of the manifold opportunities for learning and spiritual growth on Earth at this time. To create even more harmony between your High Self, Conscious mind, and Basic Selves, see my *Three Selves Attunement* in the Appendix.

After a concert at Esalen Institute, Big Sur, California

PART TWO

11

Before the Beginning There Were Miracles and Stories

After one of Serafina's special dinners, I went out to the woodhouse to get a load of wood for the evening fire. When I returned Mikael and Serafina had knowing looks on their faces and Serafina said, "We want to hear some of the early stories about your life— your beginnings—we think these would interest your readers, by showing your development."

I replied, "I've been writing them down for weeks, so I'm excited also. However, there are so many I hardly know where to begin. And then I haven't been able to decide whether to start around age 26, when they begin to be life-changing epiphanies, or to start in the beginning of my life, when they were perhaps not quite so dramatic, but at the same time formative and informative."

Serafina said, "I think that some of those stories about your grandmother in Paris and your father in the South Sea Islands are *very* fascinating, and they show the earliest influences on you and your work." I liked their suggestion, and it sounded as if it might be a pleasant, down-to-earth break for you dear readers from the high metaphysics of the testimonials. So I will begin with one of my favorite family stories about my paternal grandmother, Myra (rhymes with "era"). This took place around the turn of the century and she must have been in her twenties.

She was Irish, born of aristocratic parents, quite a beauty, and was trained in the arts, especially music and dance. Once she was invited to a ball honoring the former king of England, Edward, who had fallen in love with an American, Mrs. Simpson. He had abdicated the throne and taken up residence in Paris. Now, in those days it was considered a social blunder to arrive after the king and no one would risk doing it but that is what Myra did. She went right up to the dais where King Edward and Mrs. Simpson were seated in elegant chairs like thrones. Then, right in front of the king, she executed a deep, elegant curtsy and, drawing on her ballet training, kicked her foot over her head. Everyone in the ballroom gasped to see what would happen next. The king got up, came down from his throne, and opened the ball with Myra. My uncle Gavin, her son, told me this story and, in spite of my doubts, assured me it was true. Thinking this story over in later years, I concluded that Myra must have had some kind of relationship with them beforehand, or Edward would never have left Mrs. Simpson on the dais.

After this story, Mykael commented, "Now we know why you value stories so much and love to tell them—it's in your Irish blood." I hastened to reply, "This is true, but please remember: all the stories in this book are true, not made up—this is my pledge to you. If I have any doubts about the veracity of a story, you can trust me to tell you."

Many years later, after Myra had retired to Santa Barbara, California, the world-famous pianist, Paderewski, presented her with a piano. I remember, as a boy, seeing this exquisite instrument. It was deep green and decorated with paintings of pastoral scenes. Its legs rested in ornate pots of ivy. Once, when she went to Europe for a few months, she asked her maid to be sure to water the ivy. When she returned the ivy had grown up all over the piano, closing the lid, and the piano could not be played.

After it was restored another famous pianist, Joseph Hoffman, came to tea and she asked him if he would play for her. He was well known for the brilliance of his technique but his interpretations lacked something in warmth. After a few measures, Myra rose up saying "No, not like that—with feeling." And, sweeping him off the piano bench, she sat down and played *the same composition* with a moving interpretation.

My uncle also told me that Myra, despite her high society connections, was uncommonly unprejudiced and considerate of those from less privileged levels of society. Once, walking down the street in London, with one of her aristocratic friends, she saw Oscar Wilde, the famous gay, sitting at a sidewalk café. She abruptly left her friend saying she had to talk to Oscar. At that time in England there was strong prejudice against homosexuals but she was an independent spirit not ruled by social custom—courageous for a woman at that time. Her second son, my uncle Gavin, who was like a father to me, took after her, hobnobbing with royalty as well as merchant seamen, and felt, and practiced oneness with all peoples. I will tell stories about him when I come to my nine-year sojourn in San Francisco.

Before the Beginning

I do not have many stories about my maternal grandmother, Lilia Tuckerman, even though I spent more time with her. She was from Washington, DC society, moved to Santa Barbara in the early 20s, and was a fine painter of the Early California School.

Her work was exhibited many times, and she would easily have had more if she had pursued them, but Lilia belonged to a time when women of the upper class, regardless of their training, did not become professionals. She could have become much more widely known if her other interests, family and service, had allowed the time. She certainly encouraged my musical training. She bought me my first full-sized harp, and kept before me my potential to become a fine harpist. She held a beautiful, simple Christian faith and would take me to the Episcopal Church, All-Saints-by-the-Sea. My love for the sea evolved and 30 years later, my first major composition for the harp was a *Sea Suite*. I really enjoyed the peaceful ambience of this little church, but I had strong intuitions that they did not have the teachings quite right, and my later association with the Christ confirmed this. Nevertheless, I am grateful for this early exposure to something transcendent. Both my grandmother Lilia and my grandfather Wolcott traced their lineage to England and Scotland but added a little German and a little Turkish to my mix. I have grown grateful for both Lilia and Wolcott. They had five daughters, my mother, Florence, being the eldest.

Lilia translated much of the Bible into Braille and formed the La Vista Club for the blind. She would have her sometimes chauffeur pick me up, with my harp, and take me to the club meetings. I was eleven and just able to play a few pieces. The blind members loved the sound of the harp. Many years later, I met this sometimes chauffeur at a party, and did not recognize him until he jogged my memory. His name turned out to be Ildo and he got permission for Serafina and me to be married on the beautiful estate where he was a gardener. This is not exactly a miracle, but an amazing coincidence, suggesting that relationships once begun can last much longer than we might at first suspect.

When I was staying with Lilia as a young boy, under ten, I would think she was some kind of magician, because the cook would come into the dining room to clear away the last course *right after we had finished it*. After some years of this apparent "sorcery," I was crawling around under the dining room table and discovered a mound in the carpet. She had a buzzer in front of her right foot. Then, when Lilia was out driving, in her long Willis-Knight touring car, she always had a loaf of bread in the glove compartment for the Depression down-and-outers along the road—in those days, called "hobos."

This background in the upper class has brought an understanding of their blessings and their shortcomings. I spent the other half of my life among musicians and artists and, ever since the spiritual illuminations that completely changed my life, among enlightened people, or in service to those who are seeking enlightenment.

My father, Loring Andrews, played the guitar and the accordion and, as a young man, played his way around the world with a friend, as a ship's orchestra. His favorite stopover was the island, Rarotonga, in the Cook Islands and he took us there: my mother, my older brother, Oliver, and me, when I was about two. My very first memory is there. I am in the arms of a Maori woman, sitting against the wall, watching the dancing legs of my mother, father, and about 20 others. It is possible my love for nature began on that South Sea Island since, in those days, Rarotonga was a tropical paradise. My father was fascinated by the idea of nature taking care of her people, and curious about how living in Paradise affected their consciousness. He spent half his life around Rarotonga and wrote two books about life there and a third, the best, which was never published. I would like to share with you two of his experiences in the islands.

He made his living there by skin diving. He had the first underwater light in the islands and his slides of the tropical fish, some of them seen for the first time, are brilliantly colorful. One afternoon, as dusk was approaching, he was harvesting crab from small caves in an underwater cliff. He stuck his hand into a hole that had a white ring and was immediately seized by the open mouth of a Moray Eel! They have rows of teeth that slant backwards. He knew that he was done for unless he played dead, hoping that the eel would open his mouth to get a better grip. On his voyage around the world, he had spent five years in India at the feet of a master, and so was an experienced meditator. Fortunately he could hold his breath for five minutes, so he went into suspended animation and, sure enough, the eel went for a better grip, and he escaped, though not without some serious wounds.

Then, after he heard that on the island of Aitutaki, one of the northernmost islands of the Cook group, there was an unspoiled tribe of natives with a king, he planned a visit. Once on the beach, he must have wanted to come with gifts so he went skin diving out past the reef. When he returned to the beach, the whole tribe was there to greet him with a shout and swept him up on their shoulders, taking him into the village. You see, Loring would collect his catch on a wire around his waist and when he came out of the water, the natives could see that there were only heads behind him. No one goes out past the reef because of the sharks, and when the tribe saw the fish heads, they assumed he was "one of the chosen ones."

Back in the village, he was made the blood brother of the king. I have always wondered whether part of their motive was to learn his secrets concerning sharks. First, the veins in their wrists were pierced and tied together. Then the climax of his initiation was to be taken up very high, overgrown steps, to a crevice in the mountain. After warning him that he must not, under any circumstances, take anything, they entered a small passageway, which led to a large circular cave. Around the edges were seated twelve, unusually tall skeletons. He noticed that there were strange-looking artifacts and much jewelry and ornaments of gold. Note: if you are feeling a little skeptical at this point, let me confess that I felt the same way when my uncle Gavin first told me this story but, if you will persevere, I have some proofs for you a little later on in the story— what I call "evidential."

When Loring returned to Rarotonga there was an urgent message for him from a close friend, who was in the hospital with a serious condition that the doctors couldn't heal or even diagnose. His friend's account was that he had just been on Aitutaki, had been initiated in the cave, told not to take anything, but that he had taken something, and he was afraid this was the cause of his illness. He had heard that Loring had just visited the island. When Loring recounted his experience of initiation, his friend beseeched him to take the object back to the king. Loring returned it and his friend recovered.

Now, there are three sequels to this story. Uncle Gavin was a famous Jungian astrologer and had a student who became fascinated by the Aitutaki story. She wrote the king and in a few weeks received an answer, saying that Loring Andrews was one of their brothers and heroes and that she would be welcome to visit them anytime and that they would celebrate her with a feast. My uncle showed me this letter and it was signed by the son of the king.

Then, when Gavin was in London, he was invited to a men's club for a banquet honoring all the British possessions and mandates. He was seated at a huge table in the shape of a "U." When he was introduced and spoke of his brother, Loring Andrews, a six-foot-four Maori arose from the other side of the table, walked around, picked up my 6' 3" uncle in a bear-hug, saying, "Anyone who is the brother of Loring Andrews is a brother of mine."

Then, years later, I was reading in the magazine *Scientific American* about a race of very tall people, dating way back in history who lived in the South Pacific and who had gold. This tended to add credence to this story, and with my never-ending curiosity for the truth behind appearances, I speculate on the possible origin of these regal humans in Lemuria. I have just read Loring's last book which corroborates this theory. I have discovered a number of Lemurian power points on the California coast. Of course, these power centers are the mountaintops of, or surrounding, the continent that sank many thousands of years ago. Mountaintops are known to be sacred places where the dedicated can seek and receive higher guidance. Therefore, Aitutaki could very well have been one of these sacred places and this might explain the cave of the twelve kings.

One of the stories about Loring that I especially love took place in a shop in New York, which specialized in imported instruments. While the proprietor was taking care of a client in the front of the store, Loring wandered to the back and picked up a kind of mandolin. As he strummed it, a melody came to him. The owner rushed back saying, "Where did you hear that tune?" My father said, "Well, it just came to me." Then the owner said, "That tune is known only in the small village up in the mountains of Greece where that mandolin *originated*."

This is the psychic gift known as "psychometry"—receiving impressions that have been stored in objects. Loring could also often remember music he heard in his dreams and would then work it out on his guitar. One of these was a rather strange song from the court of Hammurabi. This could be a past-life memory, or accessing the akashic records of history. It is possible that I have inherited genes from him that make possible my psychic gifts.

Though I saw my father only a few times, they were quality meetings. He would announce he was coming from the South Seas. I had a car so I would take him around to visit his wealthy friends. We would be met at the door of an elegant estate in Montecito, the upper class section of Santa Barbara, Loring still dressed in his island garb, and carrying his guitar or accordion. They would greet him, "Loring, how marvelous to see you. It has been too long. Come in and play us a tune." After he had played some island dance for a few minutes, they would be up and dancing around their posh foyer, people who looked as if they seldom, if ever, danced. When he began to play he had a far-off look in his eyes as if he were focusing on a distant reality or, and as I realized many years later, he was going into a light trance. This story also suggests some of the genes I carry from him.

When Loring was a young man, around 1924, he studied the Spanish-style guitar and played in a small orchestra at the El Paseo—a long-standing, and still open, restaurant in Santa Barbara. It occurred to him what fun it would be to have a day-long Fiesta, celebrating the city's rich Spanish heritage. People could dress in Spanish costumes and dance in the streets. It was enough of a success that it became an annual festival and for the past 60 years has drawn huge crowds from the surrounding counties. Now it lasts for five days and there are mariachi bands all over the city, a colorful parade, and pageants at the Spanish Mission depicting scenes from Santa Barbara's history. For many years, when I was still living in that beautiful city, Loring would ask me to send him the commemorative issue of *The News-Press* that was full of pictures and stories of "Old Spanish Days."

Here is another story about Loring that I cannot resist telling you. There came a time when it became difficult for Loring to make a living on Rarotonga, so he followed the exodus of young people to Auckland, New Zealand and the first job he found was in a meat-packing house. When Queen Elizabeth and Prince Phillip visited there, she wanted to go out on the town but, of course, she would be recognized if Prince Phillip had accompanied her. Somehow Loring's qualifications of breeding, education, being a writer, and a very handsome man, preceded him and he was selected as her escort. She disguised herself, and they had a wonderful time dancing in the local pubs. Loring said that during their conversations they actually found a common ancestor.

So, beyond the musical genes I received from my father, and the intuitive genes, I inherited a belief that life can be fun, and that in some places on earth the paradisal life continues and can inspire us to honor it and create it wherever we are. The only time Loring heard me play, he had tears in his eyes. He was so glad that I had the training in music he never had and that I would probably reach more people. I have just rediscovered the manuscript of my father's last book. It is beautifully written and full of spiritual insights about living in harmony with nature. If it were published, it might encourage readers to take care of our environment so that it can take care of us.

My mother, Florence, was a courageous adventurer, seeking life experiences that would take her beyond her somewhat conventional upbringing. However, she always retained a strong sense of what was right, and was often asked for counseling from her extended family. I have a picture of her in a grass hut in Rarotonga, dressed in a sarong with me on her lap.

When I was six, she married Robert Hyde, her teen-age sweetheart, and we went to live in a cave while we built our own house. Bobby, as we called him, was a writer when the Depression hit and we were trying to live by the book *Five Acres and Independence*.

We planted a large garden, but were challenged by how to deal with gophers, jackrabbits, and a fox. Then elegance came to the cave when Florence brought Anna home from the Salvation Army. She arrived with only a suitcase, containing her cooking costume, cleaning costume, and a governess costume. She obviously had been trained in a fine house and so was a wonderful cook, but also, being Irish, a very entertaining story-teller. In those hard times, she was perfectly content to serve as our full-time maid, just for food and lodging. Anna would draw my mother aside and say, "Now, Mrs. Hyde, we must plan a luncheon and invite your mother's best friends, the Jeffersons, the Hamiltons, the Fallettis and the Pecci-Blunts—don't you think we should go over the menu?" My mother would always humor Anna, but of course, could never invite those aristocrats to the cave. My grandmother *never* visited the cave. If she took me and my brothers out to lunch my mother would dress us up and we would be picked up at the entrance to our driveway.

Years later, I asked my mother where Anna slept and she said, "Well, we never really knew." Whereupon I burst out laughing and said, "Mom, I'm thirty-two and you can tell me where Anna slept." She answered, "No, actually she came after the rains in the spring and we were in the house before the rains in the fall and then she slept in the cave." Of course, she couldn't sleep in the cave with us, so at night, after her chores were done, she would disappear, sleep under a tree, and appear at the mouth of the cave to prepare breakfast. The weather in Santa Barbara tends to be mild in late spring and summer. Sometimes she would prepare Crepe Suzettes over the campfire in the cave. When Anna left, we were all broken-hearted. One summer we made wine and stored it in barrels in the cave. She was getting drunk and sick from pilfering wine off the top of the barrels, which had a preservative floating on top. The morning after she was discovered she was gone—she was so embarrassed. My mother would have gladly forgiven her. She said that for years she would study the faces as she walked around town hoping to see Anna. And she wanted to write a description of Anna for the Reader's Digest *Most Unforgettable Character* page.

One day Bobby suggested to me and my two brothers that we take up a musical instrument, "something to fall back on in difficult times," he said. As I remember, Gavy, age seven, chose the cello; Andy, age twelve, chose the drums; and I, nine, chose the record player. Bobby had a large collection of fine recorded music. But soon we discovered that just up the road lived a 16-yr.-old girl who played the harp. So I was sent to her house, with my hair in my eyes and my belt hanging out, to ask her if she would teach me. She said yes and ushered me into her living room for my first lesson. I remember, even at nine, how beautiful I thought she was. In 1935 we were still in the difficult times of the Depression so we couldn't afford a harp, but her father bought me an Irish Folk Harp so that she could have a student. Fortunately, Marjorie Ann (now Chauvel) was receiving excellent training in one of the best methods of harp playing in the world. So at nine, I began to study this exotic and challenging instrument, and I continued with her for many years.

During these Depression years, I also learned a lot about surviving on the basics. Bobby was uncommonly resourceful and had an eye for things people were not using that could be turned into something useful. He made a map of the vacant lots in town that had wild fruit trees on them and he would know when they were bearing. And when the olive trees on Olive Street were ready to pick our family would be the first in line with our tarpaulins and rods of bamboo to shake the branches.

After a stint in an aircraft plant during the Second World War, Bobby and Florence bought 50 acres in the foothills of Santa Barbara and founded one of the first bohemian communes. It was a rich life for my teens and college years until I enlisted in the Air Force in 1951. Bobby encouraged and guided the rugged individualists whom we attracted to the community to build their own houses. I built two: a concrete block house with a friend and a house of 4"x16"x 30-foot pier timbers mostly by myself, with some house-raisings involving friends. I remember serving them yogurt and apple butter. We made our own wine, rigged up the first hot tubs in California, and put on the first Renaissance Fair, which was then expanded by Phyllis and Ron Patterson.

As bohemian as she was, my mother was a paragon of virtue, ethics, and true morality, and I learned a lot from her example. She actually practiced the Christian ethics of her mother, loosening them up somewhat, but never using the religious words that my grandmother might use because Bobby was an atheist. They were both active in the local NAACP, and after my two brothers and I left home, they took on six Mexican-Indian foster children, all under twelve. I love the Rodriguez children and the Latin peoples, for their beautiful hearts, their dedication to family, and their music. Bobby was very authoritarian and didn't show much love for his stepchildren, but he was very creative and I learned a lot from him: how to build houses, fix things, play chess, and make wine.

My older brother Oliver, was first a painter and then, for most of his life, a contemporary sculptor. For many years, he headed the sculpture department at UCLA. in Los Angeles. Just before I discovered the Overtone Series, the scale that represents the Law of Resonance that permeates all of nature, I was "playing" the metal "tines" that extended out from his metal sculptures. So when I discovered the scale of nature, I gave him a set of numbers that he could translate to inches for these extensions, but as far as I know he never tried it. At the time I felt that much of his work was arresting but a little skeletal, with these sharp projections, and I hoped the Overtone Series would connect it with nature and provide a little warmth. Eventually Oliver graduated to building fountains and I thought the water element added that magical, flowing quality of The Mother to his work.

My younger (half) brother, Gavin, is a writer like his father, Bobby Hyde, and has continued Bobby's interest in chess and the equally complicated and challenging Chinese game of "*Go.*" He is also a national master of Scrabble and, of course, an authority on the dictionary. In addition, for most of his life, he has had a deep interest in spiritual matters, so we often have stimulating metaphysical talks.

I am deeply grateful for these family relationships, and their positive, formative influences on my life and work. Not that there hasn't been a good deal of what my masters call "sweet abrasion." Not only have I learned valuable lessons from my family, but also I have had opportunities to prove the effectiveness of higher principles; so I've been polished by these challenges. In gratitude and love, I give all of my family, who are really my brothers and sisters, "the salute of light and love."

12

Early Preparation as a Healer

Then my friend said, "After reading *A Harp Full of Stars*," I always wanted to ask you about your background and training. It must have been unusual to prepare you for the life of a professional harpist as well as a music healer and the other modalities of healing you employ."

I said, "Now that's a huge question which might take another book to fully lay out for you, but I will touch on some of the highlights that shaped my development, hopefully enough to provide a general picture, because, if it interests you, it may interest our readers. Others have raised this question, and especially about the factors that have guided my growing understanding of spiritual matters. I also hope that this subject might be, in some way, inspiring to apprentice healers."

First of all, I had a very difficult childhood, much physical and psychological oppression, which took years to process, learn from, and transcend. I have found that such children, if they receive some love and don't go too far under, often turn toward a Higher Source of Love and Wisdom. It is as if each of us has memory of Divine Love stored somewhere deep within us. This turning to a Higher Source can happen also to adults who have "lost" a love. In my case, it set me on the path of the seeker. So, as I look back, countless times I have felt a higher hand pointing the way, saying, "See that, don't see that; hear that, but don't hear that."

Then my deep desire for healing meant finding out what was really going on behind appearances in the world and what was going on with people, and this has become a habit leading to all kinds of revelations. One of them was the amazing discovery that we are meant to have the answers to every sincere question, if we are ready to receive them.

Since an early age I have enjoyed a deep rapport with nature. At 16, my first transcendent experience, discovering a sunlit valley after the rain, resulted in a long poem. As I have reported, my grandmother had a simple but beautiful Christian faith and would take me to church. I didn't understand what the priest was saying and I also had an intuition that he didn't have it quite right. However, I loved the ambience of peace and sanctity there at All-Saints-by-the-Sea. Later I was baptized and confirmed there. Through boarding school and college, when I wasn't hard at work learning the harp and music theory and composition, I was fascinated by psychology. I can remember many late nights discussing this complex subject with an older, student friend who had had some training in it.

Next came a three-year stint in the Air Force. I played my harp for the broadcasts of the Air Force Band in San Antonio, Texas and then the Symphony in Washington, D.C. While I was in basic training in Texas, around 1952, when I was 24, I had one of the major illumination revelations of my life, what is called, by the masters, an experience of "cosmic consciousness." It gave me a direct experience of Higher Realities and the possibility that I could co-create with them. I was in the barracks, sitting on my bunk, talking to four of my buddies. All of a sudden my consciousness left there and I was immersed in a liquid of ideal viscosity and temperature. I was at the center of it and I became aware of smooth-muscle walls around me. Then I experienced "bilocation." I was about a foot away looking at the center where I had been, where I could see patterns of growth. They looked like the outlines of ice cubes.

It was a very intense experience that took place in another time. I couldn't tell how long I was gone, but it couldn't have been but a few minutes because, when I returned, no one seemed to have noticed my absence. I felt changed and as I thought it over I realized that I had been regressed to my mother's womb, when I first entered this life, in order to remember my purpose in incarnating. The trauma of coming down the birth canal often causes the entity to forget this purpose and it may not be remembered until later in life. My purpose was, roughly speaking, "to serve the Light."

Then the band was sent to Hollywood, minus the harp and me, and I went into the hospital with what they called a summer cold. As I was trying to sleep I would be awakened to write down a vision and there were twelve of these. They were all meaningful revelations and by the time I was released I had 1) Lost the fear of death, knowing that I would survive that transition, 2) Totally accepted the opportunity to live an earth life, 3) Knew Higher Presences were with me to guide me and protect me, 4) Experienced a heightened intellectual ability, and 5) Gained a heightened and expanded love nature. I felt sure that the "cold" was arranged to put me into a peaceful place, like a monastery, where I would be taken care of so I could have the visions.

Following this, I was in ecstasy for a month. When I looked into someone's eyes I could see everything about them, and I saw it all with love. On two successive nights, when I went to sleep I relived my womb experience, each time in a different, very intense color: yellow and then green. I felt these were centering the experience in my Solar Plexus and Heart chakras. I got a room off the airbase and began a journal to try to describe these life-altering experiences. I had a terrible time with this, since they were fundamentally non-verbal. I grew to realize that this difficulty was a good sign that a person had had the experience. I remembered certain books I had heard about years before and they helped me understand the experience, especially *Cosmic Consciousness* by Bucke. I was grateful to my uncle, Gavin Arthur, who made me aware of "cosmic consciousness" years earlier. What I've learned from this is indelibly written on my being and I can even recall the feelings if I jog my memory. I am deeply grateful for this illumination.

When the Korean War was over I was released from the Air Force. I returned home and built my second house, mostly by myself, with a few house-raisings by friends. I had built my first house during college with a friend. By this time I had had three excellent harp teachers and then two summers in Maine with the great master, Carlos Salzedo. He founded an improved method of playing the harp, discovered 30 new sounds on this ancient instrument, composed many fine pieces using them, redesigned the harp, and even organized harp festivals of over 60 harpists.

So after I finished the house I went to Cleveland to study with a primary artist-student of Salzedo's, Alice Chalifoux. She was a wonderful teacher and person, and encouraged my sensitivity in interpreting music. I earned my Masters in Harp with a minor in Composition by presenting two different concerts in the same summer. My first job was four years as Head of the Harp Department at the University of Texas, where I organized harp festivals, the last one drawing 50 harpists nationwide and Salzedo. I arranged music for this group as well as a quintet of students. I still have a recording of the 50 harps playing together and it really sounds as if you are *entering heaven.*

In the 60's I was in San Francisco, where I met with some of the leaders of the "back to nature" movement. In my early years I had spent so much time sitting behind my harp, I deeply needed to get reconnected to nature and people. I learned a lot from the great Alan Watts who, more than anyone, introduced Zen to America. My association with him lasted for 10 years, and we gave some workshops together. Then even more of a spiritual mentor was my uncle Gavin Arthur, Chester Alan Arthur III, grandson of the president. He introduced me to people from all walks of life and from many different cultures, but especially psychics, healers, and spiritual teachers.

He took me to experience Rev. Florence Becker, one of the greatest billet readers in the world. She would sit, blindfolded, before a pile of envelopes, mix them up, select one, and then read the word on the front of the envelope. Then, after a moment, proceed to answer the question written inside. Both uncle Gavin and I had answers given that were "right on" and you could tell the others in the audience were impressed with what came through. One time, just before she opened my envelope, she made motions like playing a harp, and asked, "Do you do something like this?" Attending these evenings at The Golden Gate Spiritualist Church, over a period of years, I learned a lot about what was really going on with people that would help me later when I did personal counseling.

As I look back, this was the true beginning of what I now call the Spiritual Renaissance. I was excited to be part of the "New Age." Eventually the term "New Age" received such a bad rap in the media, a lot due to the not-so-spiritual "camp followers" who gave it a bad name, that we don't use that name anymore. Besides we are *in* the New Age—it is upon us—the time we have been anticipating for 30 years is *now*. And we mustn't forget that the leaders of the spiritual movement of the 60's, the ones that held to the higher ideals, are courageous heroes. And they should remain so in spite of the efforts of those in our society who would denigrate these visionaries in order to better control us. The term "New Age Music" suffered dilution also when main stream jazz discovered that it was making money and appropriated the term. Of course, the jazz musicians had to incorporate some of the New Age qualities in their music, adding a little more peace, harmony, and upliftment and titles along these lines, which I thought was a good thing. If there ever was a true and accurate report of the actual effect of the dissonant and frenetic music on the listener, produced by the earlier jazz musicians, many of them would be shocked and embarrassed—especially when they learned that they might be held responsible for the vibrations they put out into the world.

I'll never forget the day I fully realized this responsibility. I couldn't practice for a week, even though I was alone in my studio. Eventually I realized that it is the same for every one of us and then I could resume practicing. But it changed how I worked, slower and more carefully. I learned then that the fastest way to learn anything is slow and sure so that you don't develop bad habits that are hard to break. Everything we do is creating a habit. If you practice something seven times wrong and then stop the first time you get it right you are going backwards. If you want to learn it, you don't stop until you've done it at least more times right than you did wrong.

It was in San Francisco that I began gradually to get the idea that perhaps the highest destiny of music, and the arts, is to bring peace, to raise consciousness, and to heal. My uncle Gavin took me to see a demonstration by a fine, professional pianist, who had retired from touring to work with young children with disabilities. The subject was a boy around nine who was spastic and I was amazed how he had progressed just through playing the piano. As these little revelations increased, I began to realize they were probably due to higher guidance from the beings in spirit who might be preparing me for a higher octave of work with music. If I hadn't developed the concept of healing with music I might not have responded to the somewhat bizarre events that radically changed my life into that of a healer.

While in San Francisco I went once a month to a very high healer, Evelyn Sullivan, recommended by many of my best friends. She had a separate ascended master working through her for every day of the week. I received much healing from her, not to mention learning a lot about healing and some of the higher beings in spirit dedicated to this service. Just before I left that fair city, so rich in the arts, the celebration of life, and many varieties of spirituality, Evelyn was given a vision of my potential as a healer, it actually turned out to be more of a prediction. This was 1969 and I moved my family to Raleigh, North Carolina, to take up my position as Musician-in-Residence at North Carolina State University.

This turned out to be the climax, and end, of my career as a professional harpist. I arranged 10 different concerts involving harp in two years and was presented in a debut concert in Town Hall, New York, which changed the course of my life. But I hasten to add that during those two years I would journey often to Virginia Beach to study the work of the great clairvoyant, Edgar Cayce. On these trips I learned much that prepared me for the life of a healer. I joined a Cayce study group and began reading books about Cayce's life. I was excited about the great wisdom that was revealed in the 14,000 past-life, and general readings he channeled. In *A Harp Full of Stars* I reported the unusual events that took place in Virginia Beach and launched me into the life of a healer.

For my concert in Town Hall I prepared one of the most challenging programs and I planned to have three days to practice just before the concert. I shipped my harp ahead but they lost track of it at Kennedy Airport. *How could they lose track of a harp in its case, measuring two by three by six feet and weighing two hundred pounds*? I was fit to be tied. My harp arrived only one day ahead of my performance. Fortunately I was able to get through the concert, even though I was under great strain. Now remember that, although I had already been studying healing for some months, I had never heard of a harpist devoted to healing and had only heard of a handful of musician-healers. Right after the Town Hall concert I made the decision that I would rather play for one person at a time, if it could bring deep healing, than live out of a suitcase on tour and play for 5,000 people for entertainment.

Two smaller miracles took place in New York while I was there for the Town Hall Concert which helped to mark it as a very special time. Remember that I was only there for about a week in a city of eight million—a city so crowded that its inhabitants shun speaking to strangers when in public. I boarded a bus to go down to Town Hall and struck up a conversation with the lady sitting next to me. She asked me where I was going and when she learned I was a harpist, she said, "My uncle was a harpist." When I asked who he was, she said, "Harpo Marx." *She was Chico's daughter; he was Harpo's piano-playing brother.*

Then Gerry Goodman, a harpist who graduated with me from the Cleveland Institute of Music, was living in New York at the time. I was hoping to reconnect with him but he was not listed in information, and I didn't know how to find him. I was walking across the street and there he appeared *walking toward me.* We greeted each other with a hug, and when I told him about my debut concert, he said he would have loved to attend but he was leaving in two days on his own concert tour. Are these not amazing cases of synchronicity? The odds against these two meetings happening are unbelievable. I have experienced so many of these, and heard of others, that it has become clear that there are laws of attraction bringing people together, which are mostly hidden unless we train ourselves to notice them. Perhaps some of them are "coincidences," but for the ones reported in this book, that is not an adequate explanation. Of course, another explanation is that our Higher Guidance, or our guides, Masters, and angels have a hand in these occurrences.

Once I had turned this life-changing corner in my life, I began traveling to other cities all over the East, where a growing circle of friends would set up a week of individual sessions. Most of these were Past-Life Readings, but some focused on general healing, or whatever they wrote down that they needed. I remember sometimes doing *twenty in a week.* From the beginning I would take their full name and birth date, translate them into notes, say my affirmations, meditate, and

The Nature and Effects of Music

then I would play the music I would be given clairaudiently. Soon I had learned so much about the symbolism for the alphabet that my sources were using that I would add an analysis of my client's names. The responses were positive and occasionally really impressive. I was excited to have my own special way of healing with my harp and with music. The music was beautiful and I felt it as it passed through me. I was never tired after a session, only occasionally a little lightheaded for fifteen or twenty minutes. Later I learned how to close my upper chakras, which open as I prepare for a session. The *Name Analyses* proved to be consistent with, and supplemental to, *Numerological Name Analyses*, but the new method focuses more on the symbolism of each letter and how it relates to the other letters in the name.

So these and other experiences led to tours to 12 countries to present concerts, lectures, workshops, and individual sessions. I have actually made 16 trips to Europe, during which I've experienced five powerful memories of my past lives, from which I have learned much. There have also been tours to Japan, Australia, and across the United States and Canada. Along the way there have been many miracles of healing and I'd like to recount one of the most remarkable of these for you.

I was asked to take part in a conference in Greensboro, North Carolina. I believe it was a Spiritual Frontiers Fellowship gathering. A number of the mavens of the Spiritual Renaissance movement were presenting, among them Patricia Sun and David Spangler. He was one of the founders of Findhorn, the conscious community in Scotland. My concert was scheduled at the end of the week, on Friday evening. As I prepared to go on stage I asked my Higher Guidance, "It seems to me that everything has been said, and quite well, so what can I add to this wonderful week?" The answer came "You have been asked to *celebrate it* in music." Then I got so high that I couldn't decide whether to tune to the Tempered Scale or the Overtone Series. With twenty minutes before the curtain opened, I excitedly said to them, "Please, just tell me." Immediately I heard, distinctly, "The Overtone Series" I was so high when I entered the stage I had to keep from laughing. I kept my words to a minimum and the music was extraordinary. And this was only the beginning.

I always like to ask the clairvoyants in the audience what they experienced—to get an idea of what we accomplished. I talked to five of them and they *all* agreed that when I started playing 500 *monks came down out of the ceiling* and offered healing to the audience. There were about that many in attendance, so there was one spirit being for each person. I have assumed these were Ascended Masters, although some of them could have been from the angelic realms. Because of what they had witnessed, the psychics had asked many people what they experienced and there were many reports of healing—and of many different kinds.

I was so gratified. I realized that the whole event had been under Divine Guidance and that I hadn't needed to be anxious before going on stage, but that perhaps my anxiety was getting my nervous system up to the necessary pitch to play the concert. As I thought about this mass healing later, I had a revelation. It was much like some of the miracles reported in the Bible, such as the healing of the 5,000, so one of the lessons is: miracles are not confined to the Bible and history. It is known that masters and angels do not die and pass on as we do, so the same beings that accomplished those ancient miracles are still with us. What a revelation. And, of course, the Supreme Love/Light that makes it all possible is ever with us. The question then came to me, "What is required of us to call forth these miracles?"

Here is another special, and formative, experience: Around 1962, when I first moved to Mill Valley, just over the Golden Gate Bridge, north of San Francisco, I learned the most valuable technique for healing oneself from an apprentice master. He called it etheric healing. First let's find our outer bodies. As I have mentioned, this is not that difficult—it just takes a little practice. If you are right-handed extend your left, receptive arm out in front of you and bend your hand so it's parallel to your chest. If left-handed reverse this. As you move your hand slightly toward your chest you will feel a sudden increase in density—you can actually begin to pat it. It can help if you ask your body to show you where this outer body is. This is your Mental Body and it extends out from your body in all directions. Next bring your hand slowly toward your chest, asking to feel your Emotional Body, which extends about twelve inches out from your body. Coming gradually inward you will feel your Etheric Body extending about four inches out. This is your true physical body and your physical vehicle must conform to it. Now the size of these bodies is changing throughout the day, depending on how they are activated by your will, emotions, and the events in your life. For instance, if you're experiencing a powerful emotion, your Emotional Body might expand or shrink a couple of inches. You can check this out.

I have done healings through my hand on my own outer bodies and, since it is possible to feel and locate the outer bodies of others, on their outer bodies as well. A further realization: when you are in public, sitting next to another person, your Emotional and Mental Body,

The Nature and Effects of Music

but not so much your Etheric Body, are *interpenetrating*. If you are concerned about what you might be picking up, you could either decree some kind of protection beforehand, or do a cleansing immediately afterwards.

To continue, my friend explained that if a small cut, bruise, or sprain gets lodged in your Etheric and Emotional bodies, it takes much longer to heal. What lodges it in the Etheric Body is the emotion of hurt: shock, disappointment with oneself, pain, and the crying out of these. If you can catch it soon enough and heal it consciously it's much, much faster. So the technique is comprised of these steps:

1. Stop what you're doing and settle your emotions down to zero, holding the idea that you're going to heal the hurt consciously.

2. Placing one or both hands over the place, and say aloud if possible, (or silently if necessary): "In the Name and Power of the Living Christ (or some such High Name), I decree and accept perfection of form and function in this etheric _____. Please return to the perfect blueprint for this_____."

3. Continue to hold your hand(s) over the place. You will probably feel an increase of energy in the afflicted part and it will feel better and better.

4. When it seems to have reached as high a pitch of intensity as it's going to, stop, and take your hand(s) away. Assume that healing has been accomplished and go about your business. *Do not allow doubt* to creep in or you can undo this restorative work.

The first time I tried this technique I had run down some stairs too fast and seemed to have sprained my ankle. I actually heard it "crunch." I went through the above steps and in a few minutes my ankle felt fantastic, warmer and more vibrant than any other part of my body. Later that evening I entertained the thought, "Well, maybe I should wrap it," which I did. *Then* I started to have some pain. You see, I had tampered with the purity and effectiveness of my decree. Since then I have used this technique successfully hundreds of times. Isn't this an example of the mind acting on its prerogative as, what Edgar Cayce called, "the builder" or as others say, "the captain of your soul." It is also an example of the general effectiveness of affirmations.

Another remarkable and valuable gift I received was how to create a rainbow dome. I was meditating in an enormous amphitheater in the Redwoods near Santa Cruz, CA Suddenly I became intuitively aware of a huge angel behind me. It was a 30-foot-tall *shining presence.*

As we are trained, I challenged it by saying, "In the Name and Power of The Living Christ, if you come in The Light, I welcome you, stay and do your work. If not, be gone in The Name and Power of The Living Christ." I heard it answer simply, "Indeed"!

Then it said, "I am an angel of the Christ Presence and I understand you are about to leave on a healing-concert tour of the United States. We wish you to know that The Christ Presence has been stepped up on this planet and that we will be with you on this tour. Also, we have a gift for you to share with your audiences. It is a technique for calling forth a rainbow dome over one's head." I consider a rainbow one of The Creator's most beautiful miracles but had never heard of such a thing as a rainbow dome. Have you? Here's how the angel directed me:

Stand with your arms outstretched to your sides. Put your right palm across and onto your left palm, or the left onto the right if left-handed. Gradually move your right hand back to its original position, unfurling a regular two-dimensional rainbow. Then rotate your body, keeping your arms out, first to one side then the other, completing a circle, and creating a three-dimensional rainbow dome. You can ask it to remain over you for a certain length of time, blessing you with all the colors, and the symbolism you give them. On most of the concerts and workshops on tour I shared this new technique—to the delight of the audiences.

On an earlier tour of the U.S. I was half-way through a concert and my harp began falling apart. Some pedals stopped working and I could see a crack appearing between the base, which extends about four inches up from the floor, and the sounding board of the harp. I kept playing, trying to avoid the strings affected by the ailing pedals. The situation grew worse and worse until at the end of the concert I ended up at the top of the harp playing the only two notes that were still in tune: B and F#—a perfect fifth. I came off the stage in shocked disbelief. My Higher Guidance must have been able to ascertain which pedals were going out and guide me which strings to play—it was a miracle. Fortunately that was the last concert of the tour and the next week I shipped the harp to the factory in Chicago.

Around 1976 I had a significant revelatory experience I would like to share with you. I should preface this story by saying that as my life progressed, these experiences seemed to get lighter, even showing, at times, that the Higher Beings have a thorough knowledge of our human sense of humor. I had just attended a meeting of a metaphysical study group in Washington, D.C. and was driving home to Middleburg through a bright, moonlit night. At the meeting we were studying a paper that intrigued and impressed me greatly. It presented the concept that in order to be able to create creatures such as myself with identity and individuality, what they were calling "personality," The Creator must embody these attributes within Himself. In this case it was the Divine Father aspect, and you will see why. This made sense to me. Then the thought came "Well then, The Creator could come to me focused as a person. My next thought was, since, as you remember, I never had much time with my dad, "Then maybe He could come to me as my dad."

As I look back this is a pretty outrageous thought, but then at these special times we seem to be free of the usual constraints, and also probably under Higher Guidance. So, rather shyly, I said "Dad?" and immediately I definitely heard Him answer, in a low, resonant voice, "Yes?" Well, I was a little overcome and at a loss for words, but finally I shyly said. "How's it going?" He answered, "Well I have been busy creating, you know, and I'm very pleased with a couple of new planets I'm working on. The first is exploring many varieties of my Feminine Aspect. You might describe it as extra-flowing, super liquid, mucilaginous, or oleaginous. You might not be ready to appreciate all of this as you might find it too "oozy," but I'm excited by the extension of these qualities." After all I did ask Him. I was able to see and feel some of these textures. Then He continued, "The second planet is expanding the spectrum of what is possible with crystals and color. You probably would appreciate this more and I will expand your range of vision, so you can see more of the designs, structures, and patterns." I was dazzled by the incredible beauty of these forms and the harmony of their integration with light and color. Then He said, "You might assume otherwise but actually there is more variety here than on your planet, where you enjoy quite a bit of proliferation." I was feeling more and more relaxed with Him, as if He were my father showing me His worlds, and I thanked Him.

Then He said, "How is it going for you?" I answered, "Well, I get up in the morning and make my lists, then often I lose an hour or more trying to decide which is the most important item with which to start." He said, "I can understand that, and here's something you might try. Make your lists and then start *anywhere* on the list because, you know, it's not so important *what* you do, but more important *the consciousness with which you do it*. It's all fine with me, but your consciousness and its evolution make more of a lasting impression on Me and The Creation." After thinking that over briefly I said, "Dad?" and there was no answer for two or three minutes. Then he said, "Sorry, I forgot what I was going to say."

Imagine my shocked disbelief. Never in my wildest imagination have I considered the possibility that The Supreme, one of whose qualities is All-Knowing, could have a lapse of memory. Has such a thing ever crossed your mind? He allowed a few seconds for that to sink in, then he added "Well I didn't actually *lose track* of what I was going to say, it was more like *I misplaced it*. When you say you've forgotten something, have you actually lost it or is it still lodged somewhere in your memory?" I had to admit that this was true. So his shocking statement was becoming more like a teaching. Then He said, "I have an entire, vast universe to keep track of and just at that, what you call 'moment,' even though I am everywhere, my concentration shifted to another part of the galaxy." I said, "I understand." and I felt I did at the time, but I'm not so sure I fully understand this now.

As I began to recover from my shock, I realized two things: First, up until this point in our conversation I had held in reserve a certain amount of skepticism, as we all should, with out-of-the-ordinary, and especially inner-plane experiences. But, knowing that I never could have thought this one up, convinced me that our conversation was genuine and that probably He said it with this effect in mind. The second was that He said it also to come down to my human level not only with the concept of "forgetting" but with humor to which I would respond. In this He certainly was All Knowing. It was outrageously funny to me and I burst out with something akin to a long, pent-up laugh.

We talked further and, by the time I arrived home, I was absolutely convinced that I had had a wonderful meeting and dialogue with the Source of All Dad-ness. He showed compassion and love for me but also honesty and helpfulness. He was predominately masculine in vibration with me, even though he referred to his Co-Creator, The Divine Mother Spirit and a world celebrating her flowing qualities. It filled a void of many years standing in me and I treasure the memory of it. Our meeting proved to me again that everything we experience has its origin in Spirit, and so it reminded me of the great law "As above So Below." By the way, you never heard it the other way around, did you, "As below So Above"? It also caused me to remember, because I had intimately experienced it, that we are all, men and women, children of the Divine Father and Mother. Also that any of us who find ourselves in the role of father have the perfect example of fathering ever accessible to us if we will just ask and tune in. He loves us and is ever-ready to co-create with us— it is one of His greatest joys and fulfillments.

My hope is that these accounts and stories give some picture of the miraculous experiences and events which illuminated my path toward service to The Light. They are possible for anyone.

13

The Nature and Effects of Music

As we were walking along Mykael said, "The amazing quotations in your chapter of testimonies bring up a question that I think many of your readers, and especially the musicians, may be asking: 'What are the qualities of music that evoke these responses? What is going on in us as we listen to music?' I think this might enhance the reader's experiencing of music, especially music that is potentially healing, but also expand the knowledge of music for those who haven't had the opportunity to study it. It should also be of special interest to the growing body of apprentice music healers."

After some thought I answered, "Now that would be a challenge as it means translating an experience which is fundamentally non-verbal into words, but you have come up with an important aspect of this book. I have spent much time thinking about this subject, philosopher as I am, and I will see what I can bring forth.

First of all, every individual's responses could be different, depending on their nature and what they're going through at the time, but I will come up with a typical model—the possible sequence of the fundamental qualities of music to which the listener might respond. Also, this model, in the initial stages of listening, would be the same with uplifting, healing music as with debilitating music. Of course, we will have more to say about uplifting, healing music. Let us remember: music is not so much a *representation* of life patterns and higher patterns, as a *direct expression of their vibratory aspects*. Music is like shorthand for a vast spectrum of life.

When the music begins one might first become aware of a foreign element entering one's consciousness. Let us assume, at the outset, that music's powerful nostalgic effect hasn't reminded one of an unpleasant experience. So as the music enters one's vibratory field it could begin to loosen any excessive focus on the problems and challenges with which one is "locked up." It could be a welcome distraction from getting too wrapped up in oneself, a message to the listener that they are part of a larger continuity or context. Another general message might be: "Perhaps help is on the way." Whether or not one is ready to hear these messages is, of course, another question.

Important to remember here is that the minute we are hearing music, even though it emanates from a source, instruments, voices, or speakers, we are enclosed in a sphere of sound, filling space as it expands.

Next one might respond to music's basic attribute of *pulse*, that is, its *regular beat*. If you've had a stressful day full of rushing around, changes of pace, surprises, or emotional "ups" and "downs," this *flow* aspect of music can bring you great relief. I can hear one of my mentors, my uncle Gavin, saying, "Life must *flow*." So music's flow aspect, through its regular pulse, offers the listener the quality of "continuity," which can be most healing, especially if the flow of the listener's life has been experiencing a number of sudden starts and stops, which could cause some "short circuiting."

Next, let us remember that, in addition to hearing with your ears, your entire body registers the vibrations of music. In fact, your Etheric, Emotional-Astral, and Mental Bodies, and even higher bodies respond as well. This is why music containing jagged rhythms and carrying negative thought forms and emotions, put there by the composer or the performer, is more harmful than you might think.

Then we have the actual patterns of the music and here are the basic aspects of music whose healing effects we will be trying to illuminate.

PULSE or BEAT

METER—the grouping of the PULSE into a repeating number of beats, two, three (like the waltz), four, five. six, seven, eight, nine, and sometimes 12.

PITCH—the frequency of each note

MELODY—notes in sequence

HARMONY—notes sounding together

RHYTHM—the actual variations on the pulse of the notes of the music

LOUDNESS level and its gradual changes

TEMPO—speed of the beat and its gradual changes

TONE QUALITY—called TIMBRE, from the French, sounding like the "tamb" in "tambourine"—the unique, individual sound of the instrument or voice, which is a result of the materials and design of the instrument.

Isn't it some kind of miracle that we humans can respond to all of these at once? Doesn't this suggest that, in some way, *we are music*? It is true that every aspect of us is tuned to some frequency or pattern of frequencies. I know from years of experience that often the healing is accomplished by stimulating or relaxing certain acupressure points or organs of the body. Listeners at concerts often report feeling certain notes they are hearing resonating in specific parts of their bodies. They also report streams of vibration coursing through their bodies and sometimes just outside their bodies, in their outer bodies. So these are effects the listener could feel.

Now, music is the art form that is the least tied to an object. You need a vibrating instrument to produce the wave forms, but then they travel through the air to the listener in the form of pure vibrations: actually alternating condensations and rarefactions of the molecules of the air. So no physical object has touched the body. However, in this subtly abstracted form, music can express, and sometimes represent, all the patterns of life, including the patterns in our subconscious. It can also express patterns from the higher, spiritual realms. So as we take in and accept these more perfect patterns they superimpose on the patterns that aren't working so well, are "anti-life," and transformation can begin.

Let me go through the basic aspects of music outlined above and touch on the unique gifts each one offers to the listener. All music expresses through a universal language of vibration, given slight variations arising from the listener's genetic and cultural background, and early conditioning. In addition, each of these basic aspects has a deeper, symbolic meaning, which I will share with you. Of course, most musicians are not in that deep a rapport with their muses—their higher guidance—to bring forth this symbolism. Not that there aren't musicians who are so inspired. My guides and masters revealed this symbolism to me over a period of years and have proven that they are using it in the music I am given. It is certainly operating in all the testimonies in the earlier chapters of this book as it is a "universal language" which we all understand to some degree. I have played successful concerts in countries where I could not speak the language.

When I began my healing work I was given the system of translating letters into pitches and soon after that my sources revealed the symbolism of each letter and pitch. I printed it in the Appendix of *A Harp Full of Stars* and I have re-printed it in the Appendix of this book. All the Interpretations of the music on my personalized CDs use this system and it has proven its value. I have also analyzed 1800 names, without one client saying it didn't fit them. In *Stars* there is a whole chapter devoted to this new system of Name Analysis, which I will be expanding in the next chapter through the analysis of a number of common words. I have even helped corporations find new names that will promote the purpose of their business. This system was given to me as "The Symbolism of the English Alphabet for the Spiritual Renaissance."

So I have no doubt that my listeners are responding to the deeper meaning of the notes they are hearing—the PITCHES. Also, since there are thousands of notes in a concert, there can be certain notes for certain individuals. Particular notes or patterns of notes can activate certain organs, since every part of the body is tuned to certain frequencies. MELODY, a sequence of pitches, could accomplish a continuing, flowing pattern of healing and this is often mirrored in the body by a flow along a meridian through a number of acupuncture points.

The symbolism of MELODY, supported by harmony, rhythm, tone quality, and the feeling qualities given it by variations in tempo and loudness, is the *actual, and more specific and detailed message* of the music. Some minds call this the "bottom line." Isn't this interesting when, in music, it's written, and thought of, as the top line? However, and let us be clear about this, once music is in the air, there is no "up" or "down." So-called "high" notes do not gather at the top of the room and "low" notes around the floor. Each note fills the room. We might, more correctly, call these "faster" notes and "slower" notes to match their frequencies.

The PULSE or TEMPO of the music is expressing the "speed of life" which can slow down or accelerate. It is of interest for healing that tempos over the heart rate are stimulating and those under the heart rate are relaxing. A METER of ¾ consists of three quarter notes to each MEASURE or BAR of the music. The duple meters, like 2/4, and 4/4, are all based on, and evoke, patterns of walking, where we swing our two legs and arms—step by step progress. So their effect is grounding and stabilizing of the listener's flow. On the other hand, anyone who has danced to the waltz, remembers instinctively beginning to turn. The grouping into three beats encourages you to transcend the pedestrian patterns and begin to ascend. So it encourages higher attunement. Do you remember how exhilarating it is to watch a movie set in the 1800's where a whole ballroom of elegantly dressed couples are turning together and rotating around the ballroom to a bright Strauss waltz? It's almost as if we are temporarily freed

The Nature and Effects of Music

from our earth ties and are remembering our origins in space and our citizenship in the higher realms.

The myriad, specific variations on the pulse called RHYTHMIC PATTERNS mirror our actual movements as we live our lives: our habits of movement, how long it takes to travel from place to place, home to work, our changes of timing on the weekend or when we go on vacation. Here's an example: our regular, repetitive patterns might fall *on* the beats of the pulse of our lives, whereas when we diverge from these patterns, the rhythm of our melody might be *between* the beats, or what we call "syncopated," which is so thoroughly explored in jazz.

Obviously, increases in the TEMPO, or speed, of the music will stimulate us. As the pulse quickens, we are excited and as it slows we are encouraged to relax. I remember that for a client who is high-strung or hyper-agitated over a challenge, I am given music that usually starts out rather fast and then gradually slows down. If it started out slow it wouldn't be able to capture the client's attention and their musical mind could wander. Quicker changes can be very effective to influence the emotions, notably a slowing at the end of a piece as the "cadence" is approaching, but also an increase in tempo as we approach the climax. Expressive music utilizes many subtle changes of tempo during the course of a composition in order to speak to the emotional nature of human beings and our constantly changing sensory input. Some of these the composer indicates in the written score, others are added by the conductor or the performer if it's a solo performance. The music I co-create with spirit is rich with these subtle fluctuations of tempo as it expresses life patterns and they are essential in capturing the imagination and involvement of the client.

Music creates its own time. It has been called "the art of time" or "psychological time." A composer wrote a three-minute symphony that seems to last an hour, and there is a two-hour symphony that seems to go by in just a few minutes. So, as one becomes involved in the time aspects of music one moves away from clock time and this can be a relief for the listener.

The grouping of pitches into CHORDS, commonly called "the accompaniment," is not accidentally called "HARMONY." Two notes sounding together is called an "interval" and the listener could respond to this as a partnership of the two qualities the notes symbolize. More notes than two, arranged "vertically," offer us the combined qualities of that grouping. In contemporary music, especially jazz, we hear chords made up of 11 and even 13 different notes and their variations. Many of these chords, and especially those found in the music that flows through me, reflect the basic chord of The Overtone Series, the natural chord of nature to which everything in the world vibrates. So in CHORDS the listener is given an example of how a wide variety of qualities can work together and at the same time support the more detailed and sequential message of the melody which, by the way, may add an additional note to the group. CHORDS and HARMONY express the "accompaniments" of our lives: family groups, groups that work together at your job, even your town, your state, your country, or any group you feel supported, or adversely affected by. The group could also be your physical surroundings: the furnishings of your bedroom, your house, even the arrangement of the houses on your street, or the plants in your garden, or the trees in your woods. Chords provide a rich and changing environment or context for the melody—a texture that often affects your emotions through its play between consonance and dissonance and these influence how you experience the melody. Sometimes the melody note is harmonious with the chord underneath by repeating one of its notes and sometimes it is a different and dissonant note. This could symbolize that, at that present moment in musical time, what is being expressed in the melody is not in harmony with its surroundings—its environment.

It goes without saying that the LOUDNESS of the music expresses its intensity and this in turn serves to emphasize how important to the musical message the composer feels those loud notes are. Variations in loudness are very instrumental in stimulating the emotions. A gradual increase in loudness can express a pattern of growth or something that is approaching, just as a decrease in loudness can express a moving away from the listener—even a dying away. It could even indicate a diminishing of importance of whatever is being expressed. Let us imagine that the music has somehow reminded the listener of a challenge which has become a debilitating obsession. The higher beings decide that a brief rest from it will actually help the client to recover a more objective perspective, so a gradual "diminuendo"—music's word for "getting softer"—is begun which will bring a distancing from the problem. To be even more effective the tempo of the music would also gradually slow up—called "retard."

It is TONE QUALITY, or TIMBRE that makes a clarinet, a violin, a trumpet or a harp each sound different, even if they are producing the same pitch. The materials of which they are made and their construction create these variations, but also the way the tone is produced: oboe, double reed between lips; violin, bow of horsehair against string; trumpet, expelled air through both lips against circular mouthpiece; and harp, finger plucking freely-vibrating string against wooden sound chamber. In addition, every instrument has its associations for the listener, some basic and universal and some very personal. Most people would agree that the violin is the most like the human voice of all the instruments, that the percussion—the drums—is the most martial and commanding, that the woodwinds lend themselves well to expressing the nature kingdom, and that the harp evokes the angelic kingdom and the devic forces of nature with its breezy glissandi, when the harpist's fingers glide along strings that are set for a chord.

On the other hand—or perhaps we should say "with the other ear"—our listener could have a painful memory of an instrument. Let's imagine that, at the age of three, she is trying to go to sleep. Her mother is upset tucking her in and as soon as she returns to the living room, father and mother have an intense argument. After 15 minutes she hears the slamming of a door and the father begins practicing his violin, unusually out of tune. This experience could create an unpleasant response to violins for years unless somehow she is able to get it out, heal it, learn from it, and release it. Of course, there are hundreds of variations of this scenario. Fortunately, there are also hundreds of positive, beautiful, and uplifting memories of instruments.

In any case, the tone qualities, or personalities of the instruments add something most special to the listener's experience. I do remember, from my class in acoustics, that tone quality can also be graphically expressed in the relative strengths of the partials of the Overtone Series to which the instrument vibrates. Someone should do a study to find out if our bodies contain similar "tone qualities" which respond to those of the instruments that we hear. I'll wager that we do—how else could we recognize and appreciate them? I have heard that if our marvelous "Organ of Corti," containing twenty four thousand filaments, and positioned within the ear, was lacking a frequency, we could not hear that frequency. And I have run into this in my workshops.

Surely, then, if you were able to listen to the highly complex and rich vibrations of a human being, with its pitches, intervals, chords and harmonies, pulses, meters, rhythms, and tone qualities it might sound like a symphony orchestra! And what if you could tune into the music of a human soul, which we now know to be Divine? The individualized CDs I bring through for people are a version of that personal orchestration and it is such a privilege to hear it just before I play it on the harp. It is such a satisfaction to be able to capture it in a recording so my clients can listen to it for months and years to come.

As they hear it they will be reminded of who they truly are. They can be set back "on track" and healing often follows.

Finally, one of the paramount effects of healing with this kind of music is that, as the listener becomes involved with the music and "surrenders" to it, shutting out the outside world, they become somewhat "hypnotized" and this increases their rapport with their higher guidance. In this expanded state, not only is it easier for their guardian seraphim, master guides, and even The Supreme, to reach them but they are more receptive to the love, inspiration, and healing being offered.

14

Revealing the Ancient Wisdom

of the Alphabet, Names, and Words

My last book, *A Harp Full of Stars* (1989) contained a chapter describing a new method of analyzing names. It was based on the secret symbolism of the alphabet revealed once again by my Sources for dissemination. Even though this code has been esoteric—hidden—it has been known by some. It was used rather extensively by such great composers as Haydn, who wrote a piece based on the name Bach, and also Brahms and Ravel.

To date I have analyzed the names of some seventeen hundred clients and have never had one say that the analysis didn't fit them. But they do say that it helps them understand who they are, their purposes in life, and the past experience and skills they're drawing on to help them accomplish their purposes. I have also helped new businesses select a name that will promote their purposes. The first letter of the name symbolizes the Purpose of Growth of the name and the letters in the body of the name indicate what it draws from the past—its potential. As a name or word is visualized in the mind, written, or spoken, it calls into manifestation these qualities. This is the underlying law that makes affirmations and decrees so effective. Of course, these effects are magnified and intensified with the addition of emotion and visualization. Actually, and this is a little known fact, many of the traumatic and challenging things that happen to us, as well as the beneficial things, we have manifested in this way, but we have forgotten how we did it.

Perhaps I should go back and describe how the alphabet code was revealed to me—and it was somewhat miraculous.

In 1973, when I first began to bring through a client's past lives in music I gradually noticed the most amazing connection. Whenever I saw a person involved in a certain activity the music would utilize the same pitches or notes, that is, in the same key. This was a pleasant shock since I knew I wasn't creating these connections consciously while I was playing. I would discover them afterwards as I was recording the Interpretation of the music. Of course, this corroborated the presence of the Sources and their higher guidance. The music for a life devoted to some form of artistic expression would be clustered around the note F♯, a life in a monastery attuning to the Divine Father—Pure Patterns of Light—would feature E, and a life exploring the physical world, Divine Mother—the Manifesting Principle—would be in the key of A.

When my system of equivalents was almost complete, with only a few gaps left, my Sources came to my aid. Ellen Spies, one of the clearest channels in Virginia Beach in the early 1970s, went spontaneously into trance and announced that the Sources would like to give me the *Symbolism of the Mystical English Alphabet for the Spiritual Renaissance*. Then they proceeded letter by letter, reinforcing what I had learned from the readings, but also filling in the letters I wasn't so sure about. It was most impressive—a detailed dictation, for which I have been deeply grateful ever since.

After the first thousand readings I began to get clients with the same names. I had already been given the code composers have used to translate letters into pitches and the Sources asked me to translate their birthdates as well as their names for more accurate identification. I later learned that, as I play the name and birth date this acts as an identification number on the client's file in the akashic records, the universal data base. When the Sources hear it they know permission has been given and can access the records of past lives. I never do a reading without permission, that is, a request. Then they choose the most enlightening and healing lives to translate into music for me and the client. Let me hasten to add here that the details of place and time—city, country, years and century—are not as important as how the client is living out their life. You could almost see these sections of music as *aspects of the soul*, sojourns of growth along a client's self-chosen pathway toward God-Realization. This plays down the attachment a person can have to *who* they were and emphasizes the *steps along the way*, evolution back to Spirit.

When the code for translation and the symbolism of letters was familiar to me I decided to test it out by analyzing words I came across around me. Imagine my excitement when I discovered that the majority of words contained letters that support the meaning of the word. Does this not suggest that the wordsmiths who originally came up with these words were inspired? It is unlikely that they all knew the table of symbolisms, although it is possible that a few did. But I also found words where the letters do not support their meaning. I was forced to the conclusion that we have *good words* and *bad words*. I have often put it this way: you could write the same book using *good words* or *bad words*. Good words would be stronger, more convincing, and flow better—be easier to read and to hear. With some of the "very good" words the letters expand and enhance their meaning. I'd like to give you some of my favorite examples.

Let us begin with a simple word: "It." The first letter is the Purpose of Growth it attracts. It translates to the pitch C♯ which is the Manifestation, bringing into form of Artistic Sensitivity. Is it not true that when we focus on an "it" we immediately become interested in how it was created and how it could be used creatively? Actually every "it" is part of The Supreme's miraculous creativity. Also we are immediately aware of The Supreme's desire to create not only "oneness" but a dazzling array of specific and individual creations—each one unique. The Creator seems to love the diversity of things as well as the Oneness of things. The word "it" expresses this. Zen Buddhism especially honors the "suchness" of things, pointing directly at reality, honoring the "its" in the world.

Then, in the system, three letters produce the pitch "A"—Divine Mother, or Physical Manifestation. They are: "A"—Divine Mother herself, "T"—the Physical Forms she uses to manifest, and "N"—the energy that comes up from Earth—for us, the "kundalini" energy that arises in our root chakras. If you look at the "T" in the word "it" you see that it has a "roof," telling you that we are not dealing with "The Light of the Higher Realms," but Earth reality. Next we notice that if we extend the "I" of the "T"—"I" is Individual Expression—upwards above the "roof" we have the "crosshairs" of telescopes and microscopes which help us focus our attention on a specific detail. So the letter "T" is three quarters of a cross hair. Does this fit with what we understand the word "it" to mean? Yes it does. In addition, the notes produced by "it," C♯-A, create the interval of the third or sixth, or "the Sense of Physical Beauty" and "An Expanded Sense of Beauty."

How about a closely related word, which contains the word "it": "r-e-a-l-i-t-y"? As I progressed in word analysis internal words became more and more significant, adding to the meaning. The Purpose of Growth of the "R" is to learn more about that which fills structures or forms, the Qualitative Aspect of Artistic Creativity. Is not reality about giving body to the pure pattern that originates in Spirit? Then what does this word draw on? The "E" of the Divine Father's Light, and then the "A" of Divine Mother's Love. Many philosophies speak of the division of God, The One, into Divine Father and Divine Mother, and their coming together in what is called "The Holy Wedding" to produce "The Creation." Then comes the "L" of Artistic Creativity, in a cosmic sense, symbolizing the outer forms, structures, or designs; the

"I" of Artistic-Creative Manifestation, the "T" of Physical Forms, and the "Y" of the Patience to Complete a Creative Project Step by Step.

Have we not seen this infinite patience in the evolution of the myriad species of our Earth? Note: The symbolism of the "I" as a pitch is Artistic-Creative Manifestation. When applied to us humans, the shape suggests an individual, standing on Earth and reaching toward, and connecting with, heaven. So it is not surprising that we have chosen this letter to represent ourselves, each one. The two interpretations aren't that far apart, when you think about it. Not only do these meanings fit the word "reality" but, together with the internal words "real" and "it" they fill out and enrich our understanding of the word. Imagine for a moment what it would be like if these symbolisms became second nature to you and you were aware of them every time you used the word?

Here's one of my favorite examples of the use of the letter "T" and especially its "crosshairs aspect": "a-t-t-e-n-t-i-o-n." The first thing we notice is that it contains all three aspects of the Divine Mother Principle: one "A," two "Ns," and three "Ts." Its Purpose of Growth is to know more about, honor, and celebrate Divine Mother Herself.

What does it draw from the rich past—and here we refer to Her rich past and your rich past experience if you are saying "MY attention"? There are two "Ts," then an "E" of Divine Father Aspect—The Light, an "N" of Physical Energy, a "T"—crosshairs—an "I" of Artistic-Creative Manifestation, and another "N" of the energy that comes up. Actually, this is a reflection of the Primal Descending Energy. Remember the great law: "As Above, So Below"—and also remember that there is no value judgment intended here. Divine Father and Mother are equals and, at the same time, always One. In a world of duality this "division" seems to help us understand how they function, but they are, at all times, ever present in, and as, the whole.

This brings us to another of my favorite words: "w-h-o-l-e." "Wholistic," and its companion "Oneness" are becoming "buzzwords" in that portion of our society that is more spiritually aware and reaching out in fellowship to other humans—but also to minerals, plants, animals, angels, and masters in spirit. Here I would like to introduce you to another aspect of letters that contributes to their symbolism: their shape, particularly their three levels which represent the three chakras: Root, Heart, and Head. The Purpose of Growth of "w-h-o-l-e," the "W," is Attunement with Outer Space and other planets. The two "Vs" in the letter "W" describe Involution followed by Evolution and also represent Universal Love in the system. "V" translates to the note D♯. D is Human Love and D♯, a half-step higher, symbolizes a higher aspect of love, universal or unconditional love. "H" stands for Continuity through Time and Patience to Complete Long-range Projects, also Cooperation Through the Heart" "O" is a planet or universe, also Creative Manifestation for the whole, "L" is Artistic Creativity of the Structure and Design Type, not that which fills the design; that is, Bones, not Flesh. The letter L is the "I," an "I Am," or event in time, with an extension of the Root Chakra on the Physical Plane—all fitting Artistic Creativity. The "E," the final letter of the sequence, the Signature of Pure Spirit—Divine Father, also represents how we as individuals evolve, through the Root, Heart, and Head—the end result of the word "whole." Now isn't this amazing, enlightening, and beautiful? Whoever came up with this word, out of the millions of possible combinations of our twenty-six letter alphabet must have been Divinely inspired.

But none of this would have come to light if we were not "curious" to know more about ourselves and the world around us. Let's look closer at this word "c-u-r-i-o-u-s." We might first notice the internal words: "cure," "I," and then "us." Are we not cured and healed of our confusion and lack of knowledge when our curiosity is satisfied about our world and ourselves? And between the "I" and the "us" is the "O" which could very well represent, with our exploration through questions and their answers, expansion of our wisdom that we can apply to ourselves and to others and even lead to the "oneness" suggested by the circle, "O." The Purpose of Growth is To Learn More about Ordinary Survival Actions—the Skills we Need to Learn in Order to Maintain Ourselves. As the letter "C" moves forward through time and space it gathers information and experience. It is strong in the Root Chakra and the Head Chakra but lacks the emotion of the heart, so it suggests the dispassionate objectivity of science. It resembles a large mouth and a capacious stomach. Does this not fit perfectly the purpose of our curiosity?

What potential qualities do we have going for us in the body of this word? "U" looks like a bowl or urn and it symbolizes our ability to receive higher guidance, the presence of mind to "look before we leap." It is one of the three letters that represent different aspects of Patience in the system, together with "B"—one step at a time, and "H"—organizing long-range projects in space and time. You might like to notice that the "H" diagrams two people holding hands to work together. "R" is that which fills the Structure, the Qualitative, or Feminine, Aspect of Artistic Creativity. The "I" is an "I Am", or an Event in Time, "O" signifies Completion and Wholeness, then another "U," and we finish with the "S" of Patience to Finish a Creative Project. Does it not require patience to process and assimilate the manifold gifts of a lively curiosity? And notice here that in "curiosity" we have added an "it" and the "Y" of inspired step-by-step patience, since the "Y" is like a glass open to higher guidance. I am just now, for the first time, noticing that this is a celebratory glass, perhaps a wine glass, not an ordinary tumbler. Wouldn't all these revelations put "curious" in the "good word" category?

Then how about "yawn"? "Y", its Purpose of Growth, is shaped like a wineglass which gets filled from above. "Y" symbolizes Drawing on Higher Guidance to Patiently Complete Worthy Projects. Aren't we taking in higher energies, or prana, when we yawn? Then the word draws on the "A"—Divine Mother, the "W"—space, we expand when we yawn, and finally the N of Root Chakra energy. Isn't the end result of a yawn to energize us? And the end result of its relaxing effect is to make it easier for us to take in pranic energy from the space around us. Isn't this amazing?

Another aspect of words I should remind you of here is that we are dealing with a *sequence* of qualities that the word initiates. In the case of a name I actually play it as a melody on my harp. You could play your name and the name of your business, providing they were good and uplifting words, and it would promote your Purposes of Growth and help you and your business draw on the qualities in the body of these names. When music is played no one knows how far out it goes in waves of resonance. This would also tend to synchronize the sequence with all the natural time frames of your life and your enterprises. These are: one day, —not a week because that's not a natural unit of measure despite the moon cycles—, a moon month, roughly twenty eight days, and a year. Then you could possibly add to these an important cycle in your astrological chart, like the cycle of Saturn—twenty eight years—and your whole life, or the life of your business, if you knew these last two. I once plotted the first four of these for a client and he said he used it to his advantage. It must have been a great name. When I worked this out I made an intriguing discovery. At any particular point in time my client was experiencing a chord—a cluster of qualities—made up of the letter in his day, his moon month, his year, and his Cycle of Saturn.

And it didn't stop here. Early in the analysis of names I realized that, once a name was translated into pitches, or notes, I could see how each letter related to the one on either side, that is, the degree of consonance, harmony, or dissonance between them. When I told clients that these disharmonies could result in possible conflicts they were usually familiar with these tensions in their lives. Similarly, they could also relate to the more harmonious pairing of letters. Most of the time, this play between "sticky flow" and "easy flow," is something the client experiences, and in the case of a word, it fits the meaning of the word. Don't we humans need to be challenged once in awhile? Aren't we somewhat lazy? In most cases, under Higher Guidance, I am able to help the client feel better about the challenges by seeing them in a positive light, as opportunities for learning, growth, and spiritual advancement. There isn't space here to give you very many examples but here are some letters that produce what is considered in music the most dissonant interval, the tritone. Perhaps you can find them in your name and they could give you a clue as to the nature of some of your most trying challenges.

The tritone consists of three whole steps. Imagine you're in the key of C and you count up from C: C-D-E-F-G-A-B. If you then played the F with the B you have the interval of the tritone and it will sound pretty dissonant, even though it's fairly common in chords, or clusters of notes, in the music of the last one hundred years. Before around 1700 it was actually forbidden in the music of the church. Of course, combining it with other notes usually renders it less strident and if it does appear alone it is almost always resolved into a more consonant interval. The notes of this tritone, F-B symbolize The World of Nature—elementals, devas—and the Patient One-At-a-Time Steps we Humans Take and therefore a tension between these two areas of your life. For the symbolism of the letters of the tritones mentioned below, please consult the Letter-Pitch Equivalents in the Appendix.

The "CR" and the "IM" (C#-G) in "c-r-i-m-i-n-a-l" are both tritones. Isn't this remarkable, since many crimes are committed by people who are suffering from deep polarities that they are unable to resolve? "C-r-i-m-i-n-o-l-o-g-y" adds a third tritone, "OG"—C#-G. Certainly anyone studying criminals and crimes will be exposed to a long list of these polarities.

If you'd like to check out your name for tritones: C-F# could also be produced by Cl and CR. If you would like to resolve this dissonance, or tension, try to substitute the letters UG, BG, HG, UM, BU, or HM. In addition to the three tritones above, look for D-G#—DS and DY, D#-A—VA, VN, and VT, A#-E—EZ, KZ and QZ, and FB—FB, FU, and FH. Of course, three of these pairs you would rarely, if ever, find: KZ, QZ, and FH. Note also that all the above pairs could appear in *reverse order*. How about "e-n-v-y" and a shocking discovery, "T.V."? Are not the majority of T.V. serials, and movies, based on the tensions of polarized situations? And it makes sense that "c-l-a-r-i-f-y" would begin with an unclear situation (CL) and proceed to strong artistic creativity—ARI.

How about "c-a-r-d-i-o": Purpose of Growth, Basic Survival Skills? The heart is quite basic to our survival, isn't it? And the "a-r-d" translates to "AF#D—Human Love. Coincidence? How about "a-r-d-o-r"—heartfelt enthusiasm, especially when in love? Its Purpose of Growth is Manifesting the Divine Mother Principle—love. And again it draws on Human Love—F#-D—and then "o" and "r", the C#-F# of artistic creativity.

To better understand the following you might like to sit at a keyboard.

I would like to give you a further realization which could help you resolve the tritones in your name. The tritone is the essence of what we call Dominant Harmony in music. The progression to Tonic Harmony—the chord built on the home note of the key you are in—is its strongest resolution. So this movement to the notes that outline Tonic Harmony alleviates and harmonizes the tension and thus provides a clue as to how the tension of your tritones can be resolved. Let's take C-F#. The F# would move up to G and the C would move down to B, outlining the G chord. G symbolizes the "How To" techniques of Survival, and the B symbolizes One-step-at-a-Time Patience. Can you see how this suggests concrete steps that could relieve the stress indicated in your name? To translate these two pitches to letters: G = G, or M, and B = B, U, or H. Possible pairs would be GB, BG, GU, UG, GH, and HG; and MB, BM, MU, UM, MH, and HM. I give you these in case you'd like to add them to your name or incorporate them in your name, to help you resolve this tritone in your life. The strongest way of adding them to you name would be right after the tritone—CRUG or CRUM, but you could add another letter between the tritone and the letters you are adding to make it more pronounceable: CROUG or CROUM.

There is another resolution of the tension in a tritone and it also follows the progression in music from Dominant to Tonic. In our first example the F# could also go down one half step to F and the C could come up one half step to Db. Db-F outlines the chord which symbolizes bringing into form Artistic Creativity. Our system for translating letters into pitches uses only sharps so we correctly translate Db into its equivalent C# and F into its equivalent E# to get their symbolism, which is the interval of the major third on C#, the Sense of Beauty of Creative Manifestation.

I realize this is becoming a little technical and might take some study and thought, but this is for the musicians, and the adventuresome word lovers among you. The letters presented to us by C# and E# are IW and OW—or their reversals, WI and WO, just in case one of you would actually like to change the spelling of your name to help heal the tension of this tritone. Another possibility would be to include the notes of resolution in a nickname, or create a new nickname. Examples: CLOW or CROW. I have found that often letters that are missing in a name have been intuitively added in a nickname. If you would like to replace your tritone with these resolutions consider C#, which translates to Manifestation of Artistic Creativity, and the W—Space Attunement or Higher Guidance.

The other serious dissonance I find in names is the half step, but there are so many of them we can't go into them here. I will have to leave them to you to heal, using the procedure outlined above. When you translate the letters of your name into pitches from the table in the Appendix, you may find adjacent notes—half notes—in your name. That's the smallest interval on the piano, including the black notes; that is, from a white note to a black note, but also from E to F and from B to C. Examples would be the letters EF, BC, ID and OD, or their reversals. The challenge symbolized by the halftone is "too much congestion"—the people or things in your environment or your life that are too close to you or closer than you can handle. But they can also suggest progressing seven to eight in the scale of the upper note; that is, completion of a series of steps in that scale. Is it not true that the last step of a course of growth is often the most challenging and requires the most effort and focus in order to finish the series?

I have learned so much over the years from this new method of revealing the symbolism hidden in my own name and the names of my clients. I have come to the conclusion that, since saying, writing, and thinking of yourself as your name is setting your goals and drawing to you qualities that will affect their realization, your naming was rarely the whim of a parent. It is much more likely that, in most cases, it was guided by the higher beings, angels and masters in spirit, who know you, honor you, love you, and are dedicated to aiding you in your optimum path toward reclaiming you divinity. In some cases where an infant got the wrong name, or was given a name for later in life, they are called by a nickname, which provides more suitable vibrations for the first part of life. I have often heard it reported that when a man marries, his wife will say, "Isn't it time you used your given name?" Up until I reached the age of nineteen I was called "Joey." When I married, at my wife's suggestion, it became Joel. The OEL symbolizes the creative manifestation of the Light for the good of the whole"—isn't this suitable for one destined to become a healer for many? My older brother was called "Andy," given name "Oliver" and my younger brother was called "Gavy," given name "Gavin." And isn't it fascinating that when my brothers assumed their true names they graduated from the tritone dissonances in their nicknames?

I hope this chapter has given you enough information to explore your own name. There is an entire chapter in *A Harp Full of Stars* devoted to the basic analysis of names, but here we have taken it quite bit further.

15

Strengthening our Weeks

and Restoring Meaning to our Days

It has bothered me for some years that we say the names of the week all the time without knowing what they mean. We have inherited these names from history, some of them ancient, and have long forgotten the symbolism they were originally meant to add to the progression of our week. These names we use every day have come down to us from various cultures and languages, shrouded in mystery; except, of course, to the dedicated philologists, students of language, among you, to whom I bow. But doesn't it border on superstition that the majority of us use them as if they had meaning to us, without knowing the effects we are creating for ourselves and others.

I was fortunate to have been blessed with a classical education in a private boarding school, but all I gleaned about the names of our days was that Sunday was obviously named after the Sun, Saturday after the planet Saturn, and I guessed that Thursday could have come from the Norse god of thunder and war, Thor. I think I assumed that Friday must have been named by the Catholics, it being the day of "frying" fish, and that Wednesday might have once been a favorite day for weddings—certainly no longer. Monday and Tuesday have always seemed devoid of meaning. It might be amusing to ask your friends what they know about these meanings but I wager you won't turn up much information and will often draw a blank.

One of the reasons we came to America was to step out of ancient, time-worn traditions and create a new, more enlightened culture. Now, in the Spiritual Renaissance, and the new era to which it is giving birth, there are many customs we must take out, examine carefully, appraise, and either update, or release, because they no longer serve our enlightened and much-expanded understanding of life.

I have probably made my point but just for fun let us imagine that a benign space being has just landed in mid-America and the first human he meets is of average intelligence and education. The American mentions a day of the week and our space brother asks him why he calls it by that sound—he's been curious about this on the way down—and the American, nonplussed, answers, "Beats me, I really don't know." To me this would be truly embarrassing.

These realizations began to fester in my consciousness until I finally heard a small voice say, "Well, would you like to come up with some new, more meaningful names for the days of the week?" So, with a good deal of thought, and reaching out to my muses for positive inspiration, I came up with new names. I've been using them for some twenty years and find that they promote a pleasing, effective, and supportive flow to my week. Of course, over that many years they have become installed in my subconscious so most of the time I don't even think about them consciously, and yet I know that they are giving a wonderful rhythm to my days. I'm confident that, after a few weeks, they will change for the better how you experience yours.

Now, take a moment and visualize yourself beginning your week. Each day has a name which has meaning for you and the sequence provides a nice continuity of qualities which sweep you along through a spectrum of seven days—*a logical, creative progression.* Since the names suggest general types of tasks they reduce the temptation to engage in all types of activities on the same day. One of the challenges I have, and many people have it, is to make long lists and then see how many items you can cross off each day. In other words, this world is so hectic and stressful our focus has become quantity rather than quality. One of my missions for the past few years has been to get people to slow down for quality because that is what the average human and the world needs. As I have mentioned, a very high Source suggested to me one day, many years ago: Make your lists if you want to and then start anywhere because, at this stage of your evolution, *the consciousness with which you do something* is more important than *what* you're doing. In other words, we need to become more "be-ers" than "do-ers."

I was able to make the new names sound almost like the traditional names so that most people won't be shocked when they hear them, even though they might notice a slight difference of pronunciation. Studies have shown that we hear, and see, pretty much what we expect to hear and see. Something entirely new, most of the time, passes us by, except for the rare individual trained in observation. But even if you're not ready to say them in public you can receive much benefit by using them in your own mind and in your "daybook."

Here are the names and the symbolism they can add to your week:

Mandane—Tunesday—Windsday—Thorosday—Finaleday—Celebray—Reverveday

MANDANE ("mahn-dain") stems from the word "mundane," things of the world, but starts with the word "ma"—the first word most babies speak all over the world—The Divine Mother Principle which brings into form the pure patterns of light that come from The Divine Father. "Man" denotes the human race, woman and man. So this name reminds you to re-enter the everyday world after the day of rejuvenation. It gives you permission to begin your week with simple steps that will lead you toward your projects or goals for the week, actions that will lay the groundwork for what you would like to accomplish, or bring to fruition, by Finaleday. See the beauty of deliberate, methodical activities done with love and care, the philosophy of Zen. Put off complex, "working through" or "completing" procedures and be content with modest but solid foundations. This is especially beneficial if you have had an intense weekend, where leaping into high-level or challenging activities could be stressful.

TUNESDAY ("toons-day") Let a flow like music come into your work and it will pick up a little speed in an effortless way. In the beginning, to call forth this quality of tunefulness, you can whistle or sing first thing in the morning or listen to some music that you like—music that has some nice rhythmic continuity and free, soaring melodies. It's still only the second day so you don't want to wear yourself out. You're not pushing, just allowing the music of life to sweep you along. You can actually imagine that everything you do on Tunesday is accompanied by inspiring music. If this is difficult then put some of your favorite music on in the background, with the idea that eventually you will be able to supply the quality of music from within.

WINDSDAY ("winds-day") Here is the arch of your week's energy. Feel the wind at your back, filling your sails, and your projects gradually rising off the ground and taking off into the freedom of the air. This can happen if you've made good preparations on MANDANE and listened to the music on TUNESDAY. You can still hear the music on WINDSDAY but it's a little louder and faster—and more expansive. It could be helpful for some people to imagine the whistling of the wind through the rigging and the soft slapping of the sails of their ship. Begin WINDSDAY by becoming aware of your breath and resolving to breathe fully throughout this day, breathing the power of the air—prana, life force—into your work. This will ease any tensions that might be building as the energy increases, and will open you to higher inspiration.

THOROSDAY ("thaw-rows-day") Whatever you're working on is airborne, but today you check the details to see if there are any adjustments you might need to make so that as much of it as possible can be completed on Finaleday. Patient, honest and accurate analysis, appraisal and adjustment are the keywords on THOROSDAY so as to make the best showing on FINALEDAY. It's kind of like the attention to detail we practiced on MANDANE: you draw your energy in and focus it, but it's a little more complicated—a natural complexity with which you've been growing. You're on top of it and your excitement is building. It's a good time to check to see if your project was a little too ambitious and whether it might be wise to put something off until next week in order to finish up on Finaleday.

FINALEDAY ("fin-ah-lee-day") Like the end of the last act of a musical, all the elements of the week, or their conclusions, enter the stage in a meaningful sequence to perform in harmony. Hopefully you will have a fast-paced, grand and fulfilling finale. So the spirit of this day is that you're on stage dancing with all aspects of your project—at least you are the conductor. In the latter part of this day you might want to assess how it all went and make some notes about what still needs to be done. Of course, there are a number of factors that can hold up the completion of your project. If you are aware of them they won't be stressful for you and you can see them as learning so as to make things easier next time: 1.Taking on too much, 2. Not sticking to the flow pattern. 3. Circumstances beyond your control such as other people not coming through, external events, or even "acts of God." Just take some notes for next MANDANE. At the very least you will have enjoyed the flow and what you did accomplish. Sometimes it's as if Higher Guidance is saying "This project needs more cooking, and we have some additional factors due to enter next week which could raise the project to a higher level of quality. But hold in the back of your mind: The sound of FINALEDAY suggests "holiday" so even as you're completing things you're anticipating the next two days, and this lends a lightness to your work.

CELEBRAY ("cell-uh-bray") Note: For some years I called this PHONEDAY because people were generally at home, but with the widespread use of answering machines, cell phones, and e-mail, many of your friends prefer you leave a message, or if it's important, call them wherever they happen to be. Without getting into the potential dangers of cell phones, we can say that they certainly have sped up, and increased, our communication. Can we step aside from the stress this can cause—at least on Celebray?

On Celebray we remember to count our blessings of the week, feel good about our achievements, and allow them to make us happy. Plan some activities that will help you release any tension you are holding from your work. Enjoy nature, get some exercise, see friends, renew relationships with your loved ones, and have some fun—celebrate!

REVERVEDAY ("ree-verv-uh-day") is so named to remind you to do whatever will be restful, restorative, and renewing. Hold the thought that you are filling up with energy for MANDANE. If you still need some activity to release tensions from the week, that's good, but just try not to work at it—let it flow easily. Recreation which is too organized or strenuous can leave you tired when you begin your new week the next morning. Reserve a little time later in the day to plan the first steps you want to take on MANDANE morning, unless these are obvious, or you wrote them down in the latter part of FINALEDAY.

Can you see how these names would organize your flow of activities along a natural, creative progression and help you make more sense out of your week? Could they keep it from getting jammed up? Once they are memorized and become more automatic you would be able to put off tempting projects that you know can't be completed by Finaleday, or at least , give them only the time that is absolutely necessary, so as not to upset your flow. Of course, you reserve the right to modify the sequence and then return to it as soon as you can. I've found that it really has simplified my life. It reduces sources of stress and promotes quality work over the "how many things can we cross off our list today" syndrome. Imagine the enhanced effectiveness if a group of people who work together were all using these names and concepts. Mutual support?

Now we come to a most vital issue: the word "week." After the clue I gave in the title of this chapter, have any of you felt a growing dissatisfaction with that word? I don't suppose any research has been done on the effect this word, sounding like "weak," has had on our success, our well-being, and even our health. If you think I'm stretching a point here, let me tell you that research has been done on the subliminal effect "other words," some of them just *within* words we use, have on us. Studies indicate that the subconscious is capable of processing thousands of bits of information and so must be reading all the words hidden within a word, and "week" sounds *exactly* like "weak." We are saying all the time "*my* weak," "*your* weak," "*this* weak," "*next* weak," and "*in a few* weaks," to name just a few. However, I should mention here that the letters W-E-E-K are strong: W (E#), Purpose of Growth: To expand into Space; then what the word draws on, the two Es, The Light of the sun, The Light of The Source; and the End Result, K, another note "E": Mastery of The Light. This may reduce the effects of "weak."

Nevertheless, consider how often we use this negative word and its shady companion "weakend." This word implies not only weakness and an unsatisfactory conclusion of the week but implies a "ceasing of the flow" of the week altogether. But life never stops, not even in the transition we call "death." There have been many accounts by people who transitioned from this life and then came back, having been told on the other side that it wasn't time yet. These are reported in Raymond Moody's *Life After Death*. With the negative programming of "weakend, it's no wonder you hear conversations like "How was your weakend?" followed by "Actually, not so bad..." We probably even program our futures when we say, "How are you going to spend next weak?"

At the end of the 1800s the New Thought Churches were founded in this country: Christian Science, Science of Mind, Unity, and Religious Science. One of the backbones of their practice and success is the power of affirmations and decrees, based on the metaphysical law "What you hold in your mind tends to manifest in your life." The book *The Power of Positive Thinking* by Norman Vincent Peale was, and continues to be, a best seller. So I see it as a vitally important question: "What effect has the constant, and widespread, use of "weak" had on our culture? And, let's face it, if this effect has been only *slightly* deleterious, the word should be replaced.

As a deep student of the healing effects of sound and music I know that sound creates a vibration on the inner planes of being and as growing co-creators with Infinite Intelligence we are learning to take responsibility for our creations. Since the Spiritual Renaissance began to gather momentum we have found many things that need to be redone: gotten out, examined, and either updated, or released. Many of them seem almost to be the work of the darker forces, and I suspect this may be true of our word "weak."

In my search for a more meaningful word for "week" I looked first to nature for how it separates into weeks and found the phases of the moon. But "phase" has a serious drawback: the phases of the moon

Strengthening our Weeks 169

don't coincide with our calendar weeks and there would be confusion as to which was meant, the moon phase or the calendar week.

Of course, if we could go ahead and make sense out of our calendar, by making each month a full cycle of the moon, then each new phase of the moon could initiate a week and we could make the most of the moon's influence. Now you have to consult the newspaper or an almanac to find the moon phases which now fall on different days of the week throughout the year. It might be some time before we could expect this kind of reorganization. A legitimate question: were there forces trying to confuse us and separate us from nature at work here?

Now, to avoid confusion we need a word that has very little other meanings, and I considered "whack." For years I've wondered what it really meant if you were out of "whack"—what were you out of? Of course, all I had to do was look it up in a good dictionary. Then I found that "out of whack" isn't a very good use of that word, but I took this as a recommendation for our purposes, especially its second meaning:

WHACK: 1. To strike or slap with a sharp, resounding blow 2. A share, or portion, separated out in a forceful way.

It's strong but perhaps we need this strength after the "weakness" of "week." The second meaning above could help us to honor the individuality of each day, even as the new names are providing a flow. "Whack" might wake us up to the vital importance of living in the *now*, which is so important at this time It would certainly wake us up from our two or more centuries of the lethargic programming of "weak."

Another candidate is "REAP." It is a little gentler, and less of a change, since it sounds like "week." During the week it would remind us to sow our seeds well and nurture them to guarantee a plentiful harvest on Finaleday, and it would remind us to "gather in" what we have accomplished. On the "reapend" it would remind us to celebrate, as they have down through history, at harvest time.

Unfortunately "Whack" and "Reap' are a bit extreme and often cause laughter in those with whom I have shared them. So the best word I've come up with so far is:

PEAK: 1. The crest or summit of a hill, ending in a point 2. The highest or utmost point of anything 3. The maximum value of a varying quantity during a specified period.

Wouldn't these qualities be wonderful to associate with our week and counteract the debilitating effects of "weak?"

While I was at it, I thought it might be of value to come up with a model sequence for a week off (a peak off). And also a "peak off" in which you wanted to accomplish a lot in your own personal work. First the peak off:

NATUREDAY (Mandane) Ah, sweet solitude. A day of sauntering among the trees, leaves, flowers, grass, streams and lakes, or the sea. Especially notice their sounds. Everyone else is at work—you'll mostly have it to yourself. In the evening review and write down your inspirations.

SPIRIDAY (Tunesday) Accompany everything you do with music that will bring you peace, harmony, upliftment, healing and ecstasy. Count your blessings and allow them to make you happy. Contemplate the possibility that everything is alive. Make it a time to renew your oneness with whatever you call the Source of All Life. Evening: review and make notes.

DANCEDAY (Windsday) Give permission to your body to move and stretch, and don't forget to breathe as you do it. Do some vigorous walking and dancing to your favorite music. Evening: as above.

HEARTDAY (Thorosday) A day to connect and show your love to family and friends. Make a call or write a note, or even do something nice for someone close to you. Even do something nice for yourself—write yourself a nice, supportive, and loving note. Express your generous side—give a gift. Evening review.

GRATISDAY (Finaleday) A whole day when you're free to do whatever you're moved to do, but do it filled with gratitude. Review.

SONGDAY (Celebray) Hum, vocalize, chant, decree. Read something you find interesting out loud and then try singing it. Have you ever improvised a song about yourself—what's going on in your life? This can be a very enlightening experience. Just so you'll feel freer, I suggest you be alone the first time you sing this song.

MY-CHOICE-DAY You are free to repeat any of the days of this "peak," whichever was the most rewarding, or whichever didn't go as well as you would have liked, and you have ideas about how it could go better—be more fun and rewarding.

Can you imagine the richness and inspiration you could feel after this peak?

Then, with some slight rearrangement, consider: A Personal Accomplishment "peak":

MUSICDAY (Mandane) Fill this day with background music that you find stimulates and lends continuity to your work.

SINGDAY (Tunesday) Fill this day with vocalizing about your work to lend it flow.

DANCEDAY (Windsday) Take breaks to breathe, stretch, walk and dance. Possibly even while working or thinking about your work.

SPIRIDAY (Thorosday) As an undercurrent to your work, do it as if it were a blessing for you and those who will benefit from it.

HEARTDAY (Finaleday) Bring the principle of generosity into your work—go, at least a little out of your way to serve, or please someone—a colleague or a client.

GRATIDAY (Celebray) Do anything day, but do it well and with gratitude as if you're celebrating.

NATUREDAY (Reverveday) Trees, leaves, flowers, grass, streams, the lake, or the sea.

Not only could this peak introduce variety into your work, but stimulate new ideas, and your enjoyment of your working life.

Then here are some once-a-month days:

REVIEWDAY Take a clear, honest, but loving look at your life. An excellent exercise here is to measure what you do for "standard of living" or "status" against the energy and time you put into "lifestyle"—what you love, what feeds your soul. Do you put so much time and energy into "status" that your "lifestyle" is suffering? And consequently your happiness and possibly also your health through the accumulation of stress?

APPLEDAY Eat nothing but apples (no juice). Cleanses and rids the body of toxins. If you have a cold or are sick, do for three days followed by one-third cup of olive oil. Recommended often by Edgar Cayce, I have used this for years and often kicked a cold in one or two days, rarely more than three. Also gives your digestion a new lease on life.

BED DAY Permission to spend an entire day in bed, resting and recuperating. Alone or together.

HUG DAY Permission to hug anyone if you have the slightest inclination. Just don't force it on anyone. If you're not sure they'd like it, ask.

WHOLING DAY (HARMONIDAY) A day of integrating your Physical, Emotional, Mental, and Spiritual aspects. Also spend some time integrating Past, Present, and Future. This could be done in meditation and through writing. Also integrate Work, Home, and Play.

SHED DAY Permission to spend a whole day without clothes, or as few as possible. Shed all the roles you play, while you're at it. You can always take them up again. Engaging and revealing question: "Who are you without the roles you've taken on?"

SNOWJOB DAY For your best friend or lover. Plan an entire day, from the time you get up until you go to bed, of what they would most like on a day off and only tell them what's next. Or, each one can plan one-half of the day. Wonderful surprises. A great way to show you care. A snow-job day is perfect for Valentine's Day or your Anniversary. These have been some of the best days my wife and I have ever spent together.

I have found it exciting to introduce you to these possibilities of breathing new life into your days and peaks. After using the new names for a few peaks they will become part of your subconscious and then, even when using the traditional names, you will think of them with the new symbolism. But the word "week" will sound worse and worse. Isn't it always this way with something new? It takes courage to change habits even when you know they will be worthwhile. I have found that after any day that resembles a day off, when you return to your routine the next day, everything goes better and faster.

After you give some of these a "go," I invite you to come up with names that might be even more inspiring for your particular temperament and type of activity. Of course, you have the right to make exceptions: to put the names aside if you have a good reason. But isn't it inspiring to have choices? Just imagine: if you were getting a little bored with your routine, you could set up a month where the names of the days in every peak provided a different slant on your activities. It could also be dotted with two or three special once-a-month days, including of course, a "snow job" day. Just the new names for the days of the basic peak are guaranteed to add a meaningful flow to your life.

For myself, I am eagerly looking forward to experiencing some of the special days I brought forth for this chapter.

16

What is This Thing Called Love?

> "What is this thing called love?
> This funny thing called love
> Just who can solve its mystery?
> Why should it make a fool of me?"
>
> -popular song by Cole Porter

Certainly the time has come to address the question "What is love?" What do we mean when we use this very general, catch-all phrase "I love you?" Up until the 1960s perhaps it was enough to hear these words and know that their speaker was feeling something nice, which is certainly one of the sweeter condiments of life on Earth. To be sure, if you knew quite well the one who said "I love you," you might have a fair idea of what they meant, but what if this particular time the meaning had expanded, contracted, or changed? Of course, the inflection, intensity, and the speech tune or music in the way they were said might give you a clue, but otherwise you probably had to rely on your intuitions. And this could open the interpretation to your own wishful thinking, the projection of your own doubts and suspicions, and all manner of difficulties in communication—and, by the way, most of the plots of the romantic novels and films, especially the tragic ones.

In the not too distant past most marriages were not based on love. Surprisingly, it has only been in the last century that the idea of marrying for love has become a widespread and noble experiment. Marriages, in all but the lowest classes, were arranged to guard property and the social power of the family, or for political and many other reasons. Even before this time, if the marriage was not arranged by the parents, the role of the sexes was so polarized that any real communication between them was not expected. Marriage was a dance between two quite different species. Any real difficulties were sometimes negotiated with outside help, but this was rare. Most of the time each spouse, and most often the woman, had to make their own adjustments, or separate, and this could lead to all manner of hardships. In these arranged marriages love either developed between the couple or it didn't—especially when there had been no original attraction. Then each one probably took a lover which, unless it was kept absolutely secret, offered a questionable example to the children.

Psychology and psychotherapy and their full exploration in books, films, and television, have presented to us the possibility of communication between love partners. But along with this expansion in the media has come, quite often, an idealism that leads us to expect that a marriage guarantees everlasting love. Unfortunately we are not adequately trained in this new conception of the art of love and relationship. Are there courses available in high school and college in the vital art of communication in the basic types of relationships—even as electives? Yet this is a course that everyone should take. Aren't there a number of courses that would provide valuable tools for life that should be given in school? The teachers could be those fortunate few veterans of the art of living who often turn out to be wise parents.

In the expanding, world-wide, spiritual community there has been for some years the awareness that the human race is experiencing an initiation and opening of the Heart Chakra—unconditional, or Christ-like, Love. So to use the word "love" alone is no longer enough. More and more enlightened people are asking those who use it in their presence, "Well, I appreciate that very much but what are you really feeling and just what, out of a rich spectrum of possible meanings, do you mean by it? I'd like to savor the emotions behind what you said. As wonderful and welcome as its general quality is, it is intriguing and leaves much to be desired. I'd like to know more."

An apropos, although basic, analogy is with food, since love is a kind of food. What if you said to your partner, "I'm hungry but I'm not interested in telling you what I'd like to eat, so long as it's food?" Or if you said, "I'm going to feed you now, but I'm not going to bother asking you what you would like, or whether you'd like what I have to serve you. Just be content that it is, in fact, edible food." This is an especially apt analogy in our times, when a large percentage of available food is suspect, if you're looking for nutrition without side-effects.

Therapists describe the unbelievable tangles their patients get into when they each had a different conception of what they meant by their professed love. And yet, because they needed and wanted love and wanted the relationship to work, they would suppress the miscommunication and staunchly defend the simplistic view, to others and themselves, that they loved each other. Despite the value of keeping your mind positive, the kind of repression I am describing here will eventually come out, usually painfully, and could have been avoided by a more honest and detailed expression of "I love you."

Now there is nothing wrong with men and women, or any two people, loving each other differently as long as they are really trying to communicate, as accurately as possible, the nature of what they're feeling, thinking, and believing. I think this is long overdue, especially now that we have entered the Spiritual Renaissance. So I will devote the next three chapters to various aspects of this question with the hope that these insights will begin to enrich the expressions of love by you, my readers. Isn't it entirely possible that when you begin to uncover your true love feelings, an aspect of your love will emerge that you never expressed before and this could be so sweet for your partner. It could even rekindle flames that have been burning low.

I remember a time in my life, and many people I've interviewed can remember such a time, when the word was so lacking in meaning for me that I was reluctant to use it at all—and this could be difficult for my partner. I felt it was over-used, too easy and too simple —a "cop out." Fortunately, I was expressing love in other ways: I guess my hope was that "love in action" would make up for my lack of "verbal love." In later years I have learned to use this word more easily and either fill it with some emotion or qualify it by adding words. So, for those who can relate to this reluctance to use words, here's a way to begin: first express how you're actually feeling, then tack on "So, I love you" or "This is how, or why, I love you." These might be good transition "add-ons"; so your partner won't think you *don't* love them.

So I present this analysis with the hope that it will stimulate you to make your own study. It draws on my own experience in partnering, but also my over three thousand *Attunement* sessions, *Soul-Path Re-Alignment* sessions, and *Counseling* Sessions. Most of these have been for couples where the Higher Forces working through me have illuminated the nature of their relationship with unbelievable compassion, and understanding. And this experience has prepared me to lead hundreds of workshops in relationship.

Let us begin with a spectrum of seven varieties of meaning for the phrase "I love you." These will start with the basics and then progress through higher and more universal meanings, vital to our understanding of world harmony and peace. I'm sure you will be able to relate to these; but if you feel that something has been left out, please feel free to add it to one of these, or even add more to the list. Examine your expressions of love and, when you feel ready, discuss them with your partner, avoiding criticism but with the excitement of opening up new avenues. It's time we initiated some dialogues about this time-worn phrase. We're re-defining relationships, so let's expand our vocabulary. As you recognize your own feelings in this list, you will be reminded to express them when you say "I love you." So as I present each one, imagine that you have just said, or your partner has just said, "I love you" and this is a possible meaning for that statement:

1. I admire you. I like or love some quality or qualities you exhibit. I think you are a good person with attributes such as healthy, energetic, youthful, beautiful, loving, open to life, poised, talented, skilled, experienced, humorous, compassionate, spiritual, and so on. Keep in mind that, for these first two and #6 and #7, in addition to your love partner it could be a close friend to whom you are speaking.

2. I'm attracted to you, drawn to you, want to be in your presence. I feel a magnetic pull toward you. I really enjoy how I feel when I'm around you. I hope this feeling is mutual, that you have similar feelings, as I like to be wanted.

3. I desire you, want you—not necessarily sexually—and want you to be continually in my presence. So I desire to develop a more permanent relationship with you. I like who I am when I'm with you. I intend to do whatever I reasonably can to be the kind of person who will hold you.

Comment: Of course, this can lead to difficulties if you change yourself and act in such a way as to compromise your integrity in order to hold the other person. This will eventually rise to the surface and have to be dealt with. On the other hand, in certain cases, this can mean evolution for both of you, when your partner is setting a good example and following it means growth for you and brings out your higher qualities. After all, learning from each other, if it's done freely, is one of the great treasures of togetherness.

4. You arouse me on many levels. You "turn me on" and you stimulate my sexual nature. I feel that you are a person with whom I could have wonderful, satisfying sex and I desire this. The vision I have of mutual fulfillment could be mostly physical, or include the emotional and mental, or even higher, more spiritual dimensions. It could even include past-life memory of various types of shared relationships. These varieties are explored in the next chapter.

Comment: I am also using the word sex, here, in a very broad sense. Whenever any two people are interacting there is a certain amount of kundalini energy generated. Even when two love partners are having sex there is also a general spectrum of the use of this basic energy from the Root Chakra—the energy that rises. The old masters said that in order to reach enlightenment, you must raise this kundalini energy up the spine to the head, as that kind of energy is involved in illumination. There is also a form of sex in India, called tantra, the goal of which is not a climax but raising the kundalini energy together. In our relationships in the West sex is all mixed up in a very wondrous and miraculous way, although sometimes we get our signals crossed and need to sort things out. Then a few sincere and honest words between us can really help avoid misunderstanding. The Victorian taboos should be pretty much relaxed by now, so it's time partners enjoyed this kind of realistic communication. This list will help and there is more about the fine art of communication in the next chapter.

5. I am remembering the ideal vision we had for our relationship and the commitment we made to that vision and to each other. I'm feeling thankful for shared experiences in the past, appreciating your presence in my life right now, and relishing the contemplation of a rich future together. I'm excited by the prospect of my own growth, and yours, through our relationship. Thanks for your commitment and loyalty.

Comment: This is an important one because sometimes, when the going gets rough, what my guides and masters call "sweet abrasion for growth," it's hard to feel the love in the moment. Then it can be so steadying to be able to remember past love shared and you're valuing of it. So if at those times you can say "I love you," holding the memory of your shared vision and express gratitude for your partner's persistence, this could be a very high and healing expression of love.

6. I feel you are a true friend. I love that we have so much similar back-grounds, tastes, and attitudes that we can share. I really like doing things together, even when other aspects of our relationship might be challenging and bringing us growth. I value *us*, what we do, and what we can share and create together.

Comment: This could be said to a friend, but if it's a partner it shows that you feel your friendship will help to see you through. Marriage counselors say that the one thing that is most helpful in saving a marriage in jeopardy is a developed friendship they can hold on to as they sort out their "challenges." In times of crisis, we often need to be reminded of this aspect of our relationship, even though it is fundamental.

7. I value you highly just as another human being, a fellow child of The Supreme Being, a brother or sister. I feel a growing awareness of your divinity and potential. I respect your particular pathway of

evolution and want you to know these considerations should help resolve any tension or conflict that might arise between us.

Comment: The masters say brothers, sisters or brother/sister is our primary relationship. Then, if you include past lives, we have had many other temporary liaisons, long or short, which are really like workshops to develop the art of loving. We are also reminded that whenever we are tempted to limit our love to one person, there is a danger. We need to remember that *everyone* is our brother or sister. A committed relationship can have this dimension of universal love, and you also can have it with everyone. This is the highest meaning of "I love you" but it is rare in this culture as so many have turned away from The Light. We need to listen for it, treasure it in others, find it in ourselves and express it. And as I observe those around me it seems that over the past few years people are being gradually nicer to each other. Have you noticed this?

Now, so you can fully appreciate these seven positive aspects of the word "love," here are five negative, or sick, possible meanings of the phrase. If the truth be known these are more prevalent than you might think and they are sometimes mixed in with the positive ones and therefore tend to be hidden and harder to notice. The speaker would rather you don't recognize these. Since none of us are perfected souls yet, they are possibilities we should be aware of—but not be *expecting*, which could attract them. Also, we could well test ourselves for these. If any of them are lurking just below the surface, they can really confuse a relationship and steal from the effect of the innocent and positive love expressions.

1. My feelings for you are probably the opposite of love but I hope that if I say "I love you" you will stay with me so I can act out these feelings. I really think you are inferior, so it makes me feel better having you around. I don't mind taking a little abuse from you if you will let me hurt you also; then I can release some of my frustration and anger at others on you. I think this could work out for us. Is it a deal?

2. I'm attracted to your strength. Please take care of me: I'll do loving-type things for you if you will. I know I'm inferior and insecure so I'm attracted to your superiority and we'll make a match. This will prove that my parents and others were right about me, because it will "work" for us. You have something I want and I'll act as if I love you to get it, but God help me if I'm discovered.

3. I'd like to develop some power over you. It would make me feel stronger if I could control you and make you dependant on me. I feel you are my friend when you do what I want you to do. When you don't, I feel that our relationship is in danger.

4. How about some mutual sexual stimulation? Wouldn't that be fun, and relieve our tension? But no fair prying into my inner life, who I really am, or the rest of my life when I'm not with you. Let's keep it physical. Our mental, emotional, and spiritual aspects might not jibe. I must love you without any commitment; then we will know it's the real thing—spontaneous. Even if we should create a child that would be your responsibility. I hope you can enjoy me taking from you. I promise to be dashing and lovable, but I might not always be "around," or what they like to call "faithful."

5. I'm attracted by the "danger of the unknown" with you. There are things about you I don't think I'll ever understand and this is confusing. You're so different from me. This fascinates me but it scares me. It also threatens my desire to bend you to my will. If I can persevere in our relationship perhaps I'll prove that, contrary to most reports, I'm worthy .

I see these insights as a beginning. You could, when you notice the general emotion of love arising, pause a moment to see which one of these thirteen meanings is actually behind it, but you may find more than one. Then, as your awareness develops, you can make much more meaningful your expressions of love. Then, better still, with some deeper soul-searching, you could come up with your own personalized list. At least, now you will be able to listen more closely to your friends and loved ones and enrich your understanding of what they mean when they express their love in words. If they only say "I love you," you can show your appreciation and then gently ask them to elaborate.

Here is a simple way you could begin to experience and learn these expanded meanings: Set up two chairs facing each other. Sit in one and imagine your partner sitting in the other. Have the following list with you. Visualize your partner looking you straight in the eyes and saying each one with a pause in between for you to savor your responsе. Then, after you've gone through the list, see how you feel. You could also practice saying each one to your imaginary partner. You could also invite your partner, if they're interested and willing, to sit in the other chair. Then you go through the list, asking them how each one felt and how they felt afterwards. Then reverse roles.

After each one you add: "And this is what I mean when I say 'I love you'"

1. I admire you. I like all your wonderful qualities.

2. I'm attracted to you—I want to be in your presence.

3. I desire you—I want you to be in my presence more permanently.

4. You arouse me on many levels, including sexually.

5. I'm remembering and savoring our ideal vision of our relationship —our past, present, and future.

6. I feel you are a true friend and companion—I love doing things with you.

7. I value and respect you just as another human being, a fellow child of The Love/Light.

There's no question about it: greater self-awareness and clearer communication are enormous factors in leading us out of the horrors of the Dark Ages into the light of honesty, sincerity, healing, play, joy, creativity and mutual spiritual encouragement. The giving and receiving of genuine love will certainly ease the opening of the Heart Chakra of the human race and even affect the minerals, plants, and animals, and give the angels joy.

An afterthought: Why is it so much easier to "fall" in love than to separate? We all know the incredible anguish, and time and money spent during this second, deeply challenging ritual. Is it possible that if the couple had been practicing the insights described above, separation could be made much smoother? They would know much sooner if their love would not justify the enmeshing of their lives. Or, if it had been a long relationship, the love that they were sure of might sustain them through a more gracious untangling. Some couples have demonstrated that they could work out an amicable settlement, without handing over half their savings to a lawyer. Did loving communication help them do this?

I had a client who was going through a divorce and was terrified of meeting her husband for lunch. The past few times had been disastrous and painful. I suggested that, before she left for lunch, she sit down, calm herself and go into a contemplative state. Then concentrate on the love that they had shared and the things they had accomplished. Then reach out to him from her heart, sending unconditional love to his heart. It worked like a charm. He was friendly and polite and they were actually able to work out some issues and come to some agreements. At least it was a major change in the tenor of their relationship and a new beginning. I theorize that one reason this worked is that it bypassed the husband's mind. I've had success with other clients with this technique and have used it with some success myself. Does this not suggest another form of loving: long distance, or remote, or "inner planes" loving?

17

Expanding the Definition of Love

We're sitting around, Serafina, Mykael and I; they say some nice, appreciative things about the last chapter, and then one of them says, "But, you know, that leaves some questions. And since love is so important at this time, could you tell us more about the varieties of love of which we humans are capable? This was deeply thought-provoking, exploring what we might mean when we say 'I love you.', but what are the basic varieties of love?" Then the other says, "I think, nowadays, your readers would be interested in expanding further their concepts of love." And I say, "Well, that would be my great pleasure. I wrote a whole paper on this very subject on which I could draw. It divided love into Physical love, Emotional love, Mental love, Soulic love, and Spiritual love. And Mykael says, "The two that intrigue me the most, because there is probably not so much known about them, are Mental love, and of course, Soulic love.

MENTAL LOVE

Taking Mykael's cue, let us talk first about the nature of the mind. It is an amazing processor, but we must recognize that there are no real life patterns in the mind. It does help you to *manipulate and deal with* a wide variety of life patterns. It can utilize the laws of logic, that is, clear thinking. It can predict the future by projecting the possibilities which could unfold from an idea or action. It can make analogies, by noticing that *this* is like, or similar to, *that*. Then, with the help of the subconscious, it can help you remember ideas from the past. It can also bring forth wisdom from Higher Sources and even channel information from your guides and masters. But I realize now that the masters who help us in this way must have studied deeply how to translate higher thought into human, earth-life terms so that we can understand it. Somewhere, associated with the mind is our free will, the part of us that actually makes the decision to do something and hold to it. This depends on our self awareness, our ability to step outside of ourselves and observe ourselves—what the animals don't have. I suspect this capability is an attribute of our human consciousness.

The mind can help us in so many ways. Let's face it, this book concerns itself with a wide spectrum of subjects and it is through the mind that these are set down into words. And is it not a miracle that words can be found that stand for, or evoke, so many subtle, higher realities of consciousness? Even when we talk to friends, it is through the mind that concepts are formed *about* something. Then, the mind is very good at symbolism and finding words that could stand for real-life realities. Another ability the mind has, through repeated affirmations, is the creating of a powerful thought-form which can set in motion an intention. This in turn can, especially when combined with an emotion, lead to manifestation in one's physical world. Of course, here you are telling the mind what you want it to do, since it has no volition of its own.

Mental love includes the joy and excitement of sharing ideas. An example would be: you are invited to a dinner party and you meet a new person. He's a wonderful conversationalist. He has stimulating ideas which are enough like yours that you're interested, but he gives new slants on them. This would be a form of mental love because you are sharing ideas and you want to see him again because you enjoy this, what has been called, "intellectual rubbing." This can be very stimulating, exciting, educational, and even enlightening.

One of the most intriguing functions of the mind suggested by the masters is that it functions as the mediator between your High Self and your Body Consciousness. Isn't that interesting to contemplate? And this brings up a question that clients and students often ask me: "If we are basically three selves: High Self, Conscious Mind, and Body Consciousness—the "subconscious" or Basic Selves—it must be important to achieve harmony between them. But this can seem like such a daunting task, as they are so different. How can we accomplish this?" It is true that many of our problems arise out of lack of communication and harmony between these three levels. This can be a perplexing challenge until you realize that by far the easiest way to accomplish anything is to *decree and accept it*, using the mind's capability to create your reality. Some years ago I wrote out the affirmation that follows, which I say every morning. I have noticed more and more harmony in my whole being since I have been saying it. Of course, invoking whatever you call The Highest is a big part of its effectiveness, since there is no problem for Infinite Intelligence, when the motive is to promote life.

> In the Name and Power of _____, (I say "The Living Christ") I decree and accept, between my High Self, my Conscious mind and my Body Consciousness: understanding, cooperation, harmony, love, and bliss. Manifest, Manifest, Manifest, Now.

SOULIC LOVE

I've chosen the name "Soulic Love" for the feeling we have for, or relationship we develop with, those we have known in past lives. If you think about it, you have probably had the experience where you meet someone for the first time and after just a few minutes you feel a strange rapport with them. Then, after a few hours of getting to know each other, you're saying to them, under your breath, "Oh, there you are. I feel I know you. Where have you been all my life?" Through time, the development of this kind of relationship, with its deep communication, can be quite a blessing—even an ecstasy.

Often it blossoms into a love relationship, or at least, a deep friendship. We have had many past-life relationships with those who are close to us. When I do a past-life reading for a couple they usually will have had one, out of three, where they were married or lovers. But they will have had others where they were sisters, brothers, mother-son, father-daughter, or at least co-workers. It is this wide variety of past-life connections which has led to my realization that our true, fundamental relationship is fellow children of the universe—The Supreme. All the other relationships, though filled with potential to grow and evolve, are then temporary. I have found, further, that it helps any relationship to keep this fundamental connection in mind. This principle can encourage you to develop a friendship— a most valuable aspect of a love relationship

Soulic love can also include a similarity or complementarity of soul-purpose, destiny, or life plan. This is shown not only through the series of lives with which you are resonating but is also mirrored in the Sub-Purposes, the initials of your name, chosen by your High Self for the *present* incarnation. This is becoming increasingly important as more souls turn toward the Light. Relationships of the Spiritual Renaissance are those in which there is a sufficient rapport on the physical, emotional, and mental levels to allow for two more to be added: sharing their spiritual seeking, or at least honoring each other's path of seeking, and then even doing Lightwork together. It is truly inspiring to see couples now who are harmonizing all of these levels.

One of the most puzzling "soulic loves" is the sudden attraction we can feel for a soul we have seriously wronged—yes, perhaps even taken out of life. Ever since then, through the intervening incarnations, we have been looking for this person to have an opportunity to resolve the situation. When we meet them, it is as if we say "Oh, there you are, at last. Please don't go away until you can forgive me—I beg you!" The "victim," who has been holding the blaming and deep down would love to be rid of it, can have a similar response to the meeting. And this powerful attraction has often been mistaken for love and even resulted in marriage. How long it will last is another question. If there is forgiveness and learning, or if the "victim" cannot forgive, there is usually separation so that they each can pursue their chosen path toward self-realization. I should add here that my sources take a positive attitude toward *everything* that you have done in past lives; they see it all as potential growth in consciousness.

I should add that a good relationship, one that has the potential to last, will have both deep love shared before and some negative karmic patterns to resolve, because we are all about the business of growth. My sources call this "sweet abrasion for soul-growth."

Many shorter relationships are motivated by negative karma. Not that there aren't short meetings with those we've known before, even intimately, and with whom we've developed good karmic patterns. These come to lift us up and encourage us on the path. In the three thousand readings I have done, roughly one in seven have been a deep, and more or less ideal, love relationship. After one of these, we are called upon to be examples to partners who need to open up their ability to love. Is it not true that in most unions there is one that is more able to express love than the other? Once you have received such a love, you are more able to give it.

At this point Mykael interjects, "What about 'soul-mates' and 'twin-souls'"? I answer, "Soul-mates" refers to two people who have had a number of past lives together. They have developed a fairly deep understanding of each other, have worked through a good bit of their differences, or at least how to handle them, and could enjoy a committed relationship. One of the special cases of past-life karma that creates a good measure of oneness is when two people meet who have basic selves who have been in the same person. When they meet there is an instant feeling that they intimately know each other. Of course. They were in the same body. I experienced this once, there was actual proof of it, and I have heard of other cases. Even in these relatively harmonious relationships there are challenges for growth. To tell the truth, once you open yourself to a long-term relationship with a soul-mate, the commitment can make you more vulnerable, but again, this should create more opportunities to learn and grow.

Over the years I have had a diminishing belief in the concept of "twin-souls." I don't think it's healthy to entertain the idea that there is one love partner who is more special than all others—especially if that special one isn't around in this incarnation, or you meet them only briefly. Those who entertain the concept of twin souls say that you don't necessarily meet your twin in every incarnation. Doesn't this sound like a formula for a strange, underlying loneliness and couldn't it make it more difficult to give all you can to the one you are with? It's elitist—the concept that some people are more special than others. Also it runs counter to the belief that we are all One, and to the belief that we are brothers and sisters, fellow children of the Creation, and "equals in the eyes of The Most High."

EMOTIONAL LOVE

This is the successful and pleasurable sharing of emotions: the ability to allow oneself freedom, within some discipline, to enjoy and express a wide range of emotions to another. Of course, we must also feel responsible for expressing them. Included here is the ability to find non-hurtful ways of expressing negative emotions out of consideration for your brother or sister. Ideally, Emotional Love includes the strength to risk the expression of the deepest love feelings for their own beauty, apart from the other's response to them. It also includes the capability of responding to the positive emotions of another without the fear of losing oneself. There is growth and power in the ability to surrender to what is beautiful in another and flow with it, share it. The inability to do this is usually a weakness at some level of one's being. A definition of an ideal relationship that I have always liked, is the model one times one (1x1), a whole times a whole, where each one is relatively complete in themselves. One-half plus one-half or three-quarters plus three-quarters describe a co-dependent situation, which can become challenging and where a strong stress from outside can cause a collapse.

Certainly a life without emotions would be not only missing some of the joys of life, but seriously lacking in a very basic kind of communication. Is it not their emotions that tell us how intensely our mates care about something? How important it is to them? Also, we know that negative emotions can play a large part in ill-health, just as can negative thoughts. However, with study and practice our emotions can become more and more positive, expressing unselfish love. Have you noticed that after a bout of negative emotion: frustration, anger, suspicion, when the emotion has subsided, the love, which is on a higher level, is always there, waiting for you? Remember: we always have a choice if we're willing to look for it.

PHYSICAL LOVE

Physical love is the enjoyable interaction of the senses through touching. Even though it is the most conditioned, or specific, aspect of love, it is often the vehicle for expressing mental and emotional love, and even in certain cases, Soulic Love. There are many aspects of Physical Love which may be idealized, that is, shared as beautiful: physical helping, physical supporting, the healing touch, teaching physical skills, preparing food, playing games, and finally, the varieties of sexual love-making. All these can be viewed from a spiritual perspective, since they are given and sanctioned by The Love-Light we call God.

Reaching back to the Victorian Era, Physical love has been the most maligned aspect of love; but we are finally digging ourselves out of centuries of distorted understanding. Farther back, in the Dark Ages, sex was limited by the church to only 40 days of the year. With this suppression people would visit each other in their dreams, but if this was "proven", a person could be put in prison. There was even a name for the offender: "succubus" or "incubus." Even today we are seeing the results of forbidding priests to marry.

Physical love is impossible without realizing the incredible beauty of the body, honoring its intricacy and complexity, and the thousands of functions it keeps in harmony simultaneously. The liver alone has 500 functions—how about this for intelligence? If we could observe the wonders of our bodies, we would be in absolute awe, but most of the time we take them for granted. The ancient wisdom tells us that each body is like a universe, a microcosmic replica of the larger universe, and it is this wondrous instrument with which we make love.

All of this is taken care of by our subconscious or so called "animal" aspect, which we have been taught to put down. How can we call it "sub," when it takes care of thousands of processes our minds alone could never accomplish? A clear look reveals that animals don't make love the way humans do at all, and yet when someone exhibits selfishness in love we call them "animal." If animals could talk, especially the paragons of loyalty, the dogs, I wonder what they might say about our using them as scapegoats.

Once we realize what miracles our bodies are we can start giving them some appreciation and love. They will show us how and we will be richly rewarded. We could stop complaining when a few functions aren't working quite as well as the other 10,000, and start appreciating the 9,995 functions that are working well. Your body deserves love, it needs this positive reinforcement, and appreciation and love will help it to operate more smoothly, and be more radiant. Touching is its way of loving. We are constructed so that touch contact between two people, unless they block it emotionally or mentally, is healing for both parties. This contact generates energy beyond the sum of the two. Studies have shown that a circle of people holding hands raises energy more comparable to the square of the number of people.

So Ideal Physical Love is the capability of loving your own body-temple and another's —to be able to combine knowledge of technique and another's body with spontaneity. It means creating an art of loving them which will combine loving their generic qualities as well as their individual and unique qualities. Their generic qualities are those they share with the rest of their sex. Loving these enables the lover to let the beloved stand for all those of their sex and promotes faithfulness. Physical love includes also the ability to respond to another's touching, to surrender to being loved—and this applies to men as well as women. Many men love to be loved but never ask or stop long enough to allow it. To be sure, in general, men tend to be more active and women more receptive but with the growing liberation of women we are seeing women calling forth their masculine side and men developing their feminine side. So it would make much more sense if henceforth each one of us is understood as both, in some measure. We can no longer think of a person as simply a "man" or a "woman." Have you noticed the serious difficulties to which this wrong concept has lead us? We are more like "man-woman" and "woman-man." So, wouldn't it be much more realistic, and richer, to think of the masculine in each person loving the feminine in the other person?

Actually, as I do in my workshop, you can also explore the other two relationships: "sisters" and "brothers" as well. I have found in my counseling of couples who are about to split up, that this exploration can rekindle the flame of love. I have them devote a whole weekend to exploring each of these relationships: masculine/feminine, brothers, sisters, and feminine/masculine. The reversal comes last since it is the most unfamiliar and therefore challenging. To tell the truth, men and women, in fact any two people, are acting out these four relationships most of the time, they just don't notice it. Same sex relationships may be more aware of this variety going on. Observing these four relationships, and then developing them can lend variety and richness to any couple's loving and certainly enhance Ideal Physical Love.

Two last considerations here: Ideal Physical Love is impossible without the knowledge and feeling that a sexual climax is a Divine blessing, a supreme form of healing, a death-rebirth experience that re-affirms life. Another way of describing it, which many people experience, is that during foreplay they feel a summing up of the gestalt, or mandala, of their lives, reaching a climax of intensity, then exploding out into space. What comes back is a pure, unconditioned, cosmic energy ready and available for a fresh beginning, retaining the last gestalt in memory for reference. In a higher sense it is a celebration of the two aspects of Deity: Divine Father Principle, Sun (yang); and Divine Mother Principle, Earth, (yin) and their harmonic, loving interaction.

Now, of course, sex can range through many degrees of openness, starting with sex as exercise and relief of tension. Although limited, there is nothing wrong with this function of it. Tension-release is a fundamental rhythm of life. But what Ideal Physical Love remembers is that, while this first level of physical loving, which we might call cellular, is beautiful in itself, as one replica of the universe makes love with another replica, we wouldn't get the two bodies together without some thoughts and emotions. Pure physical love is extremely rare. The more we open ourselves to the interaction of Mental and Emotional love with Physical Love the richer and more fulfilling it can become. Each level can stimulate and enhance the others. Let us remember that it is in the act of physical lovemaking that all the levels can be integrated and harmonized. And it is in the successful practice of Ideal Love that time and space can be harmonized and temporarily transcended.

As we try to develop and blend these aspects of Ideal Loving, there a few guidelines that are most helpful to keep in mind. These are respect, compassion and forgiveness, gentleness, brother-sister caring, true interest in the other's growth, and non-attachment to the other's response, so you can enjoy the act of giving. Of course, once in a while, we should assess how things are going. In addition, there is taking responsibility for one's sexual actions. This includes the mental, emotional, and soulic levels. This is especially true for men, so focused as we are in the practical world. Then there is the importance of cultivating freedom from possessiveness and jealousy. These last two are dangerous enemies of healthy Ideal Loving. The love that has the most meaning comes out of freedom, realistic honesty and sincerity. Finally, throughout this complex and challenging, but infinitely rewarding dance of Ideal Love you must honor your own Center and Divinity, your unique individuality as well as the Divinity and unique individuality of your partner. With these guidelines we are beginning to touch on some of the higher concepts that go to make up Spiritual Love.

At this point I looked up and Mykael and Serafina were lost in thought. Then Mykael asked, "What about Spiritual Love? You touched on it in another chapter when you were answering the question 'What do you mean when you say the words, I love you?' but I'm wondering if we could go a little deeper, or should I say higher."

I replied, "I would enjoy opening up that subject, but first let me report on a little study I made about physical lovemaking:

Once your eyes are closed and the light is off, just where is your body? I mean as a shape or physical design? It's gone, or at least radically changed. Hasn't it become the 'shapes' of sensations, emotions, or even ideas? Isn't it more like waves, or colors, or perhaps the varying intensities of the flow of music?

Another revelation that clear and honest perception brings concerns frequency. If you make love for the national average of three times a week, even if you take an hour each time, this would total three hours out of 168, or 1/56th (2%) of the time. Even if you just take our waking time it comes out 1/37th (3%) of the time. So what's all the fuss and fretting about excess? Our faithful bodies are working for us all the time, even as we sleep, doing all kinds of complicated actions for us simultaneously and we're reluctant to give them 3% of the time for their kind of lovemaking? Even when they are willing to be the instruments for the blending of the other kinds of love? This is somewhat ridiculous, isn't it? And it shows the hold that some of our more wayward religious leaders and our conscious minds have gotten on us. It also suggests the work of the Dark Forces to take us away from The Love/Light by making us feel shameful about our Creator-given capabilities and their miraculous beauty and potential to heal.

I have dwelled on Physical Love because I feel that it is the least understood and respected of all the aspects. This must be why it has received such emphasis, pro and con, in our society struggling toward enlightenment.

> We only transcend something by mastering it. If you do wish to transcend sex, first master it. You cannot release it as long as you feel there is something unspiritual about it. Evidence indicates that some forms of love and sex go right up the planes of ascension. You have heard that The Supreme is love. You could also say that the Supreme is sex in the highest sense of that word. In the planes and planets in duality—that's us—The Creator, The One, splits into The Creator, The Two, Divine Father and Divine Mother. Then the creative interaction of these two great Polar Principles creates all of these worlds and everything in them.

To make love on the levels I have presented here is to engage in a sacred and miraculous ritual—as sacred as the love that is ever being exchanged between Sun and Earth.

As we have said, life on this planet is experiencing the opening of the heart chakra, so love is becoming more and more important to our survival. And this suggests the possibility that the more dedicated souls among you might be interested in moving beyond *contemplating* these various forms of loving into actually *practicing* them and moving toward fusion on all these levels of expression. If you are, I would suggest you start with one at a time, perhaps the one that seems the most difficult for you. Prepare yourself ahead of time with a little meditation where you picture yourself *practicing* that form of loving. *Precaution*: I strongly suggest you not tell your partner you are doing this, as spontaneity is so important to every form of love-making, and calculation can kill the naturalness of love. But an occasional *practicing of the art* of love can bring rewarding and exciting results. You might be pleasantly surprised by your partner's reaction plus the stimulating effect of bringing something new into your loving.

After making progress with each one, you could move on to practicing them in pairs. Then three? Then four? Then five? You'll probably have to set aside a longer session time for these last two—perhaps a whole day. To fully appreciate the possible effect of this, just imagine how it would feel if your partner, within the space of a few hours, at least touched on how they loved you, mentally, emotionally, soulicly, spiritually, and physically.

As I review the relationships in my own life, the earlier ones often focused on one or another of these aspects. Then in mid-life often they were combining two or three. Serafina and I have been together for 30 years. We have had many past-lives together, playing various roles, and now are trying, with some success, to harmonize them all including Spiritual Love.

SPIRITUAL LOVE

As I have briefly mentioned, Spiritual Love is sharing your path of seeking enlightenment with another. If you are not on the same path, that is, the same church, the same master teacher, or the same book of Spiritual Truth, at least you support and encourage each other on their path. And you can enjoy discussing philosophical and spiritual concepts, even to the point of learning from each other.

Of course, since spiritual beliefs are so profoundly important to most people, discussion of them can easily lead to argument, and have even led to wars. Therefore, Spiritual Love requires an open mind. What also helps, I've found, is the realization that it is impossible to adequately express a spiritual concept, and especially a spiritual experience, in words. This always falls a little short of the reality. So even the best words are allusions to, or references to, or catalysts for, or signposts along the way to the spiritual revelation. Anyone who has had a life-changing illumination and has tried to put it into words knows about this. The spiritual seeker who keeps these two concepts in mind will then be able to freely listen to, or read, discussions of higher truth without getting locked in to the concepts as absolute truth. This is one thing the Asian Wisdom has kept in mind for centuries. They refer to The All That Is as "That Which Cannot be Named." Actually, we can be thankful that the limited mind of man has been able to translate cosmic consciousness experiences as well as it has, so that our speaking and writing can occasionally stimulate a direct experience of The Supreme Beingness. The few times I have been blessed to experience this Sublime Presence have upleveled my life forever.

In closing, I should touch on a realization that is vital to the smooth-running and happiness of relationships and that is the art of *communication*. First of all, a pairing that is alive, and has the potential to last, has a strong component of polarity. They have, in some measure, been attracted to each other by their differences, most importantly by the relationship between the male and female qualities in one and the male and female qualities in the other. This sex difference brings with it a challenge to communication and we can think of many other factors that can complicate communication: difference in age, upbringing, education, racial origin, daily activities, and so on. Of course, these factors also keep our interactions engaging. The second main factor is that nowadays we are all so busy we are often not relaxed enough to deal calmly with sensitive issues. Then frustration can lead to the acceleration of the emotions which, in turn, can cloud, or even completely sabotage, our attempts at clear communication. On the other hand, sometimes the emotional message is the most important message. We even hear "there can be no real communication between man and woman." So we need to learn the art of communication with someone who is, though similar genetically, basically different from us in polarity and possibly outlook. For the foregoing reasons, some guidelines may be in order to preserve peace and harmony and thus to promote the development and blending of the varieties of loving described in this chapter.

> 1. When you wish to ask your partner a question, first gauge how wrapped up they are in what they're doing, especially if the question might stimulate a long discussion. If so, either put off asking it or simply say "There is something I need to ask you when you have a minute." Then, in case they are deeply involved, say first what your question deals with; that is, help them "get out the file" they will need to be informed about your question. Don't you find

it frustrating to hear a question without any clue of its context? But it makes all the difference if your partner prefaces the question with, "Lovey" (or some such term of endearment), I need to ask you a question about your mother." And this leads to:

2. Every couple should have some time, when they can sit down and catch up with the experiences, and questions, of the day. I think one hour would be minimum—and separate from the children or other live-ins.

3. If the discussion is heating up and doesn't seem to be getting anywhere, each person has the right to absent themselves from the room, --if possible, respectfully and gracefully. This can be an art not so easy to master, but can bring great rewards. Just a few minutes break in the acceleration of emotions, to breathe and reflect, can bring fresh insights and progress. There are more insights along these lines in the next chapter.

4. Some people verbalize more clearly than others and this must be taken into account, but each of us certainly can work on developing the art of finding the words that accurately express what we wish to communicate. Many misunderstandings and arguments arise out of use of the wrong word or words, especially when strong emotions are speeding the conversation up and clouding the mind.

I was blessed with a fine education, but even at the age of 85, as I am finishing this book my Second College Edition of the New World Dictionary is within easy reach. I consult it when I have the slightest doubt about how a word is spelled or what it means. In addition, there is a great bonus for anyone who develops this habit. Did you know that the dictionary is a rich compendium of the gathered wisdom of our race and culture? If you want to learn something about who we have been and who we are, just open this treasure chest and read one page. Also, we can be sure everything in this remarkable book is true. I find mistakes every few days in the writing that comes across my desk and on my computer, in spite of "spell check." If you would like to be in the upper echelon in the use of our language and boost your communication skills, develop the dictionary habit and every time you learn a new word, write it down in your *New Word Book*. If you're having a hard time learning a new word, just write it out ten times. This works. An extra bonus for you, dear reader, is that you can uncover the deeper meaning of each word by analyzing the symbolism of each letter (See chapter 14), and this modest effort will reward you with even deeper wisdom.

5. Often, a written note is more effective than a discussion—and it allows more time to find the right words. If there is a lot to say, or perhaps a situation has built over time and the issues are subtle or complicated, then a letter could be perfect. It gives your partner time to consider things. You can always add: "Let's discuss this when you feel ready."

What we're trying to achieve here is the incorporation of the above described forms of love into our discussions so they can be more respectful, caring, forgiving and loving. Can you picture a discussion which is getting heated and then one partner remembers this chapter and begins to infuse what they're saying, and acting out, with Mental love, Emotional Love, Spiritual Love—Higher Principles that could help, Soulic Love—references to past lives, and even some appropriate form of Physical Love—like hand-holding or a hug?

Let us remember that it was the master Jesus, who brought into our spiritual striving the way of love: "Love ye one another—even as I have loved you." Our highest spiritual leaders echo this, saying that this is *the way* at the present time.

18

The Keys to Universal Love:

Human to Human

I would like to share with you a growing revelation about some simple ways of understanding Universal Love—some keys to how to love everyone. First, let me share with you how this revelation began to dawn on me.

We seem to never really know what we're doing at the time that it's happening. Only later, when things begin to fit together, do we see the significance of isolated experiences. In my own life, now that I'm getting a pretty good idea of what my soul purpose is, past events make much better sense. As I look back, it is as if there was an angel over my shoulder saying, "Listen to that phrase; no, don't hear that one; notice that scene, don't see that one; learn just this one item from this experience because you will need it later." It is absolutely mind-boggling, the synthesis of guided moments that's going on, that is, if we're not blocking it—since it's all within our free will.

In 1976 I was giving some workshops in Pittsburg and there was a young man who wanted very much to talk with me. As I remember, he was about nineteen. In a busy schedule, it was finally arranged that we would have forty-five minutes together over lunch. I was feeling in fine fettle, the workshops were going well, and I just felt privileged that this young man was sharing a meal with me and talking to me. He started to tell me all his problems and I just listened and occasionally said, "Yes, that's very interesting. How do you feel about that?" I was accepting what he was telling me but I was declining to acknowledge that it was a problem. I was seeing it entirely as his pattern of growth. If it occurred to me that I'd had a similar experience, then I would relate it to him.

By the time we had finished lunch he'd really shared a lot and when he left he talked to the woman who set up the appointment, who was arranging the workshops. He said, "I've never met anyone who understands me the way Joel does." Well, I didn't completely understand him, I just accepted him. For some reason, I was in a state where I felt no need whatever to advise him or change him in any way. After that, as I was leaving Pittsburg, I thought, "That was a thought-provoking experience. I think there's something special about it." It turned out to be a seed that grew for 3 years.

Then I was standing in a garden in Phoenix, Arizona, where I was doing some workshops and readings, and it all came together and I realized, "That's it. That's the key to universal love." So I began to put these keys together consciously. I'll share the steps with you now that can lead to relating to your fellow humans with love.

The first step is to realize that, from a higher point of view, everyone around you is perfect. What they are doing, their dance of life, whatever it is, is their optimal pattern of growth. They have attracted the circumstances, people, and situations to create their own life of growth toward the Light. That is what we are all doing. There are two purposes for all the things that we do and they are: learning about life and spiritual development. When we go on up in the ascension, through planets and constellations, we don't take the memory of all of these details with us, but we do take what we learned, especially the spiritual principles. I think that this is the true meaning of the phrase, "the ground on which you stand is holy." It means that the life you have, the opportunity to grow in consciousness, is a gift from our Creator. Not only is it "O.K.," what's going on in your life, but it's the perfect, fullest and richest pattern of development for you right now. You could also say the spot on which you're standing is "holistic" ground; that is, connected to all the other holy spots on which your brothers and sisters are standing. So you are, at all times, standing in that gifted, holy, perfect place, in the holiest of instants.

Since we are self-actualizing beings, The Creator gives us this opportunity, and lays down many laws to prevent other beings from tampering with our right of free will—of course, within the patterns of destiny we have accepted. If all your brothers and sisters are going about the perfect process of unfoldment then you have no need to change anyone. This is step Number Two. Since they are involved in a Divinely orchestrated process, they are, in a sense, Divine, and you can love them. What a relief. How much energy do you spend in thinking about how people around you should change? And how much good does it do? Don't people really change when they want to change? Of course, this may come as a result of your actions and the sharing of your experience, especially if they ask you. But almost always this happens when you have no desire or motive to improve anyone and you're just celebrating.

All good, and healthy, counselors and healers have learned that they don't heal anyone—that clients seek them as catalysts for their own healing process. Healing takes place when, on all levels involved, the patient's highest blueprint for health is brought into union with the Light, or the Christ, or the Holy Spirit, or The Great Mystery, or whatever you wish to call the highest expression of life force. For the healer it is simply a privilege to serve in this process. He meets his brothers and sisters in a space of mutual Divinity and receives healing and insights in the same areas as they do. The patient has temporarily given some of his power of self-actualization to the healer. This is why experienced healers usually only work with requests. It's not wrong to pray for someone who has not requested it but they may not accept it and the time and energy might be wasted. Even where there has been a heart-felt request and the healing action has gone well, still must the seeker work through whatever has been dredged up from the past and accept the healed state on all levels.

Step Number Three: in order for this to work, you must have the right to absent yourself from another person's presence. In other words, you might not be able to handle with love what someone else is doing. Presumably, if you know that a person is perfect, then you can love them because they are The Divine, realizing *Hirmself*. As I have said before, I call The Supreme "Hirm," that is, "Him-Her." It's really a challenge, putting two concepts together in a language that goes horizontally and this is the best I've come up with so far. The Supreme is realizing Hirmself in all of us and this makes us Divine, but how are we going to remember this? It takes practice and constant vigilance. In the meantime we have to have the right to bow out of a person's presence if what they are doing is causing such imbalance in us we can't process it with love and we feel that it's knocking us off center.

Number Four might be the general rule we remain in a person's presence as long as we can maintain a loving attitude. When we feel ourselves losing ground with love, understanding, and peace, then we retreat to think it over, meditate on it and seek higher guidance. After some contemplation, hopefully, we will return to try it again. Because, if you're having a hard time with something someone else is doing, *that's where some of your work lies.* So we look to see if there is anything resonating from our past, ask for more love from the Source of Love and come back and try again, differently. But you must have the right to absent yourself. Actually you already have this right. You are always in the driver's seat of your life. Anyone who says, "Well, I have to do this because of 'them' or because of 'this situation,'" always, I mean *always*, they are in the driver's seat. It helps so much to know this. We are always forgetting it, and with the resulting loss of our power, it's one of the major ways we complicate things and add to the murk of this world. It's so much easier to blame something outside of us: "It's my karma, what else could I do?" Or, "It's my destiny." There are patterns of karma and destiny but you have agreed on these already because they are your optimal learning patterns.

Now when you make your exit this can shake up the other person so try to bow out as graciously as possible. This is an art which we need to learn, but we have to be very honest about it. You might say something like, "I can see that what you're doing is your perfect pattern of growth but right now I just can't handle it with as much love as I'd like, and as much as you deserve, so I guess I'll have to go now. I bless this situation, I know you can handle it and when I've figured it out with more love I'll be back." An idea here: in case the emotions are so high it's hard to remember this last statement, you could have some printed up and, as you exit, hand one to your partner. Now, sometimes this statement can drive people "up the wall" but how they react to what you do is *their* problem, their opportunity for growth. That's *the holy ground they're standing on.*

So these are the steps. Once you can put them into practice you can begin to love everyone and truly know and feel and demonstrate that they are your brothers and sisters. I've been working on it for a few years now and it's beginning to come—of course, I forget it once in a while, and I get that old, small, contracted, "icky" feeling—but I'm beginning to be able to maintain the universal love consciousness. When I'm projecting this peace and love people feel the vibrations of it. Something deep inside them responds and you are both protected from a lot of dissonance caused by the polarized conditions in which we live. I was recently asked to give the keynote address at a "New World's Fair" in St. Louis. I had chosen *Co-creation with all Dimensions of Life* as my topic and it included this material. Before and after my talk people were coming up and hugging me. What a wonderful experience and glimpse into what the coming Age of Light and Love could be like.

There is a nice little revelation connected with these keys to universal love and it has to do with the idea that another person is "putting out bad vibrations." I was working closely with a woman who was an excellent psychic and was opening to do full-trance medical work. It was quite stressful at times opening her channel and at times it seemed that I could feel this negativity coming from her—she may have felt negativity coming from me also. In trying to deal with it, I sought advice in a reading. The source said, "There is no negativity coming to you. There are only vibrations."

Now, this really took me aback. It really takes some thinking over: "There is no negativity coming to you. There are only vibrations." So the responsibility is solely on ourselves as to how we wish to *respond* to the vibrations that are coming to us. The other person actually has the right to dance however they like. It's a God-given right since we are self-actualizing beings, and you have this right as well. Of course you will have to deal with the karma. But how you respond to another's vibrations is your business—and all-important. So the next time you feel these hostile waves emanating from a person, try to remember they are only vibrations for you to qualify. If you are completely at peace, centered and loose, they go right through you. Of course, you might sway, or tremble, or shake a bit as they pass through, while you're learning the art of it. You see, it's only when we have a rule or put up a resistance to something that we stop it within us. Then it can hurt us, or more correctly, we feel that it can. Actually, then we have to expand our rules, which we sometimes experience as painful.

Let us imagine that a person is raging at you, doing a very, so-called "hostile" dance. You, who are coming along in learning this new approach, are standing there in the line of this barrage of energy. You're keeping in mind the formula and you can say to yourself, "Now this is a very thought-provoking dance of growth...very thought-provoking." If you're at peace and objective about it, soon the person will probably stop because they need a reaction. The other reason they're doing it is to blow off steam. They may be over-stimulated, over-aggregated, over-contracted. So it may take a little while. In either case, if you can stand there and say, "That's a very interesting pattern of growth you're manifesting. Of course, I know that you are Divine, you are The Supreme realizing Hirmself, and this is undoubtedly your perfect, optimal dance for right now. Of course, you can change it if you wish, but it's perfect right now and I love you." They might erupt in laughter at the word "Hirmself" if they haven't heard it. This unexpected surprise might actually help the situation.

It is a strong possibility that this person has probably had a difficult time giving or receiving love for quite a while and your statement is really going to give them pause. You might be the first one who has given them love for a long time and it can truly turn them around. Such is the power of love. Surely, underneath the tirade is a cry for help that might go like this: "I just can't stand it another minute without some love." If you can remember these principles, then you can begin to know that you are a Divine being standing on your Holy spot looking at other Divine beings standing on theirs—many Holy spots looking at each other.

So, these steps are a practical way to love everyone, a method for practicing unconditional, Christ-like love in relationships. Putting them into practice could help us manifest the Brotherhood and Sisterhood of Man. After all, this was a large part of the Master's message: that you are sons and daughters of The Most High, inheritors of the Kingdom of Light and Love. This also sheds new light on the golden rule of treating your neighbor as yourself. If you're both Divine and dancing your perfect optimal dances, not only is your neighbor perfect, *but so are you*, and you can treat each other as "godlings."

These precepts may sound simple but I guarantee you that if you will apply them to the next difficult situation in which you find yourself, and give them a little time, you will see that they work. Of course, someone will say, "Oh yeah, well about what so-and-so does?" All I can say is that this method has proven effective with some very extreme, dynamic dances and my hope is that its practice will bring you understanding, peace and love.

Not only that, but these keys to universal love could open the doors for the release of personal irritations that stand in the way of working together in harmony for the healing and raising of consciousness of the planet

19

What Can We Learn From All This?

One evening, not long ago, Serafina, Mykael and I were sitting before the fire, looking out across the Pacific, filled with peace and gratitude for the unlimited love and generosity of our Higher Guidance. And he said to me, "Could you share with us some highlights of what you have learned from your forty years of serving the Sources of Light and your brothers and sisters? I just feel that most of your readers are asking this question." After some thought, I answered, "That certainly is an important aspect of this book, reporting, as it does, much of what I have learned, so this is a challenging request. I'll seek higher guidance and see if the masters in spirit will help me select what I haven't already covered that might be important and useful to our readers. I will begin tomorrow. Let me bask in this rosy glow one more day."

At this point in the writing of this book I am having a realization which I couldn't have had without nearing the end of it. There have been so many almost unbelievable miracles, that I know I could never have accomplished them without higher inspiration (my High Self? Angels? Ascended Masters? Aspects of The Supreme?). I do my part, but attribute the healing miracles to this co-creation.

Now, please understand that I don't present these insights as final truth. They are simply suggestions that I have found helpful in understanding the chaotic world in which we find ourselves. They offer possible, positive, and honorable qualities to entertain which can up-level the way we interact with the world and help to insure our success in this noble venture. Think of them as ways of being that have been suggested by Spirit to ease our way through the unprecedented crisis our beloved Earth and its peoples are experiencing. It might also be helpful to review the theory of how we learn that I gave in the Introduction to this book.

By the way, I want to remind my readers that I bless all the religions because they all have truth in them. We need them, since there are so many different kinds of people in this melting pot society. On the other hand, there is a growing population of those who have found that they can tune into the All-That-Is without dependence on an organized religion. In addition there is a long list of books now available by enlightened authors who have experienced various stages of cosmic consciousness.

Let us begin with the formula I have been given for processing one's past. It sets forth four simple steps, which have proven successful in my twenty years of counseling. Although it is best to have an experienced therapist, still it would be helpful to understand these steps, and some people—who have a reasonable degree of self-control and respect for the truth about themselves—may be able to use them successfully without guidance.

After I had completed a few hundred past-life attunements, *Soul-Path Re-Alignments*, it struck me that in the *Interpretation* the Sources were taking a totally positive view of everything that a client has experienced in this or in other lives. More and more evidence came in that we are of Divine Creation and that we incarnate to learn about life, to test our innate spiritual understanding, and through challenges, grow more in conscious attunement with whatever you call the Supreme Spirit. By the way, have you ever heard of the primary commandment Our Heavenly Father gives us: "Go forth into my creation and return it to me"?

This command is also called The Grand Cycle of Creation. It tells us that the "Fall" out of heaven, or out of Paradise, is not a punishment. Rather it is an invitation to venture forth into the world of duality in order to grow through practicing our Creator-given freedom of choice, then to ascend back into the arms of our Divine and Loving Mother and Father. This is the deeper, esoteric symbolism of "eating of the tree of the knowledge of Good and Evil ("live" spelled backwards") This goes along with the admonition that The Creator is not wrathful, which is a human trait some of us have projected onto The Supreme when we forget that Infinite Power is balanced by Infinite Love. The Law of Karma, that we reap what we sow, which has much to recommend it, and operates the same way for everyone, can appear, to our limited understanding, to be unfair at times. Then we can be tempted to attribute its effects to the "wrath of God."

Processing Your Past

These stages of processing your past experiences, especially those from childhood, are positive and most helpful in learning from, and releasing, memories of stressful events. When you didn't process them at the time it was most often because you hadn't developed enough understanding, love, and the wisdom and ability to forgive. And it also may have been that no one ever suggested that you could use these experiences to learn and grow.

What Can We Learn From All This?

Preparation: if you have a spiritual practice, it will be most helpful to surround yourself with Light and Love as you embark on these exercises.

1. Agree to see everything you have experienced as learning: learning of two types:

> A. Positive: where you want to emulate a quality or add a skill to which you were exposed.
>
> B. Negative: where you now see that you do not wish to take on a pattern of behavior.

Both of these approaches are equally valuable. In this way you take charge of the situation, make it your own, and diminish the power the pattern and other people have had over you.

Example: Your father or mother was extremely hard on you. Now you can decide to imitate and learn his/her good traits and also, seeing their less-than-good traits—ones that don't promote life—you can make a conscious, deep-seated effort to avoid these behaviors in yourself. Please note that you progress either way.

2. Realize that the people in your life: father, mother, sister, brother, other family members, and teachers, were all trying to do their best, given their own unprocessed past experiences. We humans have developed the amazing ability to repress those situations which we have not developed enough understanding and love to process, so that we can function in everyday life. This is an important ability, but only a temporary solution. Unfortunately, these patterns also have a way of becoming lodged in our subconscious and then projecting outward onto others and life around us. Children are often the recipients of these negative emotions. The good news is that there isn't anything anyone has ever done that can't be learned from and forgiven, but you must have the courage to go through the process, and these steps can help you. With them, I once helped a person, in a great deal of pain, to process five of their most burning life issues, that had been making them miserable for years—in a one hour session.

Example: You go to your mother and ask her about her childhood. If there were difficult times, as there probably were, you show sympathy and compassion and say something like "You must have done the best you could under those trying circumstances." Imagine her relief, because deep down she feels some guilt at not being a perfect mother—and who is?

3. Now, as the more difficult experiences surface, you can feel deep or painful emotions. Let them run a little to help you remember, then intentionally calm them down, knowing that you are going to take charge of them. You are going to do some valuable work so that you may no longer be the victim of what happened and how you were treated. Go over thoroughly whatever comes up, taking one thing at a time and learning whatever you can, positively or negatively. You might find it valuable to take some notes on what you're learning. Don't expect to do it all at once and make time for another session. Soon it will become a habit and you will be having profound realizations standing in front of the refrigerator, or while driving. You are transmuting the lead in the sack you have been carrying around on your shoulder for years into the gold of wisdom. Eventually you will be able to forgive your—now let's call them formative mentors. And then comes gratitude, and then love, because they brought you learning and advancement. It's somewhat like the grain of sand in the oyster that ends up being a pearl.

Example: I had a very difficult and painful childhood with my stepfather and it affected my relationships with all men, especially those over me, bosses and conductors. Since I began to awaken to the principles given here, I have worked hard at processing this relationship. I would make progress, but just when I thought I'd finished with it, it would come back to me in the strangest ways. Finally after many, years, it has receded. Occasionally I see a reminder pass before me at a distance. I salute it and smile, because I now know that it has been one of the major educations of my life. Eventually I could see how a pattern started in my stepfather's upbringing, or past lives. I have long ago forgiven him, am grateful for the learning, including how I do not want to be to my children, and am grateful for the good things he gave me: how to build houses, plant a garden, make wine, play chess, and write.

4. Make a list of the changes you wish to make and commit some time and energy to making them. It is some of the most important work you can do during this Earthly sojourn. Writing and saying decrees and affirmations with emotion is very effective and saying them in a meditative state increases their power as you enlist the support of your High Self and your subconscious. You will see changes and you will begin to feel lighter as you drop some of your heavy baggage, and you will be happier, and wiser. Also, your relationships will flow better and you will enjoy them more.

If early childhood events and relationships don't explain the "sticky" patterns in your life, look to past-life experiences, if you can access them. Then call up the image and this same formula will help you to work it through. As we've said, the pattern is all important —not when it was in time or where.

Caution: Realize that this is strong stuff you are calling forth and select a good time of the week to do this work. Also, in each session be persistent until you get results. I've come to know that it's not a good idea to shake loose these old patterns, which can feel threatening, *unless* you are going to process them. Begin with small, quality steps.

Your life is largely a manifestation of karmic patterns, plus a few gratuitous gifts from your guides, masters, and guardian seraphim to encourage you on your path. The Law of Karma may seem harsh at times, but without it our actions could have no ongoing meaning and life would be chaos. A little-known benefit is that we don't have to repeat an experience if we can learn from it the first time. If patterns repeat it is because we *haven't* learned the lesson, or there is more to it. Remember, also, that you always reap the rewards of all the good thoughts, feelings and actions that you sow—those that support and promote life. Another often-forgotten benefit, which helps me when I'm wrangling with karmic law, is the knowledge that *no one*, ultimately, gets away with *anything*. It will come back around. This is one meaning of the saying "God is not mocked." Let us be thankful for this universal, eternal law, even though, at times, it may seem challenging.

I have come to realize that we humans, including myself, tend to be lazy when it comes to working on ourselves. Often our backs must be "against the wall" before we will formulate a definite plan to take ourselves in hand. But we are assured of two things: that we have this capability and that the instant we begin, help from spirit, all the way up to the Mother/Father of Love, is forthcoming. Each one of us is this much loved.

This insight leads us to a great revelation: The Free Will Plan of Evolution, which dispels so much of the mystery in what we see going on with this world and its people. But first there is a gift of inestimable value I must offer you: an introduction to *The Urantia Book*, if you haven't already made its acquaintance. Urantia is the true name of our planet; that is, the name by which it is known out in space. Truth can be found in many books but, in my opinion, and in the opinion of thousands of readers, there is nothing comparable to *The Urantia Book* because it originated in the Higher Realms of Truth. There are hundreds of study groups and thousands of dedicated readers around the world, and it has been translated into six or seven languages, including Dutch, Chinese, Spanish and French.

I have been studying this monumental revelation for almost 40 years and have found it the clearest, most detailed, and most reliable information available on many important subjects. It covers an unbelievable spectrum of topics vital to our understanding of who we are, what our potential is, life on Earth, and what's going on out in the wider universe. Readers who have studied it even longer than I have, still read and discuss it every week in study groups. I came into this life a philosopher, always wanting to know what is really going on behind appearances and this monumental revelation has answered most of my questions—and then some.

The U.B., as we call it, is known as the Fifth Epochal Revelation to our planet and the other four, going back thousands of years, are described. It is all written by higher beings. Reading it for any length of time convinces you that no human has written it. In its over 2000 pages, each of its 196 papers are signed by a higher being. It covers everything you would want to know about the Master Universe, its nature, its origin, who inhabits it, what's going on, and your nature and potential destiny. Human beings are called "Evolutionary Free Will Creatures with Ascension Potential" and our ascension path, through countless embodiments, is described in some detail. I once traced it throughout the book for a paper I gave at a U.B. conference. It leads us ever inward through universe after universe all the way to the Source and Center. There we are embraced by The Presence of the Triune Deity on the Paradise Isle, where we are prepared for greater service in the outlying universes now forming on outer space levels. What an exciting destiny.

This remarkable book combines astronomy, physics, philosophy, history and spirituality—all in harmony. Published in 1953, it predicted the dark holes in space before the astronomers discovered them.

Here is the basic plan of the book: Part I is devoted to a description of the Central Universe, called Havona, at the core of the Creation, and the nature of the highest Deity. Then follows a description of the 1 billion perfect and unique planets, the beings who inhabit them, and their nature and function. Part 2 is a description of our local universe, its organization, its beings and their activities. Part 3 is the history of our planet, Urantia, from its formation, including the birth of the first primates who could be called human and their evolution, and the true stories of the Garden of Eden and the Rebellion of Lucifer.

Part 4 (850 pages) is the life of Jesus taken right from the akashic records. These are the true records, or data base, of everything that has happened on Earth. This is an almost day-by-day account of that life, written by a panel of angels, many of whom were present at the time. Angels don't die and have excellent memories, like super computers. During the writing of this account the panel was under the supervision of the universe teaching order, the Melchizedeks. You will find its detailed accounts most enlightening, including what the Master actually said on certain days. I love this because I always wanted to know more of what *he* said. Apparently, most of the New Testament was written down a hundred years after the events took place, so I guess these prophets couldn't trust their memories as to his actual words. You will be most interested to have more information about who he really was and still *is*. In fact there is much explanation and wisdom in it that has not been accessible until now, that helps us to understand our present challenges. Long-time readers say it is like an update of the Bible for our times.

One nice feature is that it is written in perfect English with no typos. In one of my study groups, we were puzzled by the use of a somewhat obscure word. When we looked it up in the largest dictionary—yes, the one that's seven inches thick—we found that it was the fourth meaning of the word and used correctly. I cannot recommend this revelation highly enough to you. In these pivotal times we need to know as much of the truth as we can find. The people of Urantia are so loved and fortunate to have such a compendium of essential knowledge and wisdom, especially after so many eons of relative darkness. Do you remember the quote from the Bible which says, "Now you see as through a glass darkly, but in time to come you will see more clearly"? *The Urantia Book* is an example of this clarity.

Please don't be put off by the size of this book, but see it as a treasure chest from which you can take gifts for the rest of your life. If I have a few moments, I enjoy opening it anywhere and reading a passage. Just opening it I feel a rise in vibration in the room. Fortunately there is an excellent index, called the *Concordex*, in which you can access 110,000 references. I've read *The Urantia Book* probably five times and I still read it, because I continue to learn. No one could master all of it. We are told it also contains information for the pilgrims of future centuries. I have been applying these concepts to life situations for thirty years and have developed a great trust and love for them.

I would like to share with you what I consider to be one of the U.B.'s most important revelations as it explains so much of what is puzzling about what is going on around us. This is an explanation of The Free Will Plan for the evolution of humanoid creatures throughout the seven super universes that swing, in a grand circle, around Havona.

What follows is, of course, a vast simplification, but will give you the essentials and you can check them in the book. Imagine that The Supreme Creator—please use any other suitable name for the Unnameable you might prefer—after eons of creativity, had brought the central universe to somewhat of a completion. The 1 billion perfect, but unique planets and their perfect beings, swung majestically around the Paradise Isle, the abode of the Triune Deity, Paradise Father, Eternal Son, and Infinite Spirit, and all of the beings in Havona loved the Supreme, because they were created that way.

Then The Supreme had the thought, "I wonder what it would be like if I created a being that didn't have to love me, but would have the option of *choosing* to love me. In the seven super-universes, swinging around Havona, The Free Will Plan was born. But The Supreme had a challenge: If "I AM", and My Oneness, is everywhere, what are the choices going to be? And in His/Her inimitable and inscrutable and unlimited creativity, the *illusion of choice* was created and *duality* made its appearance: low-high, hot-cold, in-out, close-far, here-there, true-false, and yes-no, and so on and on. But, at the same time, the whole creation remained essentially *One*. Now, when you think about it, no human could ever have come up with the ingenuity and scope of this notion. And from that time we humans have been called "Evolutionary Free Will Beings with Ascension Potential" because we grow from Duality to Oneness through choosing.

As I deeply contemplated this amazing event, I had to ask my sources: "Does this mean, then, that there is no source of evil comparable to the Source of Good, or The Divine Presence?" And they answered, "That is true." After much contemplation, and inspiration from above, I was brought to the conclusion that the Real and Fundamental Choice is between The Supreme and *not* The Supreme or *nothingness*. Remember that the choices are, at the same time both real *to us*, important for our growth, and yet fundamentally illusionary. To corroborate this my Sources suggested I look at the words the Satanists use: "evil" is "live" spelled backwards, "devil" is "lived" spelled backwards, and centuries ago they started the practice of calling Sirius, the "God star," the "Dog star." A common practice among them is to get together and say the Lord's Prayer, and other prayers, backwards. This is really sad because one of the laws of the Free Will Plan is that "What you decree and affirm will come to pass", "What you sow, you shall also reap." So the prolonged *denial* inherent in the practice of undoing things, leads these confused souls deeper and deeper into nothingness, and farther and farther away from the intrinsic life of the Creation.

The U. B. then describes the extensive and experienced help that is called forth to save every soul on its path, because each one is precious to the Creator. However, since the Free Will Plan has no meaning unless each soul's choice is honored these practices can lead, eventually, to extinguishment, what is described in the book as "the second death," or the death of the spirit. This is the other side of the freedom to choose, the opposite of choosing to be "the captains of our souls."

Some of the golden wisdom that this Law provides is answers to the question you so often hear these days, "How could a loving God allow these awful things to take place?" They are the "downside" of the magnificent Free Will Plan. They are the "alternatives" to the choosing of the enlightened, spiritual qualities of peace, balance, oneness with life; and the choosing of alignment with The Supreme: faith, love, understanding, compassion, forgiveness, humility, radiance of spiritual light, joy, and the fulfillment of service. One of the most important, and worrisome, illusions is that we die. In fact, we are of Divine Essence. We *have* a body, but it is not what we *are*. What we are doesn't die—it is potentially eternal. Our Creator doesn't wish to lose a single soul but if we choose separation from The All That Is continually, over a long period of time, resisting all efforts to save us, this is a possibility. To put this concept another way: You will never be forced to grow and evolve. There are heavy penalties in store for higher beings who try to tamper with the free will of the creature.

So I have come to the rather startling conclusion that, contrary to popular belief and appearances, we do not live in a world where good and evil are balanced. Rather, through our Creator-given sacred power to choose, each one of us can create a more positive world around us. Further, that as each one makes these creative decisions, since we are all one, the effects go out in an expanding sphere throughout the whole world.

This ability to choose is of the greatest importance at this crucial time on our planet. The majority of our most trusted human visionaries, notably the great sensitive, Edgar Cayce, have called this "the Time of Division" and do we not see this extreme polarity in every aspect of life? Just look at our deeply divided legislature and political arena. In addition to the above, the vibrations of life are increasing, this Earth is moving into the fourth and fifth dimensions, and each one of us will be given a gilt-edged invitation to use these energies to turn toward The Light. The great increase of population is because so many souls want to be here for the many and rare opportunities being offered. However, many are not ready for this shift, and they are contracting stress-related diseases and passing on. My information is that one of our major Ascended Masters has been preparing a neighboring planet, which will stay in three dimensions longer, for these souls. There is no judgment here, since many of them may "overtake" us on up the Ascension Path. It's not how fast you progress but how deeply you absorb and live the wisdom—that's why one of my projects, for some years, has been to encourage people to *slow down* for quality.

So, to sum up this revelation from the standpoint of Higher Wisdom: in our apparent world of Duality with its myriad pairs of polarities, *both sides are true. Our challenge is how to understand them and how to use them. We need to look at each side of the polarity within its own context to see the value it might have for us.* We have examples: Our brain is capable of merging the two images from our two eyes into one image and our inner ear does the same with stereo music from two speakers. Another example that I have found most valuable: imagine a triangle between your two eyes and your Third eye, behind the middle of your forehead, and remember the admonition "Let your eye be single." Then picture the next time you are witnessing a polarized argument between two friends. If you rise to your third, single eye, you can look down on the polarity, see the value in both sides of the argument and bring peace and harmony to the situation. I have often been the peacemaker with this technique.

One polarity that has been resolved for me by *The Urantia Book* is the longtime controversy over the relationship between Science and Religion. Both of these are vital to the understanding of who we are and life on Earth. They are simply different windows through which we can look at the same reality. Science deals more with *measurable facts* and *predictability* whereas religion deals more with concepts about *the whole creation, and the value of things*. Both are true and we need them. Fortunately science has recently become deeply interested in probing to the essence of things and has announced that they have discovered some core principles that could be called *The Supreme*.

Its long-time associate, the Creation vs. Evolution controversy, which heated up considerably in the early 1900s, is taken care of in two pages in *The Urantia Book*. It explains, with its usual authoritative accuracy, that both are true. Yes, The Creator created everything, as it states in Genesis, and yes, everything was created to evolve. End of controversy. Now we can all return to more productive uses of our time and energy. I have found these examples of the resolution of polarities more and more valuable in my understanding of life.

In *The Urantia Book* there is an entire paper devoted to life on a neighboring planet which is slightly ahead of us in evolution. I've found it most valuable to see how humanoids quite similar to us have solved some of the challenges we now face. We are embarking on an Ascension Career of much vaster magnitude than we ever imagined. The cosmic adventure that lies open to us is far more rich, fascinating and glorious than our wildest "space-fiction" dreams. There is even a description of a planet of non-breathers.

The Divine Plan is for us to start at the bottom so we'll have first-hand experience of the major aspects of Creation as we ascend through the universes. While there are beings who are created perfect who must eventually descend to the lowest, in service, to fulfill their destiny, we, through our own choosing, plus ample higher guidance at every juncture, enlist in this panoramic odyssey back to The First Source and Center. Then we can be trained for the supervision of planets in the newly-forming universes on the outer space levels, still only barely visible even to the advanced astronomers. So then, Earth appears to be a kind of "hatchery" where we have our spiritual birth—for the Basic Selves, "series of embodiments,"—for us the first of perhaps thousands of ascending lives leading to possible merging with The Three Aspects of Deity—The Divine Embrace.

The foregoing relatively simple concept, The Free Will Plan, has some inspiring and important implications and consequences:

1. We will never completely understand the nature of Deity until we are received in this Divine Embrace. Nevertheless it is absolutely essential to learn all we can about Its nature, even from our remote and infinitesimal corner of the Creation. Hopefully, we can develop a desire to know It, attune to It, and be as much as we can like It. It is this will-desire on which our survival beyond Earth is based and, as we have outlined, all do not survive, according to the plan of will-progression. We are self-actualizing beings.

2. If Earth is essentially a seed-bed for creatures of Free Will beginning their long ascent, it is not necessary to master all the

activities that are going on here or to completely understand the nature of the seed-bed itself. These activities are important to you only as they serve your physical survival and your growing understanding of, and desire to be like, Deity. *What a relief.* The releasing of this and other related anxieties can free much energy in you for the pursuit of worthwhile ends. In 1,000 years you probably will not remember the details of your earthly existence but you will remember the spiritualized mind transcripts you gleaned from it—the universal, or "higher" laws you learned. Again, *what good news* —that you don't have to keep carrying around all the reels and reels of what will seem like melodramatic movies of the details of this earthly life. When you're starring in one of your movies it seems like such a serious role in your career as an actor, but have you noticed that some of the most serious roles you've played seem to fade away and become increasingly hilarious? But to replay them is restful and restorative and is actually one of the forms of recreation on higher worlds.

Now, everyone on Earth has at least four sources helping them all the time, if you will give your connection with them a chance and open yourself to receiving their higher guidance and love:

1. Your High Self, Superconsciousness, or I Am Presence, an undiluted portion of the essence of The Universal Father which has been assigned to you to bring you ever inward to the Presence of the highest aspects of Deity. It specializes in adjusting your thoughts—while honoring your Free Will.

2. Your seraphic guardian to point to things which are for your highest growth and to guide you for your protection.

3. The Spirit of Truth and Beauty, the spiritual circuit of the Creator of our Local Universe, The Comforter, what the master Jesus sent to our planet when he ascended to assume full supervision of our local universe.

4. The Holy Spirit, the spiritual circuit of his equal partner, the Creative Mother Spirit.

If you could begin and get the habit of attuning to these Sources of Love and dedicated service to you, your whole life and ascension would flow better and easier. They await you reaching out to them but they cannot circumvent your free will.

In order to give the foregoing gifts to you I have digested and condensed around 500 pages of *The Urantia Book*. Should you wish to study this invaluable revelation, please see the Bibliography in the Appendix for the address of the Urantia Foundation to find a book

What Can We Learn From All This? 215

and a study group in your area. Some book stores carry the book, or can order it, but the cost might be more reasonable through the Foundation.

I salute all those who have made the commitment to turn toward The Light and The Love, no matter what happens on this planet. If we reach out we will receive all the guidance we can possibly use, as we get to work to transmute all the negativity from our past. Have you noticed that it's the same process for the world in general: all the negativity that has been long hidden is coming out to be recognized and healed in preparation for the shift.

My personal message to you, besides the fact that I love you, is:

Relax, brother or sister. You are loved and guided beyond your imagination. The best thing is to get in on the ground floor of this "cosmic business." There is no hurry: "First things, first." Savor everything that comes to you, try to see its deeper and higher significance, and don't worry about what doesn't come to you. Learn all you can about the cosmic business right around you and the cosmic business as a whole. Your destiny is to become a spiritual "CEO" who loves every aspect of this business and promotes the growth of everyone and everything in it—this will be emulating The Supreme and the Company of Heaven.

So if this is only the beginning of millions of ascending experiences into glorious realms,

WOULD YOU WANT TO BOW OUT BEFORE YOU GET STARTED?

CHOOSE THE ETERNAL LIFE NOW!

20

Summation, Now, and Looking Forward

Two weeks later Serafina, Mykael and I were sitting on the front porch surveying the majestic blue of the Pacific Ocean. They had just finished reading the last three chapters and Mikael said, "I thought your revelations about the principles of co-creation were most valuable, and especially applicable to the present world situation." Serafina commented, "I was particularly impressed with the guidelines you gave for humans respecting and loving each other, because that seems to me to be a prerequisite for group action in these critical times." Then Mykael added, "I know you were thinking of ending this book here, but wouldn't it be of value to your readers to comment on the present world situation, the predictions and fears around the ending of the Mayan calendar, the earth changes that seem to be increasing, and some positive thoughts about the immediate future? I know you recently lectured at a conference on the island of Malta exploring that subject, and to prepare for it you collected a number of insights by some of our top intuitives. Could you share some of these highlights with your readers?"

I answered, "It would be my pleasure to shed as much light on this situation as I can. First, let me try to allay some of the fears around this special time, and then offer positive guidelines as to how we can best conduct ourselves now and in the coming months and years. Then I will quote some of the insights of our greatest visionaries. And yes, Serafina, one of the central themes of the prophecies is that it is vital that we come together to act for the good of the whole."

First of all, in my intuitive work, I have been guided never to predict the future. This is because the future is the result of our free-will decisions and the higher guidance from our guardian seraphim and masters that we elect to follow. So we are much safer putting as much guidance as we can together and then predicting a trend. Following this advice has been a major factor in earning me one of the higher reputations for the efficacy of my channeling and insights. Another thing I've learned about prophecies: most dire prophecies that come true are failed prophecies; that is, they were warnings of what could happen if we persisted in our negative thoughts, feelings, and actions. So I see a "doomsday" prophecy as a wake-up call. And what is going on at this time certainly is a call to wake up.

So we can't accurately predict events of the next few years, especially as the Egyptians and the Mayans, some of the best astrologers in the world, couldn't do this. In the Great Pyramid there are marks in the passageway leading up to the King's Chamber which correspond to major events in history, and they stop at the date May 5, 2000. Obviously, the Egyptians saw it as a significant date past which they couldn't really see events, even though there are those who say that the Egyptians also saw the end of the era around 2012 as did the Mayans and other indigenous cultures.

Next we need to deal with the fear around 2012. I see it as a "marker," or tipping point, just a way of pinpointing major changes in time. It is more like the ending of past time cycles of evolution and the beginning of new cycles; but not necessarily indicating that these changes would happen on that date or even all in that year.

By the way, I doubt if very many of us can remember anything cataclysmic that happened in the year 2000, even though it was a prediction date similar to 2012. As I remember, 9/11, the collapse of the twin towers in New York, was in 2001.

History tells us that at the end of almost every century, and especially at the end of a millennium, large segments of the population thought the world was coming to an end. They also often thought it would be accompanied by The Second Coming. It makes me wonder if their leaders played up this fear for their own purposes of exploitation of the people, as we have seen so prevalent in our own time. *The Urantia Book* gives the conditions for that event: Yes, Jesus said he would come again, but he never said when. The only clue he gave was the condition that he would come when everyone would be able to see him—in a non-physical body. Well, given the level of consciousness of the majority of earthlings, that could be a long way off. We can still look to some of our best visionaries for guidelines as to how to prepare ourselves and actions we might take. Given these realizations, let us come up with actions which will be good for us no matter what happens. Acting sensibly in this way will increase our safety. It's guidelines like this on which I will focus.

Consider that the time that really matters the most is the present moment. Very much time spent on the past or on the future is taking power from your golden present moment and the full living of your life. Memory of past times is never totally accurate and a good deal of the future is created in the present. It is possible that one of the most significant changes we are about to experience has to do with how we experience time itself. I think our valuing of past and future is going to diminish greatly, resulting in much more focus on the present time, often called the "eternal present." A poet friend of mine says, "Have your forever now."

I have been experiencing this fading of the importance of my past and future for the past two years. I like being more in my present, but it does have a down side, that I am working with, and that I should warn you about. Since all my projects have originated in my past, and since they are all more with me now, something in me is expecting me to bring them to fruition now. To avoid this stress I am training myself to work happily at my projects, even if I only accomplish a small step along the way, and to release them at the end of the day.

So one of my revelations here is that it's not so important when you pass on, but how you live each day while you're alive. You see, I'm absolutely convinced that we go on to higher planes and planets, that what we call death is only a transition—a rebirth into higher frequencies. This process is described in detail in *The Urantia Book* where it is called "Terrestrial Escape."

Some years ago, in preparation for a workshop I was asked to give, I did a study of death. I interviewed many people and found that it's not death that people are afraid of, it's the unknown. I interviewed a quadraplegic in the hospital. When I asked him what he could tell us about death he replied, "Oh, I've been there and back many times and, you know what, there's nothing there. It's more like a process." I think it was James Moody who wrote an entire book, *Life After Death*, about people who were medically "given up for dead" and a few hours later came back to life, saying that on the other side they were told that it was not time yet. They often describe going up a tunnel filled with beautiful colors and celestial music and being met by angelic guides. My uncle had this experience.

I've regressed many clients to past lives and I always take them through and beyond their transition. Almost all of these lose their fear of death because they have replaced their fear of the unknown with a more direct experience. I experienced this myself many years ago.

So when I counsel clients who are afraid of death, I ask them how their life is going now. Then I ask "Do you really have evidence that it's going to be any different when you pass over?" Then I remind them that they have had a large hand in creating their life circumstances and ask, "Why don't you get busy with affirmations and visualizations to create your own future life? What have you got to lose?" And I say the same to all of you about the coming years. Of course these affirmations are much more powerful when they are magnified by daily repetition and by many people of like mind.

A number of our prophesies suggest that many of our earth changes are Mother Earth's reaction to our negative thinking and actions. So we should take responsibility for changing our ways—not that the higher forces won't help us once we begin to take responsibility. "We must be the changes we wish to see."

A famous channel recently said, and I am deeply grateful for this quote:

> "Unfortunately, our fear just compounds the problem and motivates us to cling to the old paradigms that are surfacing to be healed and transmuted into Light."

My lack of fear about 2012 is also based on the many miracles of my healing work. Co-creating with higher beings has made it clear that they, masters and angels, reaching all the way up the vast creation to the Godhead, care about us deeply and are monitoring carefully and thoroughly what is going on here on this planet. From various sources I consider reliable, I understand that once a life wave of souls is begun, there is no stopping it, even if it would need to be incarnated on another suitable planet. This applies to those dear souls who have been involved in recent earth changes such as 9/11, earthquakes and tidal waves. My sources have never failed me when I ask sincerely, so when I asked them about the tragedy of 9/11 they replied, "First of all, understand that there is no death." So everything is in Divine Order, even though this is, at times, difficult for us to see.

We must understand that what we call "death" is a transition, with no loss of who we truly are. Wherever you go you will be given a body appropriate to that realm.

Let me share some of what I have learned from my own healing work and study. This planet is a school. We are "godlings" reclaiming and growing into our Divine Consciousness. Secondly, everything that happens to us is offering us the opportunity to learn something. Then also, occasionally, we experience expanded cosmic states of pure ecstasy, love, joy and illumination. And do we not learn from these as well?

Here's an example: Why would any creator allow us to discover anything as powerful as nuclear energy before we had the moral and ethical development to respect and avoid its potential for destruction, unless this was a school? And unless nuclear destruction would not be permanent in a world of Infinite Intelligence and Eternal Love? Of course, the students in the school can damage the school to the point where it needs to be closed for repairs for a time. This planet is so beautiful that I hope this is not the case.

I also know that if we show enough hopeful potential our higher brothers and sisters can intervene in certain areas and help us. Especially if enough of us can put aside our petty grievances and self-serving greed and act together to inhibit those among us who would exploit us. In this way we can serve the whole and its ascension. Working with these higher beings I can tell you that hardly a day goes by in my life that they don't show their ever-readiness to serve us and Life. But, because they have to honor our Free Will, we have to ask. I find this knowledge uplifting when I contemplate 2012 and the next few years..

Let me remind you here, again, of one of the greatest revelations that has come to me as I finish this book and can view the panorama of healing miracles reported herein. There is no question that I could not have accomplished them without the contribution of beings in spirit. They are miracles that require cooperation between beings in higher dimensions and the human level.

This might be a good place to comment on the various extra-sensory perceptions that we can all develop, with a little practice, that will help us relate to these higher vibrations and receive higher guidance for the challenging times ahead.

For the first 30 years of my harp career I had only slightly more than the basic intuitions we all have. With the life-changing illuminations and revelations that launched me as a healer came four basic sensitivities: clairvoyance, clairaudience, clairsentience, and telepathy. First, let me explain in what sense these are extra-sensory. The basic way these perceptions work is that the senses of sight, hearing, and touch transfer their sensory data to certain areas of the brain which interpret the data. In ESP those centers receive data directly; that is, without the input from the senses. The masters helped me to rapidly develop these sensitivities in order to transfer the healing music from the more subtle planes to the harp.

Clairvoyance is clear-seeing of visual images; clairaudience is hearing sounds or music with, what has been called, the third ear. Clairsentience is kinesthetic, or picking up impressions with some part of the body, and may include receiving impressions from an object. Telepathy is receiving concepts or words with your mind alone, that is, without the senses of hearing or reading. These words can originate from your master guides and guardian seraphim, or even space beings, archangels, Gaia, or the Elohim. Here's a tip, though, if you are opening up these sensitivities: first surround yourself with the light of protection of the highest you know.

These sources of information and guidance could be extremely valuable and comforting in the months and years ahead, not only for your survival and protection, but also to enable you to help others. A long-time student of kinesiology, I've developed the ability to muscle-test myself. This has been most valuable and has never failed me. As I may have mentioned, we are supposed to have the answers to our sincere questions.

Here's another example, from my own life, of the advantages of working with higher guidance: When the Gulf War began I couldn't believe it, because I'd seen enough war to have a basic understanding of it: that wars are started by a few selfish souls to make huge amounts of money to be paid for by human lives. War is always a failure of negotiations. Also, I had seen enough violence in films to last me five lifetimes. So, after the first gory report on television, I said to myself, "I thought we had learned this lesson. I'm not going to watch this one." But the next day I heard my master guides say "All right, but we'd like to offer you an alternative. We would suggest you watch it, while constantly asking yourself the question 'How could what I'm seeing result in soul-growth for someone?" I watched the whole war and learned much in that classroom in our school of Earth.

Now, one of the common prophesies is that we are passing into the fourth and fifth dimensions. It is clear to the objective observer that the vibratory frequencies on Earth have been increasing for some time. For some people this has resulted in a higher quality of performance but for others a decrease in quality. I find many people dangerously hyperactive so one of my missions with the co-created music, and my lectures and workshops, has been to entreat my brothers and sisters to slow down for quality. The music I co-create definitely brings peace and centeredness.

It seems obvious to me that in these challenging and pivotal times we need to know as much of the truth as we can find. So I'd like to present a few quotes from *The Urantia Book* that I think are more than inspiring in connection with our present situation. They speak of the ongoing evolution of life on Earth, even extending to a glorious future. I have consulted the Concordex under the heading "future" and selected these out of many:

> "The future can be changed by the ministry of the present creativity of the inner self."

Now and Looking Forward 223

"It is believed that, in the ages to come, the possibilities for disharmony, maladjustment, and misadaptation will be exhausted in the super-universes."

The Urantia Book also says that this is an experimental planet, as is every tenth planet, so evolution has been somewhat of a struggle here. Here are some more quotes:

"The celestial supervisors express complete confidence in the ultimate evolutionary triumph of the human race in the eventual vindication of the original plans and life patterns."

"The apparent cruelty of a perverse fate that heaps tribulation upon some suffering mortals may in reality be the tempering fire that is transmuting the soft iron of immature personality into the tempered steel of real character."

"Uncertainty is the secret of contented continuity. Sometimes ignorance is the secret of success and then it would be a colossal blunder for the creature to know the future. We suggest you heighten your taste for the sweetness of uncertainty, for the romance and charm of the indefinite and unknown future."

Comment: My former father-in-law and mentor, Alan Watts, who introduced the wisdom of Zen to America, wrote a book called The Wisdom of Insecurity. To continue:

"We incline to the belief that the eternal future will witness phenomenon of universe evolution which will far transcend all that the eternal past has experienced. We anticipate such tremendous adventures and enthralling spectacles, even as you should, with keen relish and ever-heightening expectation."

Then Mykael said, "I've been wondering what some of our greatest visionaries have been saying. Could you share some of that research with us?

Around 1973 I was living in Virginia Beach, the home of Edgar Cayce, the great American psychic. While there I studied many of his amazing psychic readings—of which he did over 14,000. He prophesied a period from 1958 to '98, which his Sources called the "Time of Division," which could also be the beginning of extreme earth changes.

Now we can see that, even though earth changes seem to have been delayed, they are increasing, This suggests that it is possible for higher forces to modify these predictions and also that possibly we grew in consciousness enough to merit their help. Have we not heard that a negative prophecy that comes true is a failed prophecy? As I have mentioned, because of the unpredictable action of free will, and of Higher Forces, only a trend can be projected. Another factor that is difficult to take into account is the fact that the Spiritual Renaissance is a grassroots movement that is spreading rapidly and exponentially throughout the world. It does not have a central office and this could well be a most fortunate situation. We certainly cannot trust the media for a true report of what's going on in the world. How often do we get to hear the good news? Doesn't this suggest that we are considered easier to control if we are kept in the dark and depressed? These considerations should give us hope for the challenges of the present turning point.

Many of the visionaries suggest that each one of us is going to be given the choice to either grow into these quickened dimensions or pass on. This could easily be what the Cayce Sources referred to as the "Time of Division." Do we not see an incredible speeding up of the vibrations on Earth over the past twenty years? Are not people talking faster and faster? And aren't there more and more people unable to stand the speed and turning to drugs, or just going over the edge, giving up and passing over?

Many of those dedicated to the Ascended Masters suggest that the Lord Kuthumi for some years has been preparing a planet, which will stay in three dimensions longer, where these souls will be incarnated. By the way, there can be no judgment of them since in the long ascension journey of thousands of lives, through various time systems and constellations, they may well pass us up at some point. I am assuming here that most, if not all, of you dear readers have chosen to ride the ascension spiral upwards at this rare juncture.

Now I'd like to shed some light on the nature of this marker. There was a very fine channel by the name of Yolanda in Florida in the mid '60s and early '70s. She channeled from some very high angels dedicated to guarding and guiding our spiritual development. She spoke of evolutionary cycles on Earth going back 206 million years so it's not surprising that her organization was called Mark Age. It is these cycles I wish to tell you about because they support the concept of 2012 as a marker. Of course there have been many predictions of the end of the 2600-year Piscean Age and the beginning of the Aquarian Age around now. Then Yolanda continues on back, each of these cycles ending around 2000:

> ➢ Twenty-six-thousand years. Since the beginning of the Fall of Atlantis, the now-sunken continent and civilization in the Atlantic. Edgar Cayce has some of the most convincing proof of the existence of Atlantis, if you have any doubts.

- Two-hundred-and-six-thousand years. Withdrawal of the Elder Race from Earth and the decline of Lemuria, the now-sunken continent and civilization in the Pacific.
- Twenty-six-million-year-cycle. The period of evolution of man in this Solar System.

I see this, as I see the exit from the Garden of Eden, as an adventure within The Higher Plan—our responses to the Great Commandment "Go forth into my creation and return it to me." So then, "Eating of the Tree of the Knowledge of Good and Evil" more correctly describes entering the world of Duality in order to grow toward Supreme Consciousness through the Free Will Plan of choosing. By the way, the true, and more complete, story of Adam and Eve and The Garden of Eden takes up four papers in *The Urantia Book*.

Now, if all the cycles of time of which Yolanda speaks are ending around now, it is a unique time in the history of life on this planet. Is it any wonder that even the highest adepts in Egypt and Central America didn't quite know what might happen next? So in this regard it is a test of faith. Dr. Calleman's extensive research on the Mayan calendar indicates that the tipping point was Friday, October 28th of last year, 2011. So now there is quite a controversy among the authorities on the Mayan Calendar concerning just when the tipping point date was. When I heard this a loud "Oops" escaped my lips and I burst into laughter as I contemplated all the fear that spread around December 21, 2012. So far I haven't heard of anything especially dramatic that happened last October 28th or even on December 21st but I do feel that Dr. Carl Calleman's vision for "Conscious Convergence," people coming together for positive change, is inspired and timely. You will see this repeated by many of the visionaries and the current "Occupy" demonstrations are an expression of this coming together.

My chiropractor, for whom I have developed a great deal of respect, just injected a very interesting possibility into this discussion. Since the Mayan culture died out so long ago, isn't it conceivable that having projected their calendar far into the future they just hadn't gotten around to, or didn't see the need to, project it further?

I consider Patricia Cota-Robles one of our highest channels and I've selected just a few quotes that speak to our present subject:

> "Contrary to outer appearances, the horrific changes that are occurring all over the world are not going to destroy humanity or the Earth. They are commanding our attention to motivate us to find a better way of interacting with each other and the Earth."

"The devastating environmental disaster in the Gulf of Mexico was a prime example. We have known for decades that oil and coal were polluting the planet and wreaking havoc in the lives of people everywhere. Time and time again awakening souls have tapped into the Realms of Illumined Truth and come up with clean energy sources and technologies that would eliminate our dependence on oil and coal. But because of the power and money associated with these industries, these new methods of energy have been suppressed and hidden from the mass consciousness of humanity. The people have come to the erroneous conclusion that we must have oil and coal to maintain our livelihoods and survive—even now with oil destroying the precious wetlands and ecosystems in the Gulf of Mexico. There were even many people there who were upset that President Obama called for a moratorium on deep-water drilling. This is a graphic demonstration of humanity's distorted perception at this time. Our lives are so interwoven with the very things that are causing the problems that we feel we must perpetuate them in order to survive. This illusion is the direct manipulation of our fear-based, fragmented human egos. Breaking the bonds of the paralyzing grip our egos have had over us for lifetimes is the next critical step in the unfolding Divine Plan. The transformations possible in the fourth and fifth dimensions can occur when we all remember who we are and our purpose for being. We are co-creators and it is time for us to reclaim our Divine Birthright, which is God's Infinite Abundance."

"An activity of Light that involves the God Selves of all Humanity and the Company of Heaven is now underway. Step back, take a deep breath, and release any fear your human ego may be using to manipulate you. Allow the Divinity within your heart to expand with an open heart and an open mind. Miracles are happening and we are receiving more assistance from the Company of Heaven than ever before. The Beings of Light have confirmed that at this very moment there are patterns of perfection in the Causal Body of God that contain practical solutions for every negative situation manifesting in Earth."

She wrote this in July, 2010, and I feel that it is timely today.

She continues:

"The exceptionally powerful Solstice and the amplified Eclipses brought an influx of Light which has helped Humanity break down crystallized negative patterns from our past. This empowered each of us to let go of obsolete behavior patterns and belief systems that do not serve our highest good."

"One of the most destructive of these is humanity's belief in separation and duality. The next step in the Divine Plan is to remember that we are one with all Life and there is no separation. Once we develop Unity Consciousness we will know there is no such thing as "us" and "them." All Life is interconnected, interdependent, and interrelated. And this means that every single thought, word, feeling, or action we express affects every facet of life on the planet."

What a responsibility. But we're all in this together—and we're not expected to be perfect. Also, if all life is interdependent, it's the famous motto of the Three Musketeers: "One for All and All for One."

Back to Cota-Robles:

"A movement called 'Conscious Convergence... A Wave of Unity' has been initiated by Dr. Carl Johan Calleman, a scholar of the Mayan Calendar and its prophecies. Its mission is to bring people together with the shared intention of cultivating a critical mass of harmonious energy that supports inner and outer reconciliation. Coming together in the spirit of Unity can heal the wounds that separate us, reconcile the conflicts that divide us, inspire ideas and actions that express our oneness, and join our hearts and minds to welcome the birth of our New World."

21

The Visionaries Speak

Grand Elder Don Alejandro is an expert on the Mayan Calendar. His message reports that the Mayan Calendar predicted that a mass change of consciousness would be required at this time through collaborative movements: movements that would fulfill the Divine Plan for Humanity's greater destiny. The striking analogy they use is that "we are One, like the fingers of one hand."

Can you begin to see the consistency of these predictions?

Barbara Marx Hubbard is a futurist, and tireless champion of what she calls Evolutionary Consciousness. She appears at many conferences and has written a number of important visionary books

> "Our crisis is the birth of a co-creative, universal humanity. It is the greatest wake-up call humanity has ever received. Despite the moral and spiritual teachings of all the great systems none have been able to move humanity toward a shared awareness that we are all members of one planetary body. The crisis of survival triggered by our planetary conditions is having this effect. We cannot go back to survive, we can only go forward. If we can converge, connect, and resonate quickly enough to support the consciousness field of the Earth, we will have a more gentle birth into the next stage of our evolution. And through this birth process we are sharing contact with life that is beyond us."

Tom Kenyon is a channel who has attracted quite a following. Here's a quote from his sources, the Hathors from Venus:

> "You are literally at the brink of the collapse of the old world and a chaotic birthing into the new. The chaotic nodes are upon you in ever-increasing intensity. We view this as the contractions of the birth of a new Earth into higher dimensions. If you are caught in one of the contractions it could be quite difficult. This is a time for intuition and instinct. Hone these abilities within you and act on the revelations that come. Each of you will be in the right place, the circumstances and the timing based on your level of evolution and what you came to Earth to experience. Move upward in consciousness even if those around you seem to be moving downward. Gaia will survive this. It is not clear at this point whether the bulk of humanity will...but there are exquisite opportunities to move upward in consciousness, both as individu-

als and culturally creative and cooperative communities. Do not be frightened by these changes but recognize them as breaks in the walls of a prison that has been erected around you. Move through the cracks into your freedom! You are creator gods and goddesses with immense power in your hands, but you have been sleeping and unaware of it. As you let go of the distortions created by your culture and wake up to the simple truth of your existence as an embodied being in time and space you will see that the great adventure has just begun!"

"The simple act of appreciation and gratitude for the simple things in your life will shift your vibratory field faster and more effectively than any sacred geometry. Share your love and affection with those close to you."

And now I'd like to include some wisdom from India, from **Sri Amma and Sri Bhagavan.** I don't know anything about these two, but I received an e-mail from them and thought it might add a slightly different slant to our theme. Since I didn't actually receive permission to quote I'll paraphrase it for you.

Our illusions of separateness have made it difficult to work together, and with nature. This self-serving divisiveness is threatening our very survival. More and more we are realizing that the whole of mankind is affected by what the few experience. We are one human, planetary family and we can no longer avoid this fact. We must see ourselves as citizens of the world ready to cooperate with all the life forms and the beings of higher realms. This will require honesty, love and also respect for the sacredness and Oneness of all life.

Now I quote from **John Kimmey**, the past elder of the Hopi Indians. Many indigenous cultures concur with these prophecies. These are highlights only:

"The Hopi Prophecy is 5000 years old. It has provided proper instruction for these times through glimpses of over 200 events that will take place during this time of Purification to prepare for the Fifth World. So far it has been 100% accurate. It says we must seek true Divine Guidance from within to facilitate union as spiritual brothers and sisters. We must return to our original ancestral condition of dependence on the guidance of Mother Earth because our survival and hers are now one and the same. Our circle becomes an *us*, greater and wiser than any one of us alone. Then we can act for the whole."

"All polarities will become extreme but we can help by healing these in our personal lives. How we govern and we are governed must change together with all economics based on exploitation. All religious chauvinism must give way to a global holistic approach, incorporating the wisdom of the East. In other words, we must become one family in order to act together to achieve common goals that will benefit everyone, including all the life-forms on Earth—we must "indigenize" our way of life. The ancestor cultures have had a track record of sustainability and harmony for thousands of years and they warn that the annihilation of these cultures would definitely eliminate human participation in the Fifth World."

I love that word "indigenize."

The Hopi prophecy also says that when the **Grandmothers** speak the World will heal.

I just heard of thirteen indigenous grandmothers from several continents who have been meeting twice a year for the past four years. Their prophecies are similar to the Hopis. They are saying that the imbalance of energy has placed all of the life forms on Earth in danger and it is imperative that we return to balance. After a long era of yang leadership our salvation is in the honoring of the Divine Feminine. This means men listening to women and the two working in harmony. They also say forgiving all people in your past will accelerate your own healing and the healing of the planet.

John Kimmey says that **Dr. Micheo Kaku**, quantum physicist, has been reporting for some time that the foremost scientists have been meeting every 30 days to discuss new discoveries, and conduct a complete revision of science.

I also like the way **Peter Russell** puts it:

"We are entering into a time of catastrophic change, possible breakdown of systems, major social disruption, but also possible positive transformations and great spiritual awakening, through letting go of old attitudes and beliefs. We need to see a shift to a more loving, compassionate way of being—perhaps even the emergence of a global consciousness. Imagine a tree in a severe storm: It needs strong roots,—for us, inner balance—; it needs to be flexible and resilient—for us, letting go of past assumptions—; and it needs other trees for protection—for us, a strong sense of community. So we need to open our hearts to kindness, compassion and love, to help see us through these turbulent times."

Peter says the exact date 2012 was not so important as we have seen a gradual increase of changes since 2000. He calls it a "Temporal Epicenter of a Cultural Earthquake" and this fits with the concept of a marker.

Eckhart Tolle's classic book *The Power of Now* hit the best seller list because of its universality and clarity about spiritual issues. This book and his more recent book *A New Earth* draw on Buddhism and Western traditions like *A Course in Miracles* to show us that only the present exists and that to experience The Supreme Being, The Holy Spirit, we must learn how to be fully in the moment. Ram Dass, the famous spiritual teacher of the 70's, who sat at the foot of a master in India, said often "Be Here Now." An excellent daily affirmation is: "This day I will be with the Presence in the Now, I will be in the Now with the Presence." I say this affirmation every morning.

A close friend of mine, **Allisone Heartsong**, for many years has been on top of some of the best channels for space beings. Here is a partial list of the main ones, who speak of benevolent assistance from outside the Earth, and their books:

- THE SIRIANS: Wendy Munro, *Journey into the New Millennium*; Sheldon Nidle, *You Are Becoming a Galactic Human*
- THE PLEIADIANS: Barbara Marciniak, *Bringers of the Dawn*
- AN EGYPTIAN SOURCE: Jani King, *Ptaah—an Act of Faith*
- THE ARCTURIANS: Norma Milanovitch, *We the Arcturians*; Patricia Pereira, *Songs of the Arcturians*
- THE HATHORS OF VENUS: Tom Kenyon, *The Hathor Material*

And now **Sheldan Nidle**, from the Spiritual Hierarchy and the Galactic Federation, reports that time is running out for the dark ones who have dominated us for so long (the "reptilians," the "Anunaki," the "fallen ones from Mars"). Their control of the world's money is crumbling and their heartless greed for power must be replaced by a leadership which is motivated by love and world harmony.

He says the stage is being set for the arrival of the benevolent space beings with a plan to redistribute the funds of Earth to benefit its people. This will mean many changes: restructuring of governments, sweeping forgiveness of debts, removal of pollution, the employment of long-suppressed technologies, and the coming forth of the truth about UFOs.

But even more exciting: we will be shown our true nature, which has been hidden for so long, as Beings of Light. He says the Divine Plan is that, then, we can transcend the Plane of Dualism. His information indicates that the space beings wish to work WITH us for our upliftment and return to full consciousness.

By the way, these revelations present an entirely different picture of the space beings than we are shown in films and on TV. These cinematic images seem to be designed to create fear in us—the common strategy to make it easier for the dark ones to control and exploit us. As we have known for some time, our government has been active in the suppression of the truth about extraterrestrials.

What we can do to prepare for the changes of these transition times? This is just a beginning as surely more can be gleaned from this book:

1. Take fifteen minutes each day to give your body, your emotions and your mind the gift of coming to peace. Journey into the innermost chamber of your heart. Connect there with the Highest that you know. Recognize that you were made from Light and Love, that they are your true nature and that you are potentially an eternal being with an Ascension Destiny—unless you choose otherwise. If your stress is accumulating, as soon as possible, take ten minutes to do some deep breathing and come to peace.

2. Accept that what we call death is only a process, a transition to higher planes of being where you will be given a new body appropriate to that realm. Once you leave this planet the universe is basically friendly.

3. For various reasons, life on Earth is going through a healing crisis and our help is needed to right the wrongs created by some of our wayward supervisors and also by our misguided fellow humans, and that includes *ourselves*. Practice casting and holding a Net of Light over anything that needs healing and balancing.

4. Cultivate and develop a deep respect for the Divine Feminine, a practice needed especially by men, since they are still more in charge of our physical environment. Balance the feminine with the masculine in you: yang and yin. Being aware of Her Presence throughout the Grand Universe means taking care of Mother Earth.

5. Take some time *off* from this hyped-up lifestyle to rest and recharge, especially in nature. Have some fun.

6. Be the change you wish to see, *and live its lifestyle.* Your example will go out into the world.

7. Cultivate and make new friends, creating a cohesive circle. Find something you can love about every one of your brothers and sisters, no matter what they look like, or how they act—they are also fellow children of The Most High. You can help them realize this in how you see them and how you treat them.

8. Eat sensibly, probably less. Before you go to sleep release *all* the cares and tensions of the day. Ask for healing and to be prepared for the coming changes. Get plenty of exercise, gentle and aerobic, that is, active. Review the priorities of your projects, to make sure they are worthy of your precious time and energy in these unique times. Phase out any roles which are no longer serving your highest purposes. Think about how you and your group could be more self-sufficient, as well as outgoing.

9. Develop the constant awareness that you are loved, nurtured and guided, and that many higher beings are ready to co-create with you. If your motive is noble, you need only ask. Be aware that you have the High Self, or I am Presence, an undiluted portion of the Highest Deity assigned to your guidance and also guardian seraphim assigned to your watch-care.

10. Make a concerted effort to connect happily with others who are promoting the uplifting potentials of these extraordinary times. Ask for the inspiration of higher guidance, and see what you can do to support this glorious birth of consciousness.

11. Then you could take this book as a manual for spiritual unfoldment. You could write down the 30 principles that you deem most valuable to you personally and meditate on one each day for a month. Then try to incorporate each one into your daily life. How would it uplift your life if you repeated this process for six months or even a year?

12. If you need some music for peace and healing, or to help you connect with your higher sources please visit my website:

www.harpofgold.com

There you will find a wealth of information about my 30 years as a pioneer healer, how to order my first book about the miracles in my healing ministry, *A Harp Full of Stars*, *Miracles through Music* and my many CDs, as well as how to order the various personalized CDs.

MAY YOU BE IN THE NOW WITH THE PRESENCE!

I leave you with a quote from a bridge in my local botanical gardens:

"NO COINS NECESSARY TO OPERATE STREAM"

And I would add:

*AND NO COINS NECESSARY TO OPERATE
THE STREAM OF LIGHT AND LOVE THAT FLOWS
FROM THE SOURCE.*

Appendix I

LETTER-PITCH EQUIVALENTS

This code has been used by composers for 250-300 years. In German the note B is written as an H. J. S. Bach used it and Haydn wrote a composition based on the name B-A-C-H. More recently, Brahms and Ravel, to name just two, both derived themes with it. At first this code may seem strange, but further study will reveal the soundness of its logic. There probably never has been as detailed a proof of its value as the research into music healing reported in *A Harp Full of Stars* and in this book. And much further corroboration would be brought to light through more detailed studies of the use of the code by the above-mentioned composers.

a	b	c	d	e	f	g
A	B	C	D	E	F	G

h	i	j	k	l	m	n
B	C#	D	E	F#	G	A

o	p	q	r	s	t	u
C#	D#	E	F#	G#	A	B

v	w	x	y	z
D#	E#	F#	G#	A#

The key to memorizing and erecting this table is to notice that the pattern of the natural minor scale is set by the first line, each succeeding line consisting of a natural minor scale starting a whole tone above the first note of the preceding line. It could also be described as four natural minor scales starting on notes of a whole tone scale beginning with A and ending when A# (Z) is reached.

NUMBER-PITCH EQUIVALENTS (FROM MY SOURCES)

Numbers 1-22 coincide with letters 1-22

23 = 2 and 3 or B and C
24 = 2 and 4 or B and D
25 = 2 and 5 or B and E
26 = 2 and 6 or B and F

Thus, for any number over 22, each digit is translated into its letter of the alphabet and then into a pitch.

Note: Some work has been done to correlate this system with Numerology with some success. I suspect that, as with all forms of divination, the two systems provide different points of view of a person which could be complementary.

Appendix I

The Symbolism Of Musical Intervals

OCTAVE: Higher significance of the qualities of the lower note. Transition from one cycle of life to a higher cycle, level, or phase. Ability to build on the past. Finishing and beginning (elision).

PERFECT 5th: Creation, actualization, manifestation. First "skeletal" building blocks of material reality.

PERFECT 4th: Mental concepts, thought forms. Rising from material reality of four dimensions to a higher plane (mental), toward transcendence.

MAJOR 3rd: The sense of beauty expressed in the external world. "Color tones" in music. Expansive (Yang). The completion, fullness and synthesis of the 5th and 4th (through the inversions of a major triad, such as C-E- G. E-G-C, G-C-E.)

MINOR 3rd: The sense of beauty felt in one's inner world (Yin). More emotional and intuitive than the Major 3rd.

MAJOR 6th and MINOR 6th: Same as the 3rds only more ambitious; a larger leap, traversing and embracing more space.

MAJOR 2nd: A building block of life, a patient step toward a larger goal (up the scale toward completion at the octave.) A physical, outer connection or relationship between two things or beings. A detail of daily living. Caution. Deliberation. (Yang).

MINOR 2nd: The same as the Major 2nd, but within: emotional and intuitive. The psychological aspect of a step. Relations between persons. (Yin) Somewhat dissonant by itself and wants to be resolved, either into the Major 2nd or into the unison.

MAJOR 7th: One's relationship with the group around one through thought, material things and works. (Yang) Somewhat dissonant by itself and wants to be resolved, usually upwards, but downwards if approached from above.

MINOR 7th: One's relationship with the group through feeling, sensitivity, awareness, psychology. (Yin) Resolved down unless approached from below.

MAJOR 9th and MINOR 9th:. Same as the 7ths, but one's relationship with the larger group: nation, race, humanity, etc. This meaning comes from the building of chords in 3rds. The 9ths would also carry the qualities of the 2nds, but much expanded into a higher octave: patient steps leading to goals involving the larger group. The Minor 9th is somewhat dissonant and wants to be resolved, probably downwards.

DIMINISHED 5th or AUGMENTED 4th or TRITONE: The relationship of polar opposites. Halfway up the scale symbolizes reaching the furthest point away from home before beginning the return. If alone: the most dissonant interval ("sweet abrasion"); if harmonized within the Dominant 7th chord, resolution of duality and the richness of completion on and synthesis of Yang and Yin, male and female. Still wants to be resolved, usually upwards.

Note: Tension/release, (dissonance/consonance) is a necessary part of life and provides much of its poignancy; it is also a constant process in art and music.

Appendix I

The Symbolism Of The English Alphabet

This chart includes information channeled from the Lords of Sirius which they called "The Symbolism of the Mystical English Alphabet:' I realized that they had brought it through in past ages but that it was being updated for the transition into the Aquarian Age. These significances have been corroborated by the 3,000 Individual Past-life readings and 1600 Name Analyses, other healing tapes, and concerts I have completed, beginning four years before the channeling from Sirius and extending to the date of this writing. The Sirius channeling in 1975 confirmed my work and provided some lower and some higher symbolisms for the letters. Any set of symbols, (such as numbers, astrological signs and aspects, or designs), must be clear and definite. Yet, they must be abstract enough to be applied to a number of different levels of being in a number of different contexts. This system has proven itself with these criteria and has, in my work, culminated in the co-creation of the new world anthem, "Unitas Eanokee; in a new language, for the peace, unification and harmony of the peoples of this planet.

Over the years I have found it logical and usable to arrange this chart in the order of the Circle of 5ths with the pitches first and then the letters to which they correspond. In this way you can see immediately that a pitch (and letters) is the Actualizing Principle for the pitch (and letters) that precedes it and a pitch (and letters) is actualized by the pitch (and letters) that follows next. Bear in mind that even an individual letter can be viewed in a number of ways: 1) physically; that is, purely as design graphics. I realized that Sirius was using a system of symbols for each stroke that makes up a letter. (These meanings can be found in the Appendix of my book *A Harp Full of Stars.*) 2) Then a letter can be responded to emotionally; the sound of the letter (and possibly the universal emotions a letter might evoke in people as they were making that letter with the body; of course, ruling out personal associations with that position. (This should be researched.) And finally 3): Looking at the letter as a human being with chakras.

It is obvious that this system was given for the capital letters. It would be more difficult to apply the symbolism of the strokes to cursive writing with its curves, but this might yield some interesting results. Keep in mind also that some of these qualities, especially the polarized ones, such as A and E, overlap a little in life, and so are difficult to find in their pure state.

In the symbolism of the alphabet I have put the information

from the Lords of Sirius first, then the symbolism which came through in the musical past-life readings.

THE ARCHETYPAL SYMBOLISM OF THE ALPHABET AND ITS CORRELATED PITCHES FOR THE EMERGING AGE

F

An individual's organized expression in thought (will) (throat chakra) and universal love (Heart Chakra) without grounding in action or application in the physical. When lower-evolved, can be lacking in practicality, common sense, or humor. Could be fanatical. Look for C's, G's, and H's and B's and other signs of grounding.

PITCH F —LETTER F

In the musical readings: THE INDIVIDUAL'S ABILITY TO ATTUNE DIRECTLY TO THE ANGELIC ORDER including devas and elementals. Then, one hopes, the inspiration can be brought into manifestation on the physical plane. The initial F: the desire to develop attunement to the angelic order of life. Within a name: past experience in this direct attunement (somewhat rare in the body of names). Earth knowledge apart from its manifestation. The angelic order can come in on this note, in this key.

C

GATHERING. The half-completed, never-ending circle of consciousness. Open mind, heart and body. Questioning, receiving. When low, may accept without thought of discrimination. May have trouble closing down. May become constipated and confused if there is not enough time to process what has been taken in. Could have the need to collect. When high, open to a "cosmos" of experience—eagerly seeking the Ascension Adventure.

In the musical readings: ORDINARY SURVIVAL-TYPE ACTIVITY. Experience in maintenance and perpetuation of the physical plane, and the desire to add to this. Accumulation of life skills from the ground up, from the simple and mundane, to the complex and sophisticated. To evolve, it's important what consciousness we bring to these acts of survival. We can struggle, or we can realize that every act is a spiritual act, and co-create with God in our simplest tasks (the philosophy of Zen). A "taking on," "eating" letter. (Note how many words describing this letter contain the letter "c.")

Appendix I

PITCH C—LETTER C

PRACTICALITY, METHODOLOGY OR TECHNOLOGY OF GOING ABOUT OR MANIFESTING   C—ordinary survival-type challenges.

PITCH G—LETTER G

Open, receiving letter (like C) but focused in a particular area or areas on the material plane (the horizontal "continuity" line). The Yang or masculine approach through the mind, logic and science. Open to all ideas related to a certain project—the student or researcher. When low, not open to other aspects of self and the outer world, such as artistic and spiritual. When high, is open to seeing the practicality of everything.

> In the readings: PRACTICALITY: HOW TO GO ABOUT SOLVING SURVIVAL CHALLENGES. Gaining experience through the logical, scientific approach (male) to "how to get things done here on the Earth plane"; especially in regard to the needs of maintaining one's self. (The note "sol" or Sun.) Usually indicates experience with money.

PITCH G—LETTER M

Contains Involution and Evolution, Descension and Ascension, supported on two legs (the Plane of Duality). Also contains the V of Universal Love planted firmly on Earth. The M of Earth Mother, also the M of matter (which derives from the same word as Mother and Matrix). We use this letter when we say "Mmmmm" to express physical pleasure.

> INTUITIVE PRACTICALITY. How to solve survival-type challenges by just "knowing" rather than figuring them out logically. The Yin, or female, approach. The intuition includes: (1) drawing on past-life memories; (2) tuning in, psychically, to whatever is involved; (3) calling on the angels and Earth Mother for guidance; (4) asking the Higher Self or Source for the answer; (5) tuning in to other minds that might have the needed information.

D

BUILDING ON PAST EXPERIENCE IN HUMAN LOVE. One-to-one commitment, physical love, sharing and growth.

PITCH D—LETTER D

MOVING (or swelling) into the future based wholly on the past. When low: bound by dogma, or convention, or established structure, or any "scientific" or "religious" system which claims it has "the truth" (Illness: digestive; if too bound up with self, having also G's, B's and L's.) The presence of a P, Universal Love, would suggest that the love nature is expanding. 1 x 1 relationships are so often subject to dogma and powerful social customs.

> In the musical readings: HUMAN LOVE COMMITMENT. Sharing space together in love, especially the nitty-gritty aspects. Growth in personalized love, dealing with yours and another's needs, self-expression, etc. A supreme workshop in these times when the whole world is so polarized, and when the institution of marriage is undergoing such reorganization and renewal. Growth in learning the true love of self and another and often, also, love of family, of life, and of aspects of God.

PITCH D—LETTER J

The "I AM" expression combined with the qualities of the "U" (the lower part of the letter). Individuality seeking spiritual guidance in the growth of the lower chakras. The desire to be open to God and to have union with materiality without action (the U is meditative). Thought tends to be systematic (the "ceiling" like the letter T—please see). Inspired development of the lower centers. The spine. (Illness: back trouble, if there isn't enough flowing exercise and physical activity. Cs, Ds, Es, Hs, and possibly Ns would help for their horizontal lines.)

In the musical readings: SPIRITUALIZED HUMAN LOVE. Idealized Christ love expressed to an individual. Bringing spiritual concepts into all aspects of the love relationship symbolized by the letter D. Practicing the Golden Rule. Unconditional Love. Giving without thought of return and total acceptance of another's evolution through love relationship.

A

PHYSICAL MANIFESTATION, DIVINE MOTHER PRINCIPLE. Materiality, Four dimensions (three plus time), Earth Mother, The Planetary Being, Yin. Receptive, Dark, Yielding, Fertile and Nurturing.

PITCH A—LETTER A

The beginning of all action: Alpha. A solid physical structure, resembling a pyramid, for the collection of energy or for the physical manifestation of the Divine Father Principle (Pure Pattern). The love of structure, form and order. A neutral letter, the energy of which is influenced by the letters around it. Will tend to bring into manifestation the qualities of the surrounding letters. An Evolution line and an

Involution line connected. More balanced and also less individual than the other letters for the pitch A: N and T.

> In the musical readings: DIVINE MOTHER, the physical plane of materiality, four dimensions, Earth. Physically manifested Light, Light in form. The ability to see that everything in this world comes from spirit. Physical consciousness. Spiritualized Physicality. (N is Physical Energy, T is Physical Form.)

PITCH A—LETTER N

A "hope" letter. The overcoming of the low self, of karma, resulting in alteration of consciousness, opening up the possibility of ascension. Action. Drive or impulse to move and become involved in life. If you make an N with one continuous stroke, you see that it is two upward strokes connected by an involution stroke. But you have a choice which way to make the vertical strokes, just as you have a choice how you want to qualify and direct your physical energy: to take you down or up. The N on its side looks like lightning, or energy applied to life.

> In the musical readings: PHYSICAL ENERGY. The energy that comes up, Earth energy. Kundalini. Survival impulse. The energy, or vibratory aspect, or expression of, the qualities of the A (see above).

PITCH A—LETTER T

LIMITATION OR FOCUS OF THE INDIVIDUAL OR AN EVENT IN TIME. Limits set on physical expression. High goals, ideals and purposes, but limited by circumstances and Karma of a group nature. "Trapped!" Repression. The "I Am" limited by laws or dogma of the mentality. This letter has a ceiling on it. But the horizontal line does keep the individual moving with the stream. When low: inability to see that the physical is of the Light, not open-minded to spirituality. When high: the ability to channel the Divinity of the "I Am" into materiality with steady purpose and acceptance of temporary Earth sojourn. Looks like the beginning of "cross hairs"—a sight that focuses on a point, or physical details.

> PHYSICAL FORM. The shapes and patterns that Mother Nature uses to express herself and the patterns of Light. Solid geometry. Clock time, measurements. The most disciplined, applied, and conditioned of the A letters. (See the basic qualities of the A).

E

PURE DIVINE FATHER PRINCIPLE. Creator, Light, Power, Creative Pattern, Heaven. Yang. The Sun. A symbol of the individual at his/her best, reaching out on three levels: Will, Throat Chakra, top line, Love, Heart Chakra, middle line, and Action, Root Chakra, bottom line. In a way, the highest letter for us since it shows the "I Am" individuality evolving through time, combining mind, heart, and application.

CONSCIOUS SPIRITUAL ATTUNEMENT WITH THE FATHER PRINCIPLE, THE LIGHT, THE CHRIST SPIRIT, and the ability to channel what is perceived into the outside world, through application of higher principles, to life and physical reality. Triune expression of individuality. When high, manifested spiritually; when low, just the ability to receive energy from the Father, the sun, and use it in life.

PITCH E—LETTER K

Ability of the individual "I Am" to channel the ancient, and contemporary wisdom and apply it in a practical manner. Ability to harmonize the principles of Involution and Evolution with Love. (These lines come out of the Heart Chakra.) Illness: Heart, when there is confusion between Descension and Ascension. When high: Cosmic Consciousness and wisdom of the heart.

THE SPIRITUAL TEACHER. The ability developed in the past to organize one's spiritual experience into concepts, or other patterns, that one can teach. Must avoid the ego temptation common to gurus: that they own the wisdom, or that they are the only channel of it, or that their version of it is the purest to be found. An opportunity to learn that "truth" is evolving, and changes according to a number of variables, and that we are only co-creators of it, filtering it through our individuality.

PITCH E—LETTER Q

The perfect circle of Cosmic Consciousness, broken and tied to Earth. Past or present practice of grey or black magic. Manipulation of others by power of mind, or knowledge of the law. Tuning into universal knowledge directly with an ulterior motive. Tapping race collective wisdom, but often tampering with it or limiting it in the process—often leaving out the love part of it, the wholeness of it (in contrast with E). Also not necessarily interested in applying the knowledge. The occultist, or magician, or the psychic interested in phenomena without spirituality. Love for self rather than co-creation.

Appendix I

B

ORGANIZATION IN SPACE AND TIME, BASED ON PAST EXPERIENCE TO MANIFEST IN, OR MANIPULATE, PHYSICAL REALITY, SELF, OR ENVIRONMENT. Its higher octave is PEACE.

PITCH B—LETTER B

Reaching out on two levels of consciousness from the solid, upright base of the "I Am" individuality: the central purpose, the "One." Self expression as the past expands or projects into the future. The first step, or steps, of building on self. Without other open letters like C, G, or E, could be self-centered, preconceived-purpose-centered, or narrow-minded, especially if lower evolved. When low, could be manipulative, reaching out only for that which reinforces self. When high, pressing forward with the assurance of experience and 'know-how' combining head and heart, also heart and root, or thinking and love, or love and action.

> PATIENCE. One step at a time. Knowing what the next step is. "Looking before you leap!" The quality of caution, deliberation, circumspection. Awareness of the passage of time, especially minutes and hours (the letter H would be longer periods of time). Also awareness of units of space, and what could fill it. Through mastering this kind of patience, we transcend time and space, and achieve peace.

PITCH B—LETTER H

CONTINUITY AMONG TWO OR MORE ACTS OR STEPS OF PATIENT ACTUALIZATION ON THE PHYSICAL PLANE. Connecting two upright structures in consciousness—"I AMs" or events in time—to form a sturdy foundation. Combining attunement upwards with attunement downwards for balanced manifestation on Earth. Also depicts two people holding hands in cooperation. The only letter you can't make with the body without another person. A cross expanded horizontally through time. "Love-Wisdom" in its highest use.

The Christ letter. The sound of this letter has been thought to contain the magical power of the breath. The H in "HU" and "Huna!" We also say, "Hu are you?" wanting to know what's behind the name.

> Patient organization in space and time to complete long-range projects, especially those that require physical acts. Also the ability to coordinate others carrying out such a project. Attunement with the materials involved. Cooperation with others. Leads to making your peace with time and space.

PITCH B—LETTER U

Openness to God. Desire for direct union with Higher Forces. Ability to receive guidance and hold it. Gathering from above, waiting for help and inspiration. The listener. Without other action and manifesting letters, could subordinate physical expression to contemplative states and would wait to be shown. When low: the beggar with his bowl.

> THE MEDIATOR. The ability to quiet the mind, the emotions, and the body, to listen to Higher Guidance. The ability to "Be still and know that I am God!" The presence of mind to stop and seek inner guidance before acting. Capability of higher attunement. Tends to listen to advice.

F#

CREATIVE, ARTISTIC ABILITIES. KNOWLEDGE OF, AND SENSITIVITY TO, FORMS, THEIR CONTENT, SIGNIFICANCE, AND GRADATIONS OF QUALITY. THE CREATIVE PROCESSES.

PITCH F#—LETTER L

First steps and actions to build physical structures or systems of thought—thought-forms). Ability to understand and recreate basic life forms (root chakra), and their archetypal symbolism.

> Sensitivity to THE QUANTITATIVE ASPECT OF ARTISTIC CREATIVITY: the lines which enclose or circumscribe forms, patterns and structures. Ability to create designs. The geometric aspect of solid, physical objects. Outer form as separate from content—pure idea as separate from its manifestation in the world. The yang aspect of artistry. In music: pitches as points, form.

PITCH F#—LETTER R

As an individual: EXPANSION OF CONSCIOUSNESS THROUGH LOVE-WISDOM. Evolution of the letter P. Both feet on the ground, but capable of being a visionary, a Rabbi, a Reverend, a spiritual teacher but probably more traditional than the letter K. Building on the past in the areas of thought and heart, and combining these, like the B; but adding to this the desire to get involved with the challenge of fresh experience in the chakras of love and action—Heart and Root.

> THE QUALITATIVE ASPECTS OF ARTISTIC SENSITIVITY that an individual can bring to the creative process. As the pure pattern is manifested, this can bring that which fills the form: body, content, texture, color—the Yin qualities. In music: the

Appendix I

spaces between the notes, tone quality, the qualities of chords sounding together, inflections that call forth emotions.

PITCH F#—LETTER X

INVOLUTION AND EVOLUTION, ASCENSION AND DESCENSION, AT THE SAME TIME, AT CROSS PURPOSES. Cancellation. (The most natural sequence is one after the other as in the letter V or Y.)

Could possibly be handled in a high state of meditation, or experiencing Cosmic Consciousness, but not in the world of action. It draws from all directions at once: above, below, from the past, and the future, converging at a point (the heart). Could suggest heart trouble for someone who takes on everything at once. Would be tempered by the presence of Bs, Us, and Hs and made more intense by Cs and Gs. Artistic creativity that comes from such experience. These cross purposes can be expressed and harmonized through art.

C#

THE CAPABILITY OF ACTUALIZING CREATIVITY IN THE PHYSICAL WORLD

PITCH C#—LETTER I

The individual "I Am" creativity. PERSONALITY MANIFESTING IN THE WORLD. A person's unique contribution, idea, goal, or purpose. An individual as a connection between heaven and earth. The potential ability to cut across all horizontal lines between planes. The ability to free oneself from the laws of the Earth plane: time cycles, biorhythms, moon cycles, group karma, thought forms of others, through the ability to attune vertically (meditation). Mobility of consciousness through uniquely human will and desire. The vertical axis of the cross.

INDIVIDUALLY MOTIVATED ACTUALIZATION OF ARTISTIC CREATIVITY. ABILITY TO MANIFEST ARTISTIC SENSITIVITY FOR PERSONAL GROWTH. Personal desire to use artistic sensitivity for growth in consciousness by bringing it into physical expression.

PITCH C#—LETTER O

The ability to complete creative projects in such a way that they are a replica in the world of the qualities of God: Wholeness, Universality, Harmony, Unity. The completion of the letter U. Expansion out in all directions from a center. The ability to draw to a seed idea or project information from all directions, and put it all together harmoniously. Cosmic Consciousness, the vision to see that the one can be an expression and manifestation of the One. Integrating the All and its expression as specificity.

> ABILITY TO ACTUALIZE ARTISTIC CREATIVITY IN THE PHYSICAL WHEN MOTIVATED BY SERVICE OR VALUE TO THE WHOLE, TO OTHER PEOPLE, TO LIFE. Usually implies greater co-creation with Higher Forces to insure universal value.

G#

CREATIVE OR ARTISTIC PATIENCE. The step or steps we take to manifest creative projects. The ability to make one particular act further a longer range artistic or creative plan.

PITCH G#—LETTER S

The kundalini (snake). The energy that rises. The individual power called forth by self-motivation, personal evolution, and renewal. Made up of two Cs—gathering letters: upper half looks forward in time, and bottom half looks backward, head and heart forward, heart and root backward. Ability to integrate past and future.

> PATIENCE IN MANIFESTING CONTINUING ARTISTIC PROJECTS. Ability to sustain the original creative impulse when it serves the development of self, when it's self motivated—the project may also serve others, but this is incidental.

PITCH G#—LETTER Y

The upper half is gathering from above (to the heart); the lower half is the "I Am" expression, or an event in time. The upper half focuses an awareness of Involution and Evolution in Universal Love, and then can express this through individuality or as an act, or an event, in time.

> PATIENCE IN COMPLETING THE CREATIVE OR ARTISTIC PROCESS WHEN MOTIVATED BY THE VALUE OF THE PROJECT TO OTHERS, THE GROUP AROUND ONE, OR HUMANITY AS A WHOLE. Selfless dedication and application. More inspired and guided than S.

D#

> UNIVERSAL LOVE, UNCONDITIONAL LOVE, CHRIST-LIKE LOVE. Love without thought of return. Higher octave of D Human Love.

PITCH D#—LETTER P

An "I Am" expression projecting into the future: experience from the past in combining the head and the heart. Less grounded than the R and more idealistic—not so much manifestation in action (no root).

> UNIVERSAL LOVE EXPERIENCED AND GIVEN IN A PERSONALIZED WAY. THE INDIVIDUAL LOVING THE GROUP, THE COUNTRY, THE WORLD, HUMANITY, ALL LIFE FORMS, THE COSMOS, GOD.

PITCH D#—LETTER V

Involution and evolution in balance. The sequence suggests the Grand Circle of Creation: out from God into matter and the return. Gathers from above. Is abstract, having no vertical or horizontal lines. This higher understanding leads to a high order of love, based on spiritual principles.

> SPIRITUALIZED HUMAN LOVE. The "All" within a person loving the greater "All." This would imply that the Holy Christ Love in the heart had been opened to a large degree.

A#

> A HIGHER ASPECT OF THE DIVINE MOTHER PRINCIPLE, THE PHYSICAL PLANE, EXPERIENCE OR KNOWLEDGE OF RELATIONSHIP BETWEEN ONE PLANE AND A HIGHER PLANE.

PITCH A#—LETTER Z

The line of evolution or ascension connecting a lower plane of existence, or level of understanding, with a higher one. Thus the last letter of our alphabet expresses the final result of the human dance of life in planetary sojourn. To place the small horizontal cross-bar halfway up adds the love of the heart chakra to the root and the head of the bottom and top lines. Could also symbolize having run the gamut from the root chakra to the crown.

> THE EQUIVALENT OF PHYSICAL FORMS AND ENERGIES ON ANOTHER, USUALLY MORE EVOLVED, PLANET. The ability to bring these into this plane through inspiration or memory. Perception of higher forms of physicality. The higher octave or aspect of the letter A. If E# is present, more ability to manifest and actualize the spiritual essence of that higher dimension.

E#

ATTUNEMENT WITH SPACE AND REALITIES BEYOND THE EARTH, AND POSSIBLY BEYOND THE SOLAR SYSTEM.

PITCH E#—LETTER W

Gathers from above from two sources: Earth and solar or solar and extra-solar. Two V's: Involution- Evolution-Involution-Evolution. Suggests possibility that a soul incarnated on a "Higher" planet, evolved, then took on incarnation on Earth (a lower planet) for further testing and growth, then may ascend up higher still. May have dual concepts about the nature of God and higher Realities. This could be confusing or just provide added higher octaves of understanding. May work with descension and ascension. Abstract and needs grounding: no vertical or horizontal lines.

ALL THE PEOPLE I HAVE WORKED WITH WHO HAVE THE LETTER W HAVE A CONNECTION WITH OUTER SPACE AND ALSO A CERTAIN PLANET.

They are the "space people" of various kinds among us. The link is through memory or present-time attunement, or both. This letter completes the grand circle of this system since the pitch E# is the equivalent of the pitch F (the Angelic Order) with which we began. I have found it true that a person with this letter may channel the outer space energies, knowledge and sensitivities, directly into this world; or the aid of the Angelic Order may be enlisted to help translate it into terms and forms the Earth humans can more readily use. These space people feel somewhat alien, depending on how much experience they've had on the Earth plane. They need to learn about how things work here so they can make their special message, or abilities, more understandable to their fellow humans. In this way, they fulfill their destiny, become accepted and evolve toward ascension.

Appendix II

AFFIRMATION #1

(For clearing one's being for higher work or just clearing away negative patterns.)

> Father-Mother God, I ask to be cleared and cleansed, in the Christ Light, the Green Healing Light, and The Violet Transmuting Flame. Within God's Will, and for my highest good, I ask and decree that any and all negativity be completely cut off from me now, encapsulated in its own light, encapsulated in the Ultraviolet Light, and returned to its source, such that it cannot re-establish within me, or anyone else, in any form. Now I ask to be surrounded and filled with The White, Protective Light of the Christ, and for this blessing I give humble thanks. I accept this; so be it; manifest on all levels, NOW!

This is an adapted version of an affirmation channeled by Bonita Brookhire, for which we give thanks. "We" may be substituted for "I" if you wish to think of yourself as a set of Basic Selves plus your conscious mind, or if you're saying this with others. This affirmation can be said in the name of another person since it's never wrong to pray for someone. They can accept the effect or reject it, according to their free will.

AFFIRMATION #2

(For achieving working harmony between your three basic levels: High Self or I AM Presence, Mind, and Body.):

> In the Name and a Power of _____ (The Living Christ), I decree and accept, between my High Self, my conscious mind, and my body consciousness: understanding, cooperation, harmony, love, and bliss. So be it. Thank you _____ (Living Christ).

AFFIRMATION #3

(To open your channel for intuitive service to others.)

> Father-Mother God, as we once more recognize Thy Presence here, Thy Love, Thy Wisdom, and we bow before these; we ask to be used as channels for (healing and attunement). We understand that The Christ Spirit does the work as It sees fit, we are only channels of love and concern for ____ We ask for the sensitivity to do this kind of work; we're open to truth only. Father-Mother God, we see thy protection of Light and Love, sur-

rounding and filling this room, surrounding and filling all those who would come IN THE LIGHT to serve (his/her highest good). We see the channel surrounded, filled, and protected with The Light, the equipment protected (if there is), and all spirits involved.

Affirmation #4

In the Name and Power of the Living Christ, I command that any entities, thought forms, emotional patterns, not for my (our) highest good be gone at once from me (us), from this house, from this property (or from me, from this car, from this highway). So be it. Thank you Living Christ. Thank you brothers of Light. Begone, begone, begone!

Affirmation #5

I am living in the ecstasy of the Creator's love.

Appendix II

CHAKRA, COLOR, PITCH EQUIVALENTS AND SYMBOLISM:

Here I have paired the basic colors up with the first seven chakras and the notes to which they vibrate. While you will find other systems and variations this seems to be the consensus in the books I have studied. It makes sense and my Sources have been using it for 40 years. Bear in mind that a chakra has more than one color, so this is somewhat simplistic (See the paintings in the excellent book by C.W. Leadbeater, the English Theosophist.)

This chart is based on the Tempered Scale on the piano, just to show the color and chakra symbolism.

Notice that we have three primary colors, red, yellow, blue, and three secondary colors, orange, green and violet, produced by mixing the primaries in pairs. This provides six colors for six chakras, the Crown (the seventh) being an octave above the Root and the beginning of our higher set of chakras. Remember, also, that you can never get exact vibratory congruence between our different senses, but your higher guidance should be able to work with these, as has mine. A greater equivalence might be achieved between chakras and colors, which are not in the Tempered Scale, but in an Overtone Series.

Root—Red—(C)—Base of Spine—Life Force—Survival—reflection of the light of the Father that enters us through the medulla oblongata.

2nd—Orange—(D)—Genitals—Constructivity—shaping the red energy for a creative purpose: Art, Sex.

3rd—Yellow—(E)—Solar Plexus—Harmonizing polarities and dualities with the mind, then in the body—Illumination of the subconscious (The Body Consciousness).

4th—Green—(F#)—Heart—Unconditional Christ Love—Balances the upper chakras with the lower, just as the green of nature balances us—Your Inner Sanctuary.

5th—Blue— (G)—Throat—Ability and power to decree and affirm one's future—To Manifest The Higher Will.

6th—Violet—(A)—Pineal gland—The Third Eye—Clairvoyance—Astral Travel—The Love of Divine Mother.

7th—Rosy White—(B)—Pituitary, sometimes above the skull—Crown—elision between lower chakras and upper chakras—higher octave of the root chakra—The Light of Divine Father.

A Report On A Laboratory Study Of My Music

PSYCHIC RESEARCH INCORPORATED
A NON-PROFIT CORPORATION USING SCIENTIFIC RESEARCH AND EDUCATION TO AID MANKIND

April 30, 1987

Dear Joel,

This is to acknowledge the contribution of your work and sensitivity with the harp in the role of sound in the structuring of water.

In the first set of experiments our laboratory did with you, we found that when you tuned with your mind into the water and played your music we found a change in the water: pH, electro-conductivity and the UV spectrum.

We further did the experiments in which you played to a crystal over the water and we noted an even greater degree of change in the water with your music. What we have found is that not only is sound Important but the sensitivity of the individual playing these tones as well.

At this time I believe this work of yours indicates that when you play your type of music a change in the electro-physiology of a body listening to this music takes place over and beyond just the beauty of the sound and tonal patterns you create.

I am deeply grateful for your help and participation in the research work we are doing I wish you the very best on your book.

Very Truly Yours,
Marcel Vogel, former scientist for IBM

GLOSSARY

AKASHIC RECORDS: "Akasha" is a Hindu word for the basic substance upon which everything that happens is recorded.

ANGELS: Members of the angelic order, generally higher in rank than devas, overlighting individual humans (guardian seraphim), nations, races, languages, the arts, and sciences, etc. There are hundreds of types, supposedly 500 million pairs on Earth at this time, not counting the resident archangel contingent. (See *The Urantia Book*, Bibliography.)

ASCENDED MASTER: A teacher from a higher frequency dimension. Some believe they have evolved from humans; others that they have their own particular origin but take embodiment occasionally. The author leans toward the latter. See "midwayers" in *The Urantia Book*. "I AM" groups channel from them.

ASCENSION: At the end of life on Earth, the essential aspects of an individual (not the body) passing into higher frequency dimensions of existence, having earned release from the wheel of karma and the need to re-embody on Earth. In this book, possible for anyone in any particular life if the major karmic lessons and the basic lessons of Earth life have been mastered (see *The Urantia Book*, Bibliography) and also possible for the body consciousness, basic or low selves, to ascend along their own path, even possible (although rare) for the two to happen simultaneously (Jesus and a few others, some in our time).

AURAMETER: A wooden handle with a wire extending from it (first spiraled and then straight) ending in a solid piece of metal (various metals are used), about a foot long. The Cameron Aurameter is longer, all metal and more sensitively suspended. Like all dowsing devices, including the pendulum, it simply makes visible the subtle energies the subconsciou or Basic Selves are picking up or what it is trying to tell you. A myriad of uses, depending on the developed sensitivities and skill of the Basic Selves.

CAUSAL BODY: Found in the upper mental body.

CHAKRA (with a "ch" as in "chapter"): means in Hindu, "coin." One of twelve vortices of energy, seven of which lie along the spine. Also called psychic centers. They, like transformers, step down the higher frequency energies coming in through the medulla and also focus energies from the root chakra, reflecting upward (kundalini) for various uses in the three lower bodies: Physical-Etheric, Emotional-Astral, and Mental. See "Seven Bodies." They gradually open, hopefully in balance and harmony, but drugs and other shocks can open them too fast with extremely challenging results.

CHRIST SPIRIT: Jesus said before the Crucifixion, "I go on so that I can send my spirit, the Comforter." It is reported that on the day of Pentecost, the apostles all felt the descent of this "Spirit of Truth." Their hair stood on end and they spoke in tongues which the many races of people present could all understand. It is this personal presence, acting for The Christ, which has always been with us— The Living Christ. *The Urantia Book* explains that the presence on Earth of the Spirit of Truth and Beauty enables us to be assigned High Selves, undiluted fragments of the Highest Deity, the I AM Presence, to lead us ever to God—to be distinguished from The Holy Spirit, the presence of The Divine Mother Spirit, the equal partner of The Christ for this local universe. (See *The Urantia Book*.)

COSMIC CONSCIOUSNESS: Expanded awareness and perceptible emanations of Light resulting from an experience of illumination; usually, but not always, around age 33-36. Marked changes in physical appearance, emotional behavior, and especially mental and spiritual upliftment and perception; heightened moral sense and feeling of love for, and connection with, all of life. See Bibliography.

DEVAS: A Hindu word meaning angels. In the West used to denote members of the angelic order holding essence patterns for, and promoting the growth of, the nature kingdoms: earth, water, fire, and air, minerals, plants, and animals (but not the human evolution). Usually smaller than angels but occasionally quite large if overshadowing a lake, a mountain, or the weather. Much larger than elementals whom they supervise. Visible to clairvoyant sight.

ELEMENTALS: Seen to clairvoyant sight as tiny points of light flitting around and through minerals, plants, animals, and the bodies of humans. Working under the devas they take on prana, or life force, and fly into the creation to discharge it. Together with the devas and angels they are called the builders of form.

ESOTERIC CHRISTIANITY: An attempt to extract and reconstruct the true teachings of The Christ from the parables and second and third hand stories of the Bible. Draws also on lesser-known gospels such as that of St. Thomas, records of the teachings from Asia, the impressive revelation from higher beings, *The Urantia Book*, and other present day channelings concerning the days the Master of

Masters walked the Earth, such as the readings of the well-documented Edgar Cayce Another important source would be the metaphysical dictionary of the Unity Church. Esoteric Christianity is for the serious student who soon develops "eyes to see and ears to hear," who believes that God presents revelations to His/Her children in all ages, and that The Christ, who is very much alive on Earth through his Spirit of Truth and Beauty, can speak to those of true humility and sincere seeking, and will speak not in archaic idioms and symbols which need to be translated, but in language we can understand. An esoteric Christian is liable to believe that the monumental works, *The Urantia Book*, along with *A Course In Miracles* and *The Way of Mastery* are probably a form of "Second Coming," since Jesus said when he came again everyone would be able to see him in a much more true and essential form, and how ready are the people of Earth for that? Some stages of preparation would seem to be in order. Happily, these seem to be more and more frequent!

EXORCISM: To clear the "bodies" of an individual of so-called "negative" patterns, taken on during a period of imbalance. Could be inharmonious physical vibrations, emotional patterns, or mental thought forms. Most effective is to call on the name and power of The Living Christ, and also to have the subject's permission—although the latter is not necessary since they can always reject the action.

FALSETTO: An additional high register voice possible for some men (and the author). There is usually a break between the low voice and the falsetto. Yodeling utilizes this break.

FREE WILL PLAN: The concept that God intends that our type of being (Evolutionary Free Will Creature with Ascension Potential) shall grow through making choices in a dualistic world—apparent good and evil). Also, that God endowed us with creativity that we might learn to become co-creators with Him/Her. The author calls God "Herm").

FULL TRANCE: A state associated with the giving over of control of the body, the emotions, and the mind to a (hopefully!) higher being, usually to channel information or to heal. The subject is usually unconscious of what comes through or takes place during full trance but in experienced channels the mind is taken somewhere and shown images so that on return he/she will have some knowledge of what transpired. Has the advantage of purity of transmission, less tampering by conscious mind of channel, but is usually much more of a strain on the body. Some full trance mediums do it relatively safely for long periods and have brought through impressive material (Jane Roberts' "Seth" ; J.Z. Knight's "Ramtha,"; and Jack Pursel's "Lazaris"). To be distinguished from conscious channels, such as the author, some of whom have developed high degrees of accuracy through dedication, training of the mind, heart, and body, and practice.

HIGH SELF: Pure spark of divinity (God) assigned to a human to point the way toward Godhood. Indwells the mind and adjusts thoughts but always honors the free will of the individual host. Has experience but not individuality, which it achieves eventually, hopefully, through greater and greater fusion with the human personality. The God within, the "I AM Presence, our link with Divinity.

HUNA: The wisdom of the Kahunas, priest-healers of Hawaii. An ancient tradition, passed down through language, containing much truth and many different techniques. Came from the Holy Land through migrations around the time of Christ. The works of Max Freedom Long have preserved much of it, and there are still a few authentic Kahunas in Hawaii.

KARMA, THE LAW OF: Cause and effect operating in our thoughts, emotions, and actions. The universe manifesting and returning to us our creativity, so we can learn from it. Both difficult and a wonderful plan since no one gets away with anything. What you mete out to others (all of life) you will also experience, so that you can know both sides: giving and receiving. We are here to learn life.

KUNDALINI: The energy that arises from the root chakra and passes along the spine, through the chakras to the crown chakra at the top of the head. Can be thought of as a reflection of the divine energy that comes down through the medulla. In the average person, coiled at the root and not too active. When awakened naturally, can motivate the subject along the path toward the Light and Cosmic Consciousness. If forced by too much desire or drugs can produce experiences which, due to lack of understanding, seem psychotic.

LEMURIA: A huge land mass centered in the Pacific Ocean, supposedly pre-dating Atlantis in the Atlantic. Many historical writings refer to it. Achievements focused more on the intuitive, artistic, and oneness, rather than the scientific and power (Atlantis). There are some places with records in California.

Glossary

LIVING CHRIST: See CHRIST SPIRIT and ESOTERIC CHRISTIANITY

LORDS OF SIRIUS: Advanced beings from the twin-star Sirius. They are supervising the growth in consciousness in a large sector of the universe of which the solar system is a small part. In their messages through sensitives on Earth they emphasize the yellow-gold Second Ray, qualities of Love-Wisdom. At this time of great change we are passing into a universe sector under Arcturus and the Violet Ray (Seventh).The author of this book has channeled from the Lords of both Sirius and Arcturus.

LOW SELF: The subconscious, the body consciousness. Called "low self" in Huna, the wisdom of the Kahunas, the priest-healers of Hawaii. Low perhaps in positioning in the body, but certainly not low in intelligence, since it regulates the 500 functions of the liver—one organ out of many—as well as the five senses and much of their higher octaves of sensing! The author calls the low self the Basic Selves (See Chapter 10.).

MASTER: See 'ASCENDED MASTER. Or could also be an exalted teacher or guide from another planet or dimension of space or a human spiritual teacher acting for the above.

OVERTONE SERIES: The natural chord of tones produced by dividing a vibrating string, or any freely vibrating object, successively into segments: 2, 3, 4, 5, 6, 7, etc. The Law of Harmonics. The Chord of Nature. The "Lost Chord." Not "tempered" as the piano.

REINCARNATION: The concept that an aspect, or aspects, of a human being last beyond the transition called death to re-embody in subsequent lives, carrying memory and karmic patterns for further evolution.

SEVEN BODIES: Found in a number of religious disciplines, they are roughly: Physical-Etheric, Emotional-Astral, Mental-lower and higher, Intuitional, Spiritual, Monadic, and Divine. The first three (your own or others) can be felt with your hand, but since each successive body is larger and more rarified, the next four can only be contacted clairvoyantly.

STAR CHILDREN: Souls or perhaps Basic Selves who have come from other planets, probably outside the solar system. Occasionally a "walk in" where a body vehicle that was going to die is completely appropriated; Example: Lobsang Rampa

THE GREAT WHITE BROTHERHOOD: An organization in spirit of ascended masters dedicated to the spiritual upliftment of the human race, as well as the kingdoms of mineral, plant, and animal. Not angels but liaisons between higher spirit personalities and man. Sometimes take bodies for experience and service (such as Joseph, father of Jesus; Eknaton (or Akhnaten), who brought monotheism to Egypt; St. Francis of Assisi, the Master Kuthumi, etc.). Occasionally, humans are accomplishing such important and dedicated work in co-creation with these masters that they could be called, loosely, members of The White Brotherhood. They always honor your free will.

THE LAW OF SEVEN: Recognized in spiritual disciplines the world over as one of the Great Laws. Actually arises out of the creative combinations of the Triune Aspects of the Godhead, whatever names are used to designate them. Creating alone provides 1, 2, and 3; creating in pairs, 4, 5, and 6; all three creating, the 7th. These fundamental creative possibilities apparently set a pattern which is detectable at many levels throughout the Creation.

TIME OF DIVISION: Edgar Cayce's term for the present transition from the Piscean Age to the Aquarian Age, roughly 1958 to May 5, 2000 (the last date in the Great Pyramid). (The end of the Mayan Calendar on December 21, 2012, was another "marker") A time of extreme polarization and challenge described in most religions. In the Bible: Armageddon, the struggle between the forces of Light and the forces of darkness and possibly the return of The Christ. To an enlightened metaphysician: a healing crisis or birth pangs necessary for the emergence of a Golden Age of peace, understanding, and brother/sisterhood and possible world language and government.

TOUCH-FOR-HEALTH: An all-around system of diagnosis through muscle-testing or kinesiology which includes techniques of achieving balance by acupressure, pressing neurovascular holding points, massaging the two ends of related muscles, and tracing meridians to increase their flow. Developed by John Thie (pronounced thee with the "th" as in thing) and based on 20 years of research by Dr. Richard Goodheart, who established the connection between certain muscles and certain organs, Touch-For-Health also offers therapeutic nutrition and other related modalities.

BIBLIOGRAPHY

Andrews, Donald Hatch. The Symphony of Life. Lee's Summit, Missouri: Unity Books, 1966.

Bucke, Richard, M.D., Cosmic Consciousness, New York: Dutton and Co., 1901

David, William. The Harmonics of Sound, Color, and Vibration. Marina del Rey, California: De Vorss, 1980.

Diamond, John, M.D. Behavioral Kinesiology. New York: Harper & Row, 1979. (Published in paperback as Your Body Doesn't Lie. New York: Warner Books, 1980.)

———. The Life Energy in Music, Vols I and II. New York: Archaeus Press, 1981, 1983.

Hamel, Peter. Through Music to the Self, Shambhala, 1979. Heline, Corrine. Esoteric Music Marina del Rey, California: De Vorss, 1969.

——— Healing and Regeneration through Music. Santa Barbara: New Age Press, 1969.

Jenny, Hans. Cymatics: The Structure and Dynamics of Waves and Vibrations, Vols. I and II Basel, Switzerland: Basiliu Press, 1967.

Keyes, Laurel Elizabeth. Toning: The Creative Power of the Voice. Marina del Rey, California: De Vorss, 1978.

Khan, Hazrat Inayat. Music. New York: Samuel Weiser, 1962.

———. The Mysticism of Sound. New York: Weber 1979.

Partch, Harry. Genesis of a Music. New York: Da Capo Press, 1974.

Retallack, Dorothy. The Sound of Music and Plants. Santa Monica, California: De Vorss, 1973.

Rogo, D. Scott. A Psychic Study of the Music of the Spheres Vol. 2 Secaucus, N.J: University Books, 1972.

Rudhyar, Dane. The Magic of Tone and the Art of Music. Boulder, Colorado: Shambhala, 1982.

Scott, Cyril. Music: Its Secret Influence Through the Ages. London: Theosophical Publishing House, 1937.

Stebbin, Lionel. Music: Its Occult Basis and Healing Value. London: New Knowledge Books, 1972.

The Urantia Book. Chicago, Illinois: The Urantia Foundation, 1955.

Zuckerkandl, Victor. Sound and Symbol. Princeton University Press, 1969.

WEBSITES OF VISIONARIES

My deepest thanks go to the following visionaries, for permission to quote their wisdom. For more information on their work for the light, please visit their websites:

Patricia Cota-Robles: New Age Study of Humanity's Purpose: www.eraofpeace.org

Grand Elder Don Alejandro: cz.esoguru.com/Don Alejandro

Barbara Marx Hubbard: Foundation for Conscious Evolution: www.Evolve.org

Tom Kenyon: Hathors from Venus, www.tomkenyon.com

Sri Amma and Sri Bhagavan:

www.onenesscentre.com.au/BhagavanAndAmma.html

John Kimmey: The Hopi Prophecy, www.motherearthfathersky.org.

International Council of Thirteen Indigenous Grandmothers: http://www.grandmothersspeak.com

Peter Russell: www.peterrussell.com

Sheldan Nidle: www.paoweb.com

ABOUT THE AUTHOR

BIOGRAPHY OF JOEL ANDREWS

After three degrees and a career exploring virtually all aspects of professional harp playing, in 1971 Joel Andrews experienced a life-changing illumination. He began improvising music he was hearing in higher dimensions and pioneered some of the first music of the Emerging Age. Then followed healing sessions for individuals, international recognition through concerts, workshops, and recordings, and the many miracles of a forty-year healing ministry. To date he has completed three thousand personalized CDs, over thirty CDs for the general public, tours to seventeen countries, two books *A Harp Full of Stars* and *Miracles through Music*. All of this would not have been possible without his capability of surrendering to the guidance of higher frequency beings. He attributes the miracles to this co-creation.

APPENDIX TOPICS IN JOEL ANDREWS' *A HARP FULL OF STARS*

- The Circle of Fifths (shows the Manifesting Principle for each letter Quality and related pitch)
- Symbolism of the Strokes of Letters
- Unitas Eanokee—One World Anthem in English by Joel Andrews
- The same in Eanokee—the new language (sheet music and recording also available)
- SOHIEZ (New name for God)
- Analysis of the Higher Symbolism of Letters

FOR MORE INFORMATION AND TO ORDER PERSONAL ATTUNEMENT CDS FOR HEALING, BOOKS, AND FOR ENHANCING MEDITATION, DANCE, BOOKS, AND HEALING MODALITIES

WRITE:

GOLDEN HARP ENTERPRISES
P.O. Box 1073
Mendocino, CA 95460
www.harpofgold.com

FOR WORKS BY SERAFINA ANDREWS

VISIT:

www.SerafinArts.com

FOR OTHER BOOKS INTEGRATING SPIRITUAL CONCEPTS IN PRACTICAL APPLICATION

VISIT:

www.portalcenterpress.com

www.ingramcontent.com/pod-product-compliance
Lightning Source LLC
Chambersburg PA
CBHW030309080526
44584CB00012B/500